MRS. SIDDONS AS QUEEN KATHARINE

THE PRIVATE LIFE OF MRS. SIDDONS

A Psychological Investigation

by

NAOMI ROYDE-SMITH

"I was an honest actress"
SARAH SIDDONS

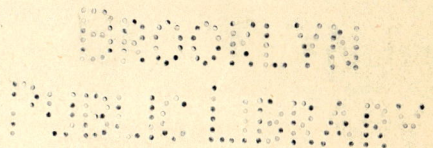

LONDON
VICTOR GOLLANCZ LTD
14 Henrietta Street Covent Garden
1933

B
S 568 R

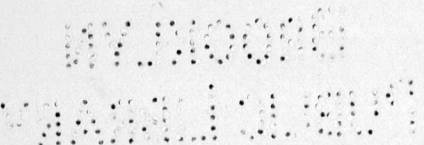

Printed in Great Britain by
The Camelot Press Ltd., London and Southampton

To
MRS. CLEMENT PARSONS

CONTENTS

Author's Notes   *page* 11

PART I
Materials for a Portrait

I. Personal   21
II. Chronological   48

PART II
The Background

I. The Road   55
II. The Town   90

PART III
Cloudy Symbols

I. Three Plays   109
II. Four Portraits   186

PART IV
The Sitter

I. Her Private Style   201
II. Lothario   227
III. Dangerous Years   256
IV. "Their fire is not quenched"   283

AUTHOR'S NOTE

Permission to reproduce the copyright photographs of Gilbert Stuart's Portrait of Mrs. Siddons and Sir Thomas Lawrence's Sitter's Chair has been obtained from the National Portrait Gallery and the Diploma Gallery respectively.

All the other illustrations are reproduced from the British Museum's photographs of drawings and engravings now in the Print Room.

LIST OF ILLUSTRATIONS

Mrs. Siddons as Queen Katharine, from a lithograph by W. Sharp from the portrait by J. Hayter *Frontispiece*

1. Mrs. Siddons at the age of 21, oil painting by Gilbert Stuart, in the National Portrait Gallery *facing page* 55

2. Thomas Lawrence at the age of 13, engraved by J. R. Smith after the original drawing by the artist 85

3. Mrs. Siddons in the character of Isabella, with her son Henry as Biron's child, engraved by Caldwell from a picture by William Hamilton 109

4. Thomas Lawrence as a young man, from a lithograph by R. J. Lane after the original drawing by the artist 227

5. Maria Siddons, from a mezzotint by George Clint after the original painting by Sir Thomas Lawrence 255

6. Mrs. Siddons's costume as Hamlet, from a water-colour drawing in Miss Mary Hamilton's collection of Costumes and Attitudes of Mrs. Siddons, now in the British Museum 265

7. Sir Thomas Lawrence's Sitter's Chair, now in the Diploma Gallery at Burlington House 283

AUTHOR'S NOTES

IN PREPARING this study of a woman about whom so much has already been written I have made use, not only of those Lives and Memoirs of Mrs. Siddons referred to in the first section of this book, but also of many of the books of reference from which these works have been compiled. In doing so I have often found that my own selection of relevant detail has lighted on facts passed over as insignificant by other writers, and have sometimes been led to conclusions and judgments which do not entirely coincide with theirs.

Once or twice accident, or the help of friends, leading me to sources untouched by previous writers, has thrown a light on a conflicting piece of evidence. For example Mrs. Clement Parsons, certainly the greatest living authority on the life and time of Mrs. Siddons, states that A. F. Cooke the actor, once when he should have been playing Norval to Mrs. Siddons's Lady Randolph was found " so flushed with the grape, as they then said, that young Henry Siddons had to read the part for him."

Boaden tells the same story, but gives the play as *Rolla*. This sounds more probable as Cooke was a heavy tragedian who would not be cast for young Norval, though Henry Siddons did later play this boy's part opposite his mother in Edinburgh. I had decided in favour of Boaden's version of the tale when, in a calendar of first nights at Covent Garden Theatre in 1803, I came upon the following notice:

"*May 4*.

"The Harper's Daughter

"A Tragedy, in five acts, by Mr. G. Lewis, and performed for the benefit of Mr. and Mrs. H. Johnston. It was taken from Schiller's play of the "Minister," and displayed much of the extravagance of the German stage. Mr. Cooke had accepted a principal character, and was announced in the bills of the day, as he had been in advertisements for a fortnight preceding.— When the curtain drew up, Mr. H. Johnston came forward, and in evident agitation of mind, addressed the house, requesting indulgence for Mr. H. Siddons to *read* the part which had been accepted by Mr. Cooke, the latter having just before sent him a note, stating that he *could not* perform that night. As Mr. Cooke had on the 29th of April, subjected Mr. Munden to a similar disappointment, much disapprobation was expressed. Mr. H. Siddons, however, left the audience no great reason to regret the defection of the actor, whose place he supplied; for though he undertook only to read the part, yet he had been so diligent, during the intervals of the acts, that he *acted* the whole with very few references to the manuscript. The play excited some interest, and was well received."

It is of course possible that young Siddons was called in to read for Mr. Cooke in all three plays, and that we have records of three incidents not of one.

The point is not of great importance as it affects a study of Mrs. Siddons herself, though it illustrates the manner in which selection is thrust upon a writer dealing with conflicting evidence from apparently equally trustworthy sources. A more relevant problem is that concerning the colour of Mrs. Siddons's hair. Horace Walpole says it was either red or that she wore red powder, when she was a young and fashionable actress, and there is a pretty story of the young Reynolds painting the children of a fashionable lady and being confused by the scent of the red French Marischale powder worn by their mother as she bent over his shoulder to examine the drawing. In most of Mrs. Siddons's portraits white powder is worn except in the Tragick Muse where the hair is, or was, of a dark reddish brown. The 1812 portrait by Lawrence shows almost black hair : but Lawrence gives his Kemble red gold hair as Hamlet, a part he played sometimes with powder and sometimes without. Lawrence's Satan, which is Hamlet in a rage and without clothes, has reddish hair, and Campbell tells us that the likeness between the brother and sister was so remarkable as, at times, almost to amount to identity. Here it seems excusable to decide that, as a young woman, Mrs. Siddons had red hair, and that its colour darkened with age so, that by the time powder was no longer worn, it had become a dark brown that looks now black in her latest portraits.

Another point, small in itself, but teasing to the searcher after some degree of accuracy, arises in connection with a letter from Mrs. Siddons to a Mr. Denison, a clergyman, published by Mr. G. S. Layard in his *Letter-Bag of Sir Thomas Lawrence*. It is dated "Feby. ye 5th 1828" and from Great

Marlborough Street. But we know that Mrs. Siddons left Great Marlborough Street after Sally's death in 1803, and lived, first at Westbourne Farm, and then in Upper Baker Street. She was in Upper Baker Street in 1828, three years before her death. I have ventured to conclude from this discrepancy that Mrs. Siddons at the age of seventy-three, and after some years of ill-health, was grown a little absent-minded and occasionally let her thoughts and her pen with them, carry her back in time. This, and other small points of a like nature have been my own justification for showing Mrs. Siddons, in the evening of her days, as an occasionally absent minded old lady.

I have used the legend current in the Wye Valley that the Blessed Martyr John Kemble was of the same blood as the actress and her brother, for its atmospheric value, in spite of the assurances of antiquarians that it has no foundation in fact. The Kembles believed it themselves, and I have recorded this belief. Legend indeed is rife about the Kemble family and I am indebted to Miss Joy Scovell for the blithe story of a verger who once showed her Campbell's caryatid of Mrs. Siddons in the Chapel of St. Andrew at Westminster Abbey, assuring her that it was a statue of the actress in the part of Portia and that Flaxman and Hinchliff's Statue of John Philip Kemble as Cato that stands near it represented her husband. When it was suggested that they were brother and sister he was very much distressed.

". Good Lord ! " he said, " and to think I've been

telling the public they were man and wife for the last seven years!"

The verger was less in error than he might have been, for the official guide, following Dean Stanley, declares Campbell's pseudo-Grecian full-length and standing figure to be "A statue by Chantry after Reynolds's picture The Tragick Muse." The statue, seated, of a figure only very slightly after Reynolds's picture, is by Chavalliaud and was erected in the open air on Paddington Green in 1897.

The story of poor Macready's angry sufferings over the business of getting Mrs. Siddons into the Abbey at all needs a chapter to itself and cannot be detailed here. I only mention the tangle as proof that even on the basis of authentic records the mushroom legend will sprout, and in the highest places: and if I cite it here it is with the lurking hope of excusing some unintentional oversight or misstatement of my own which may be detected in the following pages.

This hope is the more justified as reference to Mrs. Siddons's own unfinished memoirs, used by Campbell, convicts her many a time of slips of memory, as for instance her explicit statement that she was too busy to sit to Romney more than once, whereas in the painter's own carefully kept diary of sittings we find her name down as having sat on at least six mornings, in February, March, and April of 1783. A possible seventh sitting on May 10th may have been given to William Siddons for his own likeness.

In another connection she asserts that Thomas King was Garrick's emissary to Cheltenham when the actor-manager was considering whether he should engage her for London in 1775. Actually it was the Rev. H. Bate, afterwards Sir Henry Bate-Dudley, the friend of Gainsborough to whom Garrick wrote asking him to look at the young actress and from whom he received a favourable report of her beauty and accomplishment. King was certainly one of her earliest and most enthusiastic admirers and the confusion in Mrs. Siddons's mind, fifty years after the event, is quite natural.

I have to thank Messrs. Allen & Unwin for permission to quote several passages from the Lawrence–Siddons letters in Mr. Oswald Knapp's *An Artist's Love Story* used in the section " Lothario " of this book ; Mr. A. H. Mayhew for bringing to my attention Victor and Oulton's *Outline of the London Theatres from the years 1795 to 1817*, and for procuring for me the corrected and augmented second edition of Boaden's *Life of Mrs. Siddons* ; Miss Elizabeth Jenkins for permission to use on pages 103–4 the opening paragraph of her monograph on Lady Caroline Lamb ; my husband Mr. Ernest Milton for directing and augmenting my investigation into the literature of the theatre during Mrs. Siddons's lifetime ; Mr. W. Graham Robertson for his kindness in reading the proofs of this book for me ; and Mrs. Waggett great-grandniece of Mrs. Siddons through her father Mr. Quentin Twiss, and Mrs. Siddons-Budgen her cousin for showing me their Siddons relics and so enlivening my dim conception of their august relation. I am also very much indebted to Mrs. Enthoven for allowing me to examine her unique collection of playbills and press-cuttings relative to the professional careers of Mrs. Siddons and her family.

For the ballad of Father Kemble's grave quoted on pages 58–62 I can offer no thanks or acknowledgment as its anonymous author has given it to the world in the form of a tract sold in the streets of Monmouth on the day of the Kemble pilgrimage and in the Church of St. Francis Xavier at Hereford where the mummied hand of the martyr may be seen. It will, I am sure, afford a great deal of pleasure to readers unacquainted with the countryside whence it comes.

It would be an oversight on the part of an author attempting to treat reconstructively the life of the great English actress to omit any reference to M. André Maurois's amusing and sympathetic sketch of Mrs. Siddons's career up to the death of her eldest daughter in 1803. M. Maurois's *Portrait d'une Actrice* is an achievement all the more remarkable that it combines the solidity of fact with the ease and lightness of fiction. Much is omitted, a very little is very delicately re-arranged to fit into the charming frame designed for the completed picture. The reader who, remembering M. Maurois's work, may find mine cruder, more violent, less logical and sympathetic, is asked to remember that *Portrait d'une Actrice* stops short at the point when the more difficult passages of Mrs. Siddons's history begin, and that it has been my aim to reconcile the story of these years with the preparation for them made by her life up to this period, and to do so without sacrificing inconvenient fact to the tempting suggestions of possible and even probable interpretative fiction.

I should in conclusion like to draw attention to the charming little lyric on page 119 which blossoms in the 1694 edition of Southerne's *Fatal Marriage*. The rubric of the play states that the words were sent anonymously to the actress Mrs. Ayliff and set to music by Purcell for her to sing in the Interlude in Act IV. The words occur, with no author's name, in various editions of Purcell's songs, but I have not been able to trace the authorship in any other collection or in any anthology of English verse before or since 1694 known to me. Neither Mr. Frank Sidgwick nor Mr. Iolo Williams, to whom I have appealed, recognizes it, though they both agree with me that its quality is so far superior to that of any of Southerne's own lyrics that it is almost impossible he should have written it himself. Besides, if Southerne were the author, there is clearly no reason why he should have allowed the song to be ascribed to another's pen. I am happy to be able to embellish my book with this fragment of neglected verse, even though it was probably excised from the play when Mrs. Siddons performed in it. I shall be happier still if the researches of some authority on the seventeenth century should enable me to solve the problem of its authorship now that it has been republished here.

NAOMI ROYDE-SMITH.

PART I

Materials for a Portrait

I

PERSONAL

1

THE PLAN of this book is that of the full-length and ceremonial portraits of the late eighteenth century, the greatest period of English painting till our own day, and the period during which Mrs. Siddons lived and was actually painted by Stuart, Hamilton, Romney, Gainsborough, Reynolds, Lawrence and other less important artists. Such portraits are usually composed of a background in which, either through a window or in the partial opening of a tent, or of a pair of curtains, the sitter's victories on sea or land, or the view from his private or official dwelling-place is indicated without much insistence on detail, and with considerable licence in the selection of matters relevant to the composition as a picture, as well as to the suppression of others inconvenient to it. Against this background appear objects, actual or symbolic, such as the bowl and the dagger held by the Personifications of Terror and of Pity behind the throne of Sir Joshua Reynolds's Tragick Muse, or the volume of Milton's *Paradise Lost* in Sir Thomas Lawrence's last portrait of Mrs. Siddons. These details are arranged in such a way as to balance, to emphasize and to enrich the effect of the figure on which the main interest of painter and spectator alike is to be focused. Finally there stands, or sits, the image which has resulted from the personal encounter of the painter with the sitter he has chosen or has, at least, agreed to paint.

Such too is the scheme of the portrait I am about to attempt. If I have reversed the order in which a painter not only considers but also executes his work, it is because I am of necessity working in another medium and using a different perspective. I hope therefore that without vanity I can say I have based my scheme on that of acknowledged masterpieces since, at best, I can only achieve a composite and second-hand impression of the subject I have undertaken to execute. Thus it is that I offer, first, a consideration of the confused and restless background against which the woman I am endeavouring to present is seen, now that a hundred and more years have passed since her death, and in doing so trace the story of her youth and formative years.

When that has been established in sufficient detail to warrant the conclusions I am to draw from its existence, I propose to show, in words, three of the plays in which the actress made her most shattering appeals to the emotions of her audiences, and to group around these reconstructions of forgotten drama four still fresh and lively portraits of the woman when off the stage. These four portraits, painted by masters of their art are re-examined, not as works of art (such criticism is not only out of my province but has long since been made absolute) but for evidence about the woman whose assumption of the tragic mask so often belied and sometimes augmented her real nature.

Finally, having restated, though in my own order, matters already known and handled by other writers, I shall place the woman, who seems to me to emerge from these circumstances, these portrayals, these images, in a light, possibly a little fuller than any yet cast on her memory, certainly thrown from a different angle. In doing so I have often returned to rehandle material already sketched in, as a painter returns to his picture adding pigment to drawing, re-arranging a shadow or a drapery, emphasizing a feature as his portrait deepens into significance and completion. Sometimes the return actually reshapes a passage—as colour when it is laid on at last may change the drawing of the original cartoon.

2

It is now twenty-five years since Mrs. Clement Parsons completed the monograph which must remain the fullest and most authoritative work we are ever likely to have on the life of Mrs. Siddons. *The Incomparable Siddons* is a biographical achievement of the highest order. It includes every known fact about its subject; it is written out of a mind steeped in the history of the eighteenth century; its author had access to many unpublished letters written to and by Mrs. Siddons, as well as to the work of the four biographers who preceded her, Campbell, Boaden, Fitzgerald and Mrs. Kennard. The result is far from being the patchwork so brief a summary of it might suggest. Mrs. Parsons approached her theme with an enthusiasm, and dealt with it in a style so clear and a humour so shrewd and kindly, that, in spite of the dazzle of quotation-marks any conscientious writer must scatter over pages such as hers, her book, besides being almost rocklike in its trustworthiness, makes uncommonly good reading.

Four years earlier, in 1904, the publication of Mr. Oswald Knapp's edition of the letters that passed between Sir Thomas Lawrence, Mrs. Pennington, Mrs. Siddons and her daughters Sally and Maria in the years 1797–1799 had shed a new light on an episode in Mrs. Siddons's private life the details of which the public had hitherto accepted in the form they are given by Fanny Kemble in her *Record of a Girlhood*. Mrs. Parsons incorporated the general sense of Mr. Knapp's remarkable book in her biography and preserved her own judicial balance in the matter of drawing any conclusions from it. Possessing these two books the ordinary reader may well be satisfied that he has all he ever will need in the way of reference both to Mrs. Siddons herself (and in the case of Mrs. Parsons's book to John Philip Kemble as well) : he will also find that, in many instances I have used these two books as a palette from which to take the colours for the picture I intend to draw : and, often, when the evidence of contemporary writers differs, as that of contemporaries so often does, I have turned to Mrs. Parsons and accepted her considered judgment of the point at issue. To vary the metaphor I have treated Mrs. Parsons as a guide to the large and very well mapped out country I began to explore long before the idea of making a book of it myself dawned on my intention.

It was first, in revisiting and re-inspecting the five great portraits of Mrs. Siddons in our National Collections and at Dulwich, and next, in travelling up and down the Wye Valley in pursuit of a Kemble legend, that I began to be haunted by the vision of a thin and eager girl, too intent on the necessity for earning her own living and that of her children to realize how uneasy the stirrings of a yet unreleased and growing genius made her. Another preoccupation, setting me to re-read the *Letters* of Horace Walpole, gave me glimpses of something rather shy, astonishingly shy for the toast of three capitals, in the older and triumphant Mrs. Siddons who " continues to be the mode and to be modest and sensible—declining great dinners—saying that her business and her family take up her whole time." Then Fanny Kemble's *Record of a Girlhood* showed in Mrs. Siddons grown old, far profounder depths than the brisk little egoist who wrote of them ever realized, depths where something still at work in the heart of the marvellous old woman, stirred at times, unrecognized by anyone around her.

The train of thought pursued its way, the idea of the portrait grew. I looked up Lamb, Hazlitt, Madame d'Arblay, Horace Walpole's *Johnsonhood* and the whole literature of Bath. I spent long evenings reading the plays that held the town from 1780 to 1812. I read the life of the Rev. John Home who was cast out of his ministry for writing *Douglas : A Tragedy*. I even tried to re-read *Pizarro* (a work I had found engrossing when I was nine years old) and *Rolla*, but here I failed. I did not, at the moment, realize the reason for this inability to get on with plays not essentially duller than *Jane Shore*, or *Emilia Galotti* or *The Gamester* by Edward Moore. At this point Mrs. Inchbald stepped in, crisp and lively and of the theatre in every line, with her critical, sententious prefaces and such arrested judgments as, that the musical comedy of *Inkle and Yarico* (in which the part of a little black savage called Wowski was played by Mr. Martyn) " might remove from Mr. Wilberforce his aversion to theatrical exhibitions."

From the plays themselves it was inevitable to turn to dramatic criticism, a profession as fierce and as prejudiced in its published forms in the closing years of the eighteenth century as it has ever been, and to the more useful, laconic reporter's work of Victor and Oulton who seldom trouble to say more of Mrs. Siddons beyond that, as she was playing, the house was full. From the theatre I went back again to the painters who depicted plays and players : to Gainsborough who haunted the green-room of Palmer's theatre ; to Sir Thomas Lawrence ; to Fuseli, that violent Swiss genius ; to Haydon and Hamilton and to those pictures a Londoner must wander on staircases, or be admitted by key to a cellar, or be smuggled in to the Ladies' Dining-room at the Garrick Club to study. There was an occasional spacious day in a Library or in the Print Room of the British Museum, smiling over the lovely monographs of Lord Ronald Sutherland-Gower, or turning up small unimportant prints the curators themselves had forgotten they possessed, and looking at the little models of stage sets in the theatrical section of various exhibitions. Finally there were crevices to be filled and new vistas to be opened in poring over the rich treasure of the Gabrielle Enthoven collection at South Kensington, and in following Sir Thomas Lawrence's progress to its culmination in the Royal Collection at Windsor.

As time went on the same unacknowledged prejudice as had made me reject *Rolla* and *Pizarro,* ruled out the two fine volumes of Fitzgerald's *Life of the Kembles.* I was not very much interested in John Philip Kemble. *Rolla* and *Pizarro* were plays in which Kemble's part predominated. Nothing, certainly not Lawrence's portrait of this actor as Coriolanus, or that other one, now lost in the catacombs beneath the Tate Gallery, in which the great John Philip seems to have borrowed his sister's Gainsborough hat for the purpose of making Hamlet gigantically ridiculous, can make a twentieth century mind take Black Jack of Old Drury quite seriously. His praise has now so outworn a pomposity of style that it must be treasured sometimes for the sake of responses it was not written to provoke. Sir Walter Scott, indeed, never made Kemble more ridiculous on paper than the actor made himself in life : his criticism of Kemble's Hamlet is possibly the truest we possess :

> " He is a lordly vessel, goodly and magnificent when going large before the wind, but wanting faculty to go ready about, so that he is sometimes among the breakers before he can ware ship."

The poet Campbell, who wrote the official and unsatisfactory Biography of Mrs. Siddons, also commemorated Kemble in a poem which begins:

> *"Fair as some classic dome,*
> *Robust and richly graced,*
> *Our Kemble's spirit was the home*
> *Of Genius and of Taste."*

And these lines, though written seriously, have worn queer.

With Mrs. Siddons the case is entirely reversed. The generally received idea that she, too, was a little absurd fades into a gleam of gentle light on her purely human aspect so soon as the first stages of familiarity with her life and letters have been passed. Her portrait, though I did not yet know it, was preparing itself in my mind while I read the double story of the Kembles, and excluding her brother's monumental, but to our eyes no longer tragic, figure from the brightness she gathered throughout her life to diffuse it again in the clear light of immortality.

It was about this time that, having written a play on *The Private Life of Mrs. Siddons*, I had the singular experience of seeing her granddaughter Mrs. Siddons-Budgen act in one scene of my work. When this lady, who, by a pleasant coincidence, has two daughters whose relative ages are those of Sally and Maria Siddons, came on the stage, dressed as Mrs. Siddons is dressed in the small portrait by Lawrence (No. 785 in the National Gallery), I thought for a moment that my natural excitement had been too much for me and that I was seeing a ghost. And indeed some hereditary gleam must have fallen, or crept back, with the tall figure that leaned against the door-post on the platform of the little village hall where the Siddons Players were giving their performance. There was a breath-taking silence, while it seemed as if beauty and power were come back to the stage again and that, once more, as in the past, the makeshifts and inadequacies of a travelling player's one-night stand were about to be swept together into one magnificent and satisfying illusion. The moment passed : the little scene that followed that spectacular entrance was a small domestic comedy : there was no space in it for any tragic actress to deploy her powers : Mr. Rupert Siddons, with the handsome features of John Philip Kemble, played in it, and the two pretty daughters fluttered round candles on a supper table : it was all very pleasant and normal. The ghost had stayed for one transfiguring moment and was gone, leaving mortals of to-day to do what they could for another mortal's work.

When the little scene was over, the lady in whom for a moment the great ancestress had seemed to re-embody herself on the stage, came, as herself, and sat by me. She was wearing her everyday clothes, but two cameo bracelets still clasped her wrists and she showed them to me saying they were a part of the inheritance of such small but poignant relics as had fallen to her share. The two daughters came, the kind, proud father also : it was a tangible and yet shadowy reconstruction of what might have happened in some wayside theatre a hundred and forty years earlier, with Maria and Sally home from the French boarding-school, full of joy in their adored mamma, and William Siddons, not yet cross and gouty, come to exchange greetings with a passing friend. I came home in the company of the enthusiast who had driven me out to see the little show. She too had recognized for a flash the actual face that looks out from the toothache bandage portrait; we had held the bracelets that had once slipped warm from the wrists of the real Mrs. Siddons: it was an experience, slight in its charming way, and a little disturbing. It gave a queer hint of authenticity to the portrait that was growing more definite in my mind, peering now above the barriers of other work to be done; other books to be written before this one could be attempted.

The portrait of Mrs. Siddons had remained untouched, so far as any conscious work on my part was concerned, for almost two years when, last August, in the dog-days, I found myself in Monmouth standing in front of the meagre altar set up in the Roman Catholic Chapel there to the Blessed Martyr John Kemble who in the year 1679 was hanged at Hereford on false evidence brought against him during the Titus Oates Conspiracy. At least that is the account of his martyrdom given by responsible historians, who maintain further, that this priest was not a member of the same Kemble family as John Philip Kemble and Sarah Siddons. In Monmouth however they tell another tale. There, the story goes, Father Kemble was one of many priests who went quietly, secretly at times, from house to house in the Marches, in Wales, in Hereford- and Monmouth-shires: hiding, when the hunt was up, in the priests' chambers hidden behind wainscot, or in cells built in the thickness of deep tower walls; celebrating midnight, and secret, mass for the faithful. After Kemble's martyrdom the little wooden folding altar he carried was left unrecognized in a corner of the last house he had visited and found its way to the lumber-room, there to be discovered a generation later by one of the maids, who, being in need of an ironing-board, turned this flat, smooth, well-seasoned piece of wood to her purpose. Years went by, and while Queen Victoria was still on the throne, a young sewing-woman employed in the house, being an intelligent as well as a devout Catholic, recognized the nature of an inscription on the old ironing-board in the linen-room, and drew attention to it, with the result that the wooden table now stands in the little chapel in St. Mary's Street, with candles and a tiny altar rail before it. Above the flower vases, in the space where the altar-piece should be, a large photograph taken from a portrait of the martyr, said to be now in Belmont Abbey, has been pasted. The bearded and tonsured head of the seventeenth century priest there shown has the same dark melancholy eye; the same long, fine, by no means faintly Semitic nose; the same pallor and blackness as shows in any photograph from any painting of the eighteenth century actor and actress. I have compared a photograph of Stuart's portrait of John Philip Kemble with this of Father John: the same man might have sat for both pictures at different periods of his life. These were both Kembles of the Kemble country and, rightly or wrongly, Sarah Siddons believed herself connected by some blood-tie, however attenuated, with the gentle martyr whose business took him, as did hers, up and down the beautiful valley and through the passes across to the Welsh mountains of the country they were born in. And her portrait took on unexpected shadows and threw forth new lights, as this now beatified and half legendary figure assumed a symbolism and stood for something not, without it, quite fully explained in her character. It is what she herself believed about her connection with the martyred priest that is important as material for the texture of her spirit's dress.

Two other figures from the background of her life as we now see it, though in point of fact closer to her than that of the Blessed John Kemble, are of very much less significance here. One is the wild sister, who, with the megalomania that makes the very young and the slightly dotty equally trying to their families, pretended to commit suicide in Westminster Abbey after giving what Mrs. Parsons describes as " an objectional lecture " at Dr. Graham's Temple of Hymen. Her name was Julia Anne and she squinted. She married ; travelled to America, and settled in Wales. She has no place nor any value but that of a faint shadow in the portrait I am about to draw. When several members of the same family have gifts in excess of normal people there is quite often something left out of one of the more ordinary brothers or sisters.

The other is Eliza, " the most extraordinary creature in the world "—who may have been the infant relative of Dr. and Mrs. Whalley, but who seems, on the three occasions she is mentioned, to have been Mrs. Siddons's own child. Whoever she was, she showed herself occasionally in the stream of the actress's private life for eighteen months, between March 1785 and October 1786, and vanished beneath it, to return possibly, but not probably, as the veiled woman who wept and was unknown beside the coffin of Mrs. Siddons before it was lowered into the vault in Paddington Churchyard in 1831. If this were indeed Eliza she must have been at least fifty years old by then : but this mysterious being, so Campbell who reports her conduct tells us, was young. The mad sister, and the veiled lady, and even the vanishing child, do make a slight atmospheric difference to the portrait, though they cannot appear as figures in the background, being nothing but shadows themselves. They are not so much mysterious as obscure : they might provide hobbyhorses for a romancer : but they lose importance as materials for a picture once they have flitted across the sitter's aspect like midges against the sun. They will not be spoken of here again.

Far more relevant to the business is the almost equally shadowy figure of Mr. Galindo (we never hear his Christian name, though it began with P) who vanishes out of his wife's foaming and spluttering letter, being always abroad on some errand, or engaged in dancing attendance on the elderly actress, on almost every occasion when his name appears. Mr. Galindo colours, not his own portrait, which does not exist, but, first the portrait of Mrs.

Siddons herself by throwing up a light on her troubled, averted profile from the place at her feet where he so inconveniently worshipped, and, by an illuminating reflection, adding a touch to the detailed picture that must be drawn of Lawrence, his effortless and enduring rival.

Mrs. Galindo, like Miss Burney and Fanny Kemble, delays contemplation of the portrait for a time by the impact of her own dynamic personality. Her one short pamphlet shoots all constructive attention to bits, just as the longer volumes of the sedater and more considerable ladies lure it into their own amusing byways. To read Mrs. Galindo is to forget Mrs. Siddons, although it is exclusively Mrs. Siddons that the poor fury imagines she is exposing. But, once the first shock is over, a fresh and very vivid pigment has been added to the painting, and Mrs. Siddons vilified, emerges Mrs. Siddons purged, repentant, a more honest actress, a more exquisite woman even, than she has seemed until the subsiding of this shallow but angry flood has washed away the mist from our own eyes.

It is necessary to enumerate these two coarse figures, because they are closer to the picture of the woman herself than the great and famous men and women who must be held off, and even ignored altogether, when the study of a single figure comes to be isolated and set against, but detached from, its background. Making a portrait of Mrs. Siddons is no matter of flat washes and an agreeable pattern: such selection as must be made still leaves the background loaded with colour and with movement; the folds of the curtain looped across it from corner to corner can still be seen to bulge with the tumult they cannot altogether conceal. It is an indoor portrait : the sitter has spent the night in the theatre and comes from her drawing-room in Great Marlborough Street to pose in the artificially arranged and modulated lighting proper to the business of a portrait that really belongs to the eighteenth century and the school of studio-pictures.

In another particular also, this study I am about to offer of a single figure has, even as its subject did, shut out the great events of the world in which she lived. All artists live a necessarily self-engrossed life : those of the theatre particularly so. Having to make a mimic world in which to earn their bread, they lose to a great extent a sense of the reality of the world outside. It is difficult, on coming to the surface, after a long dive into history for the substance of Mrs. Siddons's life and personality, to realize that she was a contemporary of Nelson ; of Napoleon ; of the Duke of Wellington and of those two great pioneers of the mechanical age, James Watt and George Stephenson ; or to understand that Kemble and Sheridan, while eager to translate Kotzebue, should have passed over the publication of Goethe's *Faust* without a tremor of the pen.

It is almost incredible that, in making a study of the life of a woman who was born in 1755 and died in 1831, I should never once have had occasion to refer to the French Revolution or the Declaration of Independence.

3

It has been almost a point of honour with all succeeding biographers of Mrs. Siddons to speak ill of James Boaden, and, indeed, anyone hoping to enjoy a neat monograph on any of the persons on whom Boaden has lavished complete Works can be excused some irritation on first plunging into the quicksands of what this author quite erroneously believed to be biography—especially if such a reader has neglected to provide himself with any other work of reference. For Boaden's life of Mrs. Siddons is written largely in his *Life of John Philip Kemble*, and quite extensively in his *Life of Mrs. Jordan*, whereas, in the two large, annotated volumes of the second and best edition of the work nominally about her, chapter after chapter chats its way along with no reference whatsoever to the name on the title page. In Volume I. of Boaden's *Memoirs of Mrs. Siddons* we read of the state of Ireland in 1778; of what a pity it was that Burke did not find time to compose Garrick's Eulogy; of how Foote and Murphy each intended to write a Life of the other, but only one of them succeeded in doing it; of *The Orphan of China*; and a very great deal about Voltaire and of the sums paid by Catherine of Russia for pictures from the great English collections; but next to nothing of Mrs. Siddons. By page 176, we have come to the actor Dunstall " whose companionable qualities led him into numerous societies of which he was the admired songster " : on the following page our author " is here reminded that on the 13th of January 1779

Mr. Henderson married a daughter of Mr. Figgins of Chippenham in Somersetshire." On page 363 he concludes an account of Mrs. Abington's appearance as Lady Flutter with the remark :

> "I recede with veneration from all attempts to describe what constituted then the upper half of the figure ; but I may respectfully insinuate, that Mrs. Abington, as to surface, was not apt to allow the smallest spot to be under the undisputed control of nature."

My first attempt on Boaden was a failure. I knew too little about my subject then to keep patience with a writer who combined the industry of the bee with the inconsequence of the butterfly, and who, when he said he was going to tell one story, invariably told two entirely different ones. Later, with the main events of Mrs. Siddons's career fixed for me by staider and more considerate writers, I returned to Boaden and now acknowledge my debt to him as supplying, if not the draughtsmanship of the portrait, certainly those more brilliant and delicate touches that give finish and vivacity to a picture. Like Campbell, Boaden knew Mrs. Siddons well : unlike the poet he was not bored by having to write about her. He had admired her daily while she lived and played, and, long before she was dead, he set about embalming his careful and enthusiastic notes of her performances in any and every book he happened to be writing. As this was the method he employed with all his books, and as he admired almost anyone who could act at all, and as he appears to have written most of his books more or less at the same time, reading them with any serious pursuit in hand is rather like working in some library in *Alice in Wonderland*.

At first his style is dizzying. When forced to admit that a quite unimportant lady who had " devoted a long but not a melancholy widowhood to the occasional society of friends " had, in point of fact, died, he does so in the following periphrasis :

> " A few years only are past since I saw her borne to join once again her excellent husband in the proudest spot of the noblest mausoleum in the world, the Abbey church of Westminster."

Almost the reader forgets, as Boaden has forgotten, that this is a Life of Mrs. Siddons on which they are together engaged. The temptation to make an anthology of his inimitable phrases is strong. A Boaden Calendar might find a welcome on the shelves where the novels of Amanda M. Ros are securely treasured.

> " The dramatic honours of the lady just mentioned bloomed only in private theatricals."

> " The features of the gothic romance never lead to modern philosophy without losing much of their *picture* power, and all their sublimity."

Or, where the impulse to quote from the poets has seized him :

> " *Mark, how the dread Pantheon stands,*
> *Amid the domes of modern lands :*
> *Amid the toys of idle state,*
> *How simply, how severely great !* "

But our author does get his second wind. On page 378 of Volume I., after a shrewd analysis of Congreve's perfectly dreadful tragedy *The Mourning Bride*, Boaden pulls himself together and observing " But even Congreve may detain us too long when Mrs. Siddons is waiting " returns at last to all he has not yet told us of Mrs. Siddons in his Lives of Mrs. Jordan and of Mr. Kemble. Started in Volume II., Boaden does not stick to his subject with any constancy. His first parenthesis embraces, among other themes, Horace Walpole's tragedy *The Mysterious Mother* for no better reason than that, possessing a copy of this rarity, published privately in 1768, he is constrained to imagine what Mrs. Siddons might have made of some of what he calls its " irresistible points." One of these points is the remark taken from Cato to Labienus in the ninth book of Lucan :

> " *We want no preacher to distinguish vice
> From Virtue. At our birth the god revealed
> All conscience needs to know.*"

This is the kind of thing that makes us feel on one page that Boaden is very tiresome, only to forget it on the next where, leaving Walpole's *Mysterious Mother* for Cumberland's *Mysterious Husband*, he declares the second play to be " founded on a slighter degree of incest " than the first and observes :

> " In hearing or reading the vices of another and a distant age, we have a twofold consolation : an involuntary suspicion that the facts may never have been true ;

and a voluntary belief that our own times exhibit nothing like them."

Little by little as these convolutions wind about one another, we are brought to fuller and more complete revelations of the lady who has been quite adequately revealed in Boaden's other books. The two volumes, once read, prove themselves a more close and vivifying monograph than Campbell's who stuck to his subject with so much ill-will. For James Boaden was *thinking* of Mrs. Siddons all the time, most of all when he was fighting his way through the hosts of other memories each memory of her called up. His very discursiveness ends in creating a richer concentration on the revelations when they come.

Boaden gives us glimpses of Mrs. Siddons in comedy as well as sublime views of her in her great tragic parts. Her Rosalind, he says, " seemed indeed to be brought up by a great magician and to be forest-born—it was one of her most delicate achievements—the graceful farewell to Orlando was in such a style of comedy as could only come from a spirit tenderly touched."

This from the critic who had been among the first to recognize, in the slender and graceful girl playing at Cheltenham, the actress she was to become, adds softness and pliancy to the materials for the portrait, and is wonderfully supplemented by his account of her Ophelia:

"It might at first be thought that her figure would not express the fragility of this lovely sacrifice to her affections—but the height was diminished by lowering the headdress, and the *countenance* permitted not the eye to be discursive."

Mrs. Siddons's Ophelia was, it appears, a model of graceful virtue until the mad scenes when her acting formed " the truest delineation that was ever made from a ruined piece of nature."

" But," cries Boaden suddenly,

" I hear some very inquisitive reader exclaim, 'What ! Mrs. Siddons *sing* ? ' No, sir, it was Ophelia who sang, or rather the melancholy of the poet Collins."

For the Kembles did not, at first, act Shakespeare as Shakespeare wrote, but in the namby-pamby improved and truncated versions of Nahum Tate and the poet Collins which Garrick and his predecessors had foisted on the stage. Boaden, true and intelligent critic that he was, turned to the original play for a description of the Ophelia Mrs. Siddons presented. It is, as he very penetratingly observes, put into the mouth of a personage without a name. Garrick had excised from Hamlet one of those lovely, careless throwings-out of an almost superfluous and yet intensely relevant extravagance Shakespeare, alone among dramatists, was rich enough to offer.

" *She speaks much of her father ; says she hears*
  There's tricks i' the world ; and hems, and beats her heart ;
  Spurns enviously at straws ; speaks things in doubt,
  That carry but half sense : her speech is nothing,
  Yet the unshaped use of it doth move
  The hearers to collection ; they aim at it,
  And botch the words up fit to their own thoughts ;

*Which, as her winks, and nods, and gestures yield them,
Indeed would make one think there might be thought,
Though nothing sure, yet much unhappily."*

It might almost have been written, while the play was in rehearsal, as a direction to the boy actor, who, according to the Quarto, entered in this scene as Ophelia, playing on the lute. And it was thus Mrs. Siddons's Ophelia was played.

Another instance of Boaden's independence of judgment occurs when, having made a long and quite kind analysis of Thomson's tragedy of *Tancred and Sigismunda*, he finishes by expressing his opinion that:

> " An author, after a death wound, may keep a person alive as long as his interest requires ; but extreme length of conversation is, I believe, precluded by *nature*, and four long speeches no *art* ought to insist upon making, after the powerful hand of death is *felt* in the blow."

From Boaden, then, I have taken, not only those illuminating reflections from the splendour of Mrs. Siddons's flaming tragedy that will be found in their due position as the portrait grows ; but also a sense of the young woman's grace and loveliness and a witness to the singleness of heart and clearness of spirit that remained with her through life so that, like all immortals, she kept something childlike about her to the end. And, amongst the rest, in the Supplement to the second edition of Boaden's Memoir, I have found one of those echoes to the very seat where love is throned that gives the sense of holding a personal friendship with the lady who uttered it. Mrs. Siddons, it appears, could never laugh at the story of John Gilpin. And indeed, when, in ankle-straps and a sash, I was myself obliged to get his ballad by heart, I too considered it a most doleful tale. It was to Boswell that the great woman confided her feelings :

> " Here," said Mrs. Siddons, " is a worthy and industrious citizen, who, although married twenty years, had never yielded to the natural desire of a day's pleasure in the country. At length, with very prudential arrangement, the family set off for the Bell, at Edmonton, in a chaise and pair. Mr. Gilpin, for himself, borrows a friend's horse, to save expense ; but the unruly animal soon distresses his unskilful rider—his hat and wig are jostled from his head, and the home-made wine which he carries, by the shattering of the bottles, lays the dust upon the road instead of cheering the spirits of the party. When he arrives in sight of his family at the Bell, he is not permitted to *join* them—the horse, knowing that his real master had a house at Ware, decides upon going the whole of his accustomed route. At Ware the harassed traveller arrives, and his friend refits him with good humour, and invites him to dinner. But here his *honour* is concerned, and he resolves, on his wedding-day to dine with his wife, cost what it will. So off he sets on his return, again to ride bare-headed upon a frightened steed ; and never ends his torments until he reaches, not Edmonton, but London. And I should be glad to know what there is in all this for any *reflecting* creature to laugh at ? "

What indeed ? Dear, tender-hearted, sensible, indignant Mrs. Siddons !

4

Finally, when almost a hundred volumes had been searched and more than a hundred pictures and sketches had been looked at and put away, there came memories and ghosts to add their shadows or enhance, by the contrasts they offered, the high lights of my picture. I had seen, as a girl, Ellen Terry, flowerlike and lovely in her maturity, crying so pitifully and with such floods of real, disfiguring tears as she lay, Queen Guinevere, at the feet of Irving's King Arthur in a gorgeous pre-Raphaelite play, that all her make-up was washed into streaks and she had to leave the stage, her hands spread over her ravaged face. And these tears seemed to me, as I sat remembering them, clear and crystalline and adorable, as the tears of Mrs. Siddons's Desdemona and her Imogen must have been.

I had sat, rigid and shaken by turns, while Sarah Bernhardt, wearing huge turquoises on her tormented hands and in the belt that held the clouds of her white drapery together, moaned from the great chair of Theseus as Phèdre, sick with desire and remorse. And, remembering how the day after this performance I had wandered about the streets of Geneva, losing my way, forgetting to go home to *déjeuner*, dazed with the explosive force of the genius unleashed in the theatre overnight, I bethought me that the only play by Racine in which, so far as I know, Mrs. Siddons ever made a notable appearance was *Andromache*, and that this had been translated and reduced to the title *The Distressed Mother*.

I remembered the excitement of the days when Gilbert Murray's smooth and sounding versions of the Greek tragedies drew us all, young and eager then, to the Court Theatre, and wondered, if she had had such lines as those to speak, whether Mrs. Siddons would have persisted in her refusal to play Medea, as she also refused the part of Shakespeare's Cleopatra, saying she dared not play it as it should be played, and would not play it any other way.

I remembered too that both Sarah Bernhardt and Sarah Siddons had found a release for the superabundance of their artistic creativeness in practising the art of sculpture : but this does not seem to me to be so important a coincidence as it has done to other, possibly acuter, psychological investigators. Also it is more than probable that the French woman was the better sculptor.

I remembered the story of the Archduke who, desiring to convey his royal favour to the great Rachel, sent her during a performance a fold of paper containing three scrawled words

" Quand ? Où ? Combien ? "

and received by his own messenger and before he had left the box the written answer

" Ce soir. Chez moi. Pour rien."

And I saw how wide a chasm divided the greatness of the actress who could answer arrogance with so magnificent a generosity and scorn, and the greatness that linked the most terrific dramatic genius that has manifested itself in man or woman on any stage since there has been a credible record of the theatre, with the person of a lady in whom all domestic virtues met in a fullness that many an Anglican bishop might be not only proud but even a little surprised to observe in the walk and conduct of his most carefully selected wife.

And one night, in the semi-delirium of influenza, just as I was getting the finished portrait ready for press I found myself in a half dream wandering down narrow, dirty passages lit by candles, or by oil-lamps in sconces, on the wooden beams dividing white-washed walls, and knew I was behind the scenes at Drury Lane Theatre a hundred and fifty years ago during the performance of a play. Suddenly, down the narrow way between the wall and the wrong side of a wing of scenery, there came, hurrying towards me, a tall figure in green and white Renaissance costume wearing enormous jewels of pinchbeck and coloured glass. Her face was crudely painted in crimson and chalk white: the curls that flowed over one shoulder from under her crown were of horsehair, black and glistening. As she came I was conscious of an explosion of rage or of violent passion that had nothing to do with me—whom indeed the portent ignored.

"I am Almeyda the Queen"

she said in an extraordinary and blood-chilling voice.

When I was well enough to investigate the possible substance of this dream I verified the part as one played by Mrs. Siddons in a play *Almeyda Queen of*

Granada written by Miss Sophia Lee, a schoolmistress and author who lived in Bath and wrote another and more successful work *A Chapter of Accidents*.

Looking at all the material before me, even with everything I had been obliged to discard swept away, I realized that the background of my picture must be a little confused, a little crowded, even as the workaday years of my subject had been. I saw that the Cloudy Symbols of the professional and social triumphs I desired to place about the figure of the woman herself, must appear as the artifices and simulacra they actually were, and I realized that, when at last I came to write of the woman herself, I must move humbly and with gentleness because this woman was as good as she was great and in seeking for the truth about her I had come to know and to love her as a friend.

II

CHRONOLOGICAL

I<small>N ORDER</small> to steady the reader's mind before attempting to present the crowded panorama of Mrs. Siddons's public triumphs, and the sometimes delicate and always engrossing tangle of her private relationships, I place here a skeleton, hinged together with dates, which can be disregarded at this point by those who do not much care for precision in a reconstructed tale, and used as a reference later on, when the story returns on its own tracks, as it is bound to do.

CHRONOLOGICAL TABLE
of
THE LIFE OF MRS. SIDDONS
with
Some References to Contemporary Events

GEORGE II. 1727–1760

1755. Sarah, daughter of Roger Kemble and Sarah Ward his wife, born on July 5th at the Shoulder of Mutton Inn in Brecon.

1757. *Clive begins conquest of India.*

GEORGE III. 1760–1820

1760. *Publication of "La Nouvelle Héloïse."*

MATERIALS FOR A PORTRAIT

1768. *Royal Academy founded with Sir Joshua Reynolds as first President.*

1769. Birth at Bristol on May 4th of Thomas Lawrence, son of the innkeeper of the White Lion.
Watt takes out his first patent for the steam-engine.

1773. Sarah Kemble married William Siddons an actor in her father's company on November 26th.

1774. Henry Siddons born.
"*Sorrows of Werther*" *published.*

1775. *Birth of Jane Austen.*
Sally Siddons born at Gloucester. Mrs. Siddons plays Portia to Garrick's Shylock and Lady Anne to his Gloucester at Drury Lane and fails to please the town.

1776. Mrs. Siddons returns to the provinces and plays Lady Randolph for the first time. She sits for the portrait by Gilbert Stuart now in the National Gallery.
Declaration of American Independence.

1777. First performance of *The School for Scandal*.

1779. Maria Siddons born at Bath where Mrs. Siddons is now settled.

1780. Thomas Lawrence, aged eleven, is brought by his parents from Oxford to Bath, where he works as a portrait painter.

1781. A female child, which dies in infancy, born to Mrs. Siddons.
Birth of George Stephenson.

1782. Mrs. Siddons leaves Bath and returns to Drury Lane where she plays Isabella in *The Fatal Marriage* and is successful.

1783. Publication of engravings after the portraits of Master T. Lawrence by himself and of the same young gentleman's famous picture of Mrs. Siddons as Zara in Congreve's *Mourning Bride*. Mrs. Siddons plays Lady Randolph at Drury Lane and rivals Mrs. Crawford in that part.

1784. Reynolds exhibits his picture of Mrs. Siddons as the Tragick Muse.

1785. Mrs. Siddons plays Lady Macbeth, for the first time in London, and sits to Gainsborough for his famous portrait now in the National Gallery. Birth of George Siddons.

1787. Thomas Lawrence comes to London as portrait painter.
Birth of Edmund Kean.

1788. Mrs. Siddons plays Queen Katharine in *Henry VIII*.
Trial of Warren Hastings.

1789. First performance of Volumnia by Mrs. Siddons.
Fall of the Bastille : French Revolution begins.

1791. Old Drury Lane Theatre demolished. Thomas Lawrence is made A.R.A.

1792. Thomas Lawrence succeeds Sir Joshua Reynolds as Principal Painter to King George III.

1793. *Louis XVI and Marie Antoinette guillotined.*

1794. New Drury Lane opens with Kemble as Macbeth and Mrs. Siddons as Lady Macbeth. Birth of Cecilia Siddons.

1797. Lawrence exhibits *Satan Summoning up his Legions*.
Victory off Cape St. Vincent.

1798. *Irish Rebellion.*
Death of Maria Siddons. Mrs. Siddons plays Mrs. Haller in *The Stranger*.
Battle of the Nile.

1799. *Napoleon Bonaparte becomes First Consul.*
Death of George Washington.

MATERIALS FOR A PORTRAIT 51

1800– Kemble and Mrs. Siddons go to Covent Garden
1801. Theatre in opposition to Sheridan, where Kemble opens as Hamlet, Mrs. Siddons as Isabella.

1802. Mrs. Siddons's Irish tour. Kitty Gough Galindo and Mr. Galindo come to Covent Garden.
Peace of Amiens.

1803. Death of Sally Siddons.

1804. *Napoleon I crowned by the Pope.*
Birth of Benjamin Disraeli.
Lawrence exhibits portrait of Mrs. Siddons giving a reading at Court. Mrs. Siddons goes to Bath. Holiday in Wales, Wye Valley and Ireland.

1805. The Kembles return to Covent Garden.
Austerlitz.
Trafalgar.

1806. *Jena.*

1808. Death of William Siddons. Covent Garden Theatre burnt. Mrs. Siddons loses all her jewellery and lace and other stage properties.
"Faust" Part I published.

1809. O.P. Riots. Mrs. Galindo's letter.
Gas-light used in Pall Mall.
Birth of Abraham Lincoln.
Birth of Mr. Gladstone.

1811. *First canto of "Childe Harold" published.*
Birth of Thackeray.

REGENCY. 1811–1820

1812. Mrs. Siddons plays Lady Macbeth for the last time on June 7th, and retires from the stage.
Birth of Charles Dickens.

1813. *Publication of "Pride and Prejudice."*

1814. *First steam-locomotive, Stephenson's "My Lord," makes its trial run.*

Publication of "Waverley."

Kean plays Shylock at Drury Lane.

1815. Death of Henry Siddons. Sir Thomas Lawrence knighted.

Battle of Waterloo.

Corn Law Riots.

1816. Death of Sheridan.

Birth of Charlotte Brontë.

1819. *Birth of Queen Victoria.*

Publication of Shelley's "The Cenci" and the first two cantos of Byron's "Don Juan."

GEORGE IV. 1820–1830

1820. Sir Thomas Lawrence becomes President of the Royal Academy.

1823. Death of John Philip Kemble.

1825. *Opening of the Stockton and Darlington Railway on September 27th.*

1829. Mrs. Siddons sees Fanny Kemble's début as Juliet on October 25th.

1830. Death in January of Sir Thomas Lawrence, aged sixty.

WILLIAM IV. 1830–1837

1831. Mrs. Siddons dies in Upper Baker Street on the 8th of June, aged seventy-six, and is buried at Paddington near her villa of Westbourne Farm.

PART II

The Background

Copyright National Portrait Gallery

MRS. SIDDONS AT THE AGE OF TWENTY-ONE

I

THE ROAD

1

IN THE city of Hereford, immediately opposite to the Church of St. Xavier in Broad Street, stands the Kemble Theatre now a movie-palace glittering in the neo-Teutonic mode with black enamel and chromium plated walls, once the barn to which the Kemble Players came at regular intervals of their tour of the Kemble Circuit during the middle years of the eighteenth century. A little further on where Maylord Street and Widemarsh join one another at the Raven Inn, David Garrick was born. On an island site at one end of High Town, the open space where the Bull Ring, the Maypole and the Market Cross once made the central points of the city's communal life, stands the Old House, an ancient monument now restored to its Elizabethan richness and angularity, and still yielding fresco and painted beam and mud and wattle wall-fillings to the careful exploration of its custodian. In 1929 a Siddons Centenary Exhibition was held in the Old House, the upper floors of which are always devoted to an interesting permanent collection of Kemble relics. These include a magnificent gold snuffbox, with a Roman scene in relief on its lid, presented to John Philip Kemble as a tribute to his impersonation of

Cato, Coriolanus and other rôles in which, following his own then most courageous innovation, he had played in a toga instead of in the height of contemporary tailoring: and several alarmingly bad copies of the loveliest of all the portraits of Mrs. Siddons herself.

No one can be long in Hereford without coming upon tangible evidence of the connection of the Kemble family with the city where indeed Roger Kemble was born in 1721 and in due time became apprenticed to a hairdresser there. By the time he was thirty, his good looks; his fine manners; the great use he had made of such educational advantages as a barber's apprentice in the first half of the eighteenth century might come by, had justified him in changing his profession and he joined a company of those strolling players, who, revolving in their orbits, passed through Hereford and whirled the aspiring actor as far south as Canterbury and back again, till they came to Stratford-on-Avon. Here the manager, an Irishman called John Ward, gave a special benefit performance the proceeds of which were devoted to recolouring the painted tomb then standing dim and neglected with its threatening inscription over the grave that held the remains of the playwright whom neither Mr. Ward himself nor any member of his company dreamt of calling anything but the Bard.

The handsome young man, who persisted in claiming that his name was but a corruption of the nobler Campbell and that he was a collateral of the Kembles of Pembridge Castle and of the martyred John Kemble who was hanged on

Widemarsh Common in 1679, succeeded in marrying his manager's daughter Sally. The famous *mot* attributed to almost every theatrical manager on a like occasion : " I vowed that my daughter should never marry an actor and she has not " was probably originated by Mr. Ward who was himself prouder of his gentility than of his histrionic successes. His grave in the church at Leominster still bears the inscription :

> " Here waiting for the Saviour's great assize
> And hoping, through His merits, hence to rise
> In glorious mode, in this dark closet lies—
>
> JOHN WARD, *Gent* ;
>
> Who died Oct. 30th 1773 aged 69 years
> Also Sarah, *his Wife*,
> Who died Jan. 30th 1786 aged 75 years."

The saying that it takes three generations to make a gentleman throws a side-light here on the success of John Ward's grandson in society and, more conspicuously, on that of his majestic grand-daughter as a hostess to the critical and malicious wits and beauties of London at a time when old Mrs. Ward was still alive and able to enjoy the news of her grandchildren's ascent of the social scale.

It is certain that, all through the lives of Roger Kemble, and John Philip and Sarah Siddons, his children, some connection with the more fortunate family of the same name was assumed to exist. To-day, both in Monmouth from which the annual pilgrimage to the martyr's grave still takes place, and in Hereford where his embalmed left hand now lies in a magnificent reliquary in the Church of St. Xavier, it is possible to buy copies of the following ballad :

"THE PILGRIMS

'Twas in the shire of Hereford
  Not far from the banks of Wye,
That once at eve two strangers came
  To a village hostelry.
They took small heed of the jolly host,
  With his busy, cheerful air—
With his smile of greeting for every guest,
  And his good old English fare.

Upon some grave and solemn thought
  They both appeared intent,
And for the Sexton of the place
  In eager haste they sent.
And as the Sexton tarried long
  Those two walked forth alone,
Where the Churchyard trees wave mournfully
  O'er many a mouldering stone.

One was a man of noble part,
  With an eye of fiery pride,
With something of the Roman brow,
  And of the Imperial stride ;
And when he spoke in measured phrase,
  His full-toned voice did sound
Like the deep low murmur of the sea
  Heard in a cave profound.

The other was a lady bright,
  With such a form and face
As Grecian genius loved to dream,
  And Grecian art to trace ;

THE BACKGROUND

Much like the man, or rather like
　　His image glorified—
As if a sister goddess walked
　　By a mortal brother's side.

And now the Sexton came, and doffed
　　His cap with reverence meet,
But started at the lady's voice,
　　So thrilling 'twas, and sweet.
' Good man,' she said, ' we sent for you
　　If haply you might know
Where Father Kemble was interred
　　Many a long year ago.

' He was a good and pious priest,
　　Who in these parts abode,
And blameless to extreme old age
　　Pursued his peaceful road,
Till, in the Second Charles's reign,
　　The bigots of the time
Falsely accused and murdered him,
　　Though guiltless of a crime.'

' Oh, well,' the Sexton said, ' I mind
　　The stone above his clay ;
For all the country round retains
　　His memory to this day !
And I have heard the old men tell
　　(Who had it from their sires)
The piteous story of his end,
　　Beside their Christmas fires.

' They took him up to London town,
　　And long they kept him there,
While perjured villains were employed
　　Against his life to swear ;

And further still their spite to wreak,
  And work his body woe,
From London unto Hereford
  On foot they made him go.

' *And in a field without the town*
  They raised a gibbet high,
And there in torture, and in shame,
  This old man was to die;
But nothing shook his courage stout,
  His conscience being free,
And he went to meet his cruel death
  With a frank and hearty glee.

' *And they say he stopped upon his road*
  At some remembered door,
To smoke the friendly, social pipe,
  As he was wont of yore;
And in these parts, where custom still
  Preserves each ancient type,
The man who takes a parting puff,
  Calls it his KEMBLE-PIPE.

' *The people wept, the people moaned,*
  As round him they did throng;
The very hangman pardon asked
  For that unhallowed wrong.
" Disquiet not thyself ! " he cried,
  " Honest friend Anthony !
Thou dost me a great kindness, friend,
  And no discourtesy.

' *" For I am old, my race is run,*
  'Tis time for me to pause,
Nor would I seek a better death
  Than in my Master's cause,

THE BACKGROUND

And for that ancient Church, which still
    Upon a rock doth stand,
And which alone, in early days,
    Made this a Christian land."

'*Well, well! he was a Papist blind,*
    And that was Popish rant,
And I, thank God,' *the Sexton said,*
    '*Am a true Protestant.*
But men are men (howe'er in birth
    Or creed the difference lies),
And that old story oft has brought
    The tears into my eyes!'

The Stranger grasped the Sexton's arm:
    '*O lead us to the place,*
Where lies that holy man, for we
    Are of his name and race;
And prouder are we of the thoughts
    Which such a memory brings,
Than if within our veins there flowed
    The blood of twenty kings.

'*Is this the little mound of turf?*
    Is this the old grey stone?
Take, Sexton, take this coin of gold,
    And leave us here alone!
And, sister, 'twill not shame the light,
    Which modern schools impart,
If here we render to the dead
    The homage of the heart!'

The greatest actor of his age
    Was he, and high his fame;
The greatest actress of all time
    Was she that with him came;

And oft, upon the tragic scene,
  Their genius did control
And stir, e'en to its inmost depths,
  A mighty nation's soul.

And yet, when the half-waking Lear
  His child, Cordelia, pressed,
Or the relenting Roman clasped
  His Mother to his breast,
Or Israel for Claudio prayed [1]
  With pure and eloquent breath,
Or Heaven's own Angels bowed to gaze
  On Katherine's saintly death.

Methinks, that all those glorious scenes,
  Which Shakespere's art endears,
Drew from no higher, holier source
  The fount of sacred tears—
Than did the feelings of that hour
  When, 'mid the deepening gloom,
The Kemble, and the Siddons knelt
  At the old martyr's tomb!"

This anonymous example of modern folk-song is based on a story that when, in 1805, Mrs. Siddons, in company with her brother, took a holiday from fame and retraced in the Wye Valley the travels of their youth and hardship, they visited Father John Kemble's grave in the churchyard at Welsh Newton. Finding it in bad repair, Mrs. Siddons is said to have thereafter contributed a small sum towards its upkeep. This story, apocryphal though it may be, chimes with her known action in helping to restore once again the bust at Stratford so gaudily painted

---

[1] So the text: the reference is to Isabella in *Measure for Measure*—oddly enough not one of Mrs. Siddons's conspicuously successful parts.

through the efforts of her maternal grandfather, and in any case has its place, even as legend in the background of her portrait.

Whatever claims to gentility the arrogance of Ward the Irishman may have induced Roger Kemble his son-in-law to make in proving himself Miss Ward's social equal, there is no doubt that the status of a strolling player in the eighteenth century was as a rule little better than that of a gypsy, and that the companies of actors, wandering from town to village, from village to wayside barn, pushing the tinsel and bunting of their properties on hand-carts along the muddy roads, were often, and sometimes deservedly treated as rogues and vagabonds.

The more respectable companies usually consisted of the Manager and his family, and one or two players who were, if young, treated as children under the lady's chaperonage. Boaden has preserved for us the words of a handbill announcing the appeal of the manager of one of such a troupe for assistance on the occasion of his wife's approaching confinement.

"At the old theatre in East Grinstead, on Saturday, May 1758, will be represented (by particular desire, and for the benefit of Mrs. P.) the deep and affecting tragedy of *Theodosius*, or *The Force of Love*, with magnificent scenes, dresses, &c.

"*Varanes* by Mr. P. who will strive, as far as possible, to support the character of this fiery Persian Prince, in which he was so much admired and applauded at Hastings, Arundel, Petworth, Midhurst, Lewes, &c.

"*Theodosius* by a young gentleman from the University of Oxford, who never appeared on any stage.

"*Athenais* by Mrs. P. Though her present condition will not permit her to wait on gentlemen and ladies out of the town with tickets, she hopes, as on former occasions, for their liberality and support.

"Nothing in Italy can exceed the altar in the first scene of the play. Nevertheless, should any of the Nobility or Gentry wish to see it ornamented with flowers, the bearer will *bring away* as many as they chuse to favour him with.

"As the coronation of *Athenais*, to be introduced in the fifth act, contains a number of personages more than sufficient to fill all the dressing rooms, &c. it is hoped no gentlemen and ladies will be offended, at being refused admission behind the scenes.

"N.B. The great yard-dog, that made so much noise on Thursday night, during the last act of *King Richard the Third*, will be sent to a neighbour's over the way; and on account of the prodigious demand for places, part of the *stable* will be laid into the boxes on one side, and the *granary* open for the same purpose, on the other.

"Vivat Rex."

It was in circumstances not unlike those behind the scenes of this piteous announcement that, on the 5th of July 1755, in a room of the Shoulder of Mutton Inn in Brecon, John Ward's daughter, Sarah Kemble, gave birth to her first child, a daughter. The infant was named after its mother and grandmother and, ten days later, was baptized at St. Mary's Church, a Protestant baby, though her brothers, according to agreement, were later to be made Roman Catholics like their father.

Travelling up and down the Marches; going westward to Brecon and eastward to Stratford-on-Avon;

northward to Prescott in Lancashire where Roger and Sarah Kemble's second child John Philip was born, it is still possible to collect traces of the journeys—on Kemble's own particular circuit through Staffordshire, Gloucestershire and Worcestershire and on the tangents from it— through which little Sally Kemble was first carried as an infant in the property cart (or by stage-coach when there was enough money for such indulgence) on the earliest of those professional journeys she was never to cease from making throughout the sixty years of her player's life.

There is no record of her first appearance on any stage. She may, for all we know, have entered before she was weaned, in the arms of some forgotten Paulina to her own father playing Leontes in the second act of *The Winter's Tale*. The peeling of an old wall at Cheltenham; the demolition of a tithe barn in Worcester, may, to-morrow, bring to light the playbill[1] of some performance of *The Fatal Marriage* in which, as Biron's child, she toddled after an Isabella whose ravings she was one day to make more piteous than any yet heard upon the stage.

There is a story that some young officers of a regiment quartered at Tonbridge, having decided to amuse themselves by playing *The Grecian Daughter* in a barn behind the Old Bell Inn, in that town, co-opted the player's daughter who, too young to be politic, burst into a fit of giggles when the amateur tragedian reached what should have been

[1] Fitzgerald speaks of one such playbill of the Kemble Company found pasted on the brick wall of a shoemaker's shop in Warwickshire during rebuilding operations in 1870.

Es

his most effective scene. If this be true it shows that little Sally Siddons was possessed of that sense of humour as a child, denied to the grown woman by many of her historians.

When she was twelve, and at school, like her brother, at Worcester, her parents gave a *Concert of Music* at " the Theatre behind the King's Head " in that town. The concert was but a pretext for a play and the Kemble children's studies were interrupted in order that Sally might act the part of " The Young Princess Elisabeth " while John Philip, aged ten, appeared as " James Duke of York afterwards King of England."

About the same time " The Celebrated comedy called The Tempest ; or, The Enchanted Island, with all the scenery, machinery, music, monster, and the decorations proper to be given entirely new " was played by the whole strength of the Kemble family with " Miss Kemble as Ariel."

But though they occasionally took their children from school to take part in some benefit or extra performance, it is established that Roger and Sarah Kemble were able to provide well enough for their welfare—of body as well as of mind. When in 1767, at the age of ten, John Philip was sent to the Catholic Seminary of Sedgely Park near Wolverhampton, the outfit he brought with him consisted of :

> 4 suits of clothes.
> 12 shirts.
> 12 pairs of stockings.
> 6 pairs of shoes.
> 4 hats.

2 Daily Companions.
1 Half-Manual.
Knives.
Forks.
Spoons.
Aesop's Fables.
1 brush.
1 comb.
8 handkerchiefs.
8 nightcaps.

Little Sally was probably given an equally adequate provision when she too went to school: but the most significant witness to the soundness of her education is the indestructible evidence of those letters written by her as a grown woman. Her various essays in verse too were those of a cultivated mind and, in at least two examples, rose, as we shall see, to the dignity of real poetry. The manuscript letters, still preserved by various members of her family, and in various other collections are written in a clear and flowing hand and with a careful punctuation and use of quotation marks and paragraphing that is even now beyond the power of many a more expensively educated girl.

Mrs. Siddons's letters stand out if only by reason of their polish and fluency, from those of other contemporary beauties. Poor Emma Hamilton wrote and spelled like a nursery maid to the end of her days, and the level of most actresses' literary equipment may be judged from the letters written by the astute Mrs. Jordan, trying to steer her way between the Devil of Sheridan at Drury Lane and the Deep Sea of the Duke of Clarence who thought that a settlement of £1,000 a year should be sufficient to induce the lady to renounce the stage and settle down to playing hostess for him at Bushey House.

The various schools at which, from time to time, little Sarah received intermittent instruction until, at the age of sixteen, she became a regular member of her father's company, must have been as good in their way as those that prepared her brothers John and Charles for the College of Douai where they were sent to complete their education. But another and a more potent influence was to give the ardent and intelligent girl the final experience that, at first seeming to close the gate on any hope of a theatrical career, was to set on her still young and impressionable nature the seal of that distinction of mind and character which makes her still unique among the world's great actresses.

Every biographer who has told the tale has ascribed the stately bearing of Mrs. Siddons in later life in part to the fact that as quite a tiny child she was set in front of the Procession of Players when the time came to enter a town or village on their circuit. A drum was placed on the child's head and she was instructed to march, holding herself very straight, and as tall as might be, while another member of the troupe beat a tattoo on it to announce the arrival of the Kemble players. This, they say, like the carrying of those waterpots which is said to give Egyptian women their majesty of gait, taught the four-year-old child a carriage so firm and commanding that, when she came to play the part of queen and empress, no mock crown was too heavy, no tinsel jewels were too splendid, to diminish the glory of her bearing : but there is another and profounder trace of this childish discipline in the later years of struggle and of triumph that were to make the little daughter of a strolling player the object alternately of the fashionable world's idolatry and the gossips' malignant envy and detraction. Employed thus early " to walk under the drum " she began life with a sense that her public appearance was demanded by private necessity, and that it was her duty in life to act so that those around her might eat and live.

A contemporary of Dolly Jordan and that little queen of gold-diggers " Perdita " Johnson, Mrs. Siddons was, so far as we know, even in the days of her delicious young beauty, never subjected to offers of protection from any of the rich and frivolous admirers by whom she was surrounded. Late in her career, when her aspect had grown so commanding that most men would fear to make amorous advances towards a form so stately, the kind, foolish old king thrust a note into her hand at the end of one of her readings at Buckingham House. Opening it she found it to contain his name written in pencil, and nothing more. She did not stop, as almost any other actress of her day would have done, to wonder if this were His Majesty's way of expressing a private desire for her favours, but, concluding that the furtive bestowal of a mere autograph must be a sign of illness in its author, carried the little paper to the Queen. The readings were broken off, for a time at least, and, in later years, when the mind of George III darkened completely, Mrs. Siddons, remembering this incident, congratulated herself on having detected the on-coming of brain-disease from its outset. She had learnt early in life to set very little value on her personal attractiveness. The child who walked under the drum had been taught pride and independence, as well as common sense and a consciousness of family solidarity in addition to her fine bearing, while she stepped in and out of the villages between Worcester and Stafford at the head of her father's Players.

These lessons, as well as the native energy of her character, prompted her at sixteen to a course that, while at the moment it seemed to put an end to her theatrical career, really paved the way to her future success. She wanted to marry William Siddons, a new recruit to the travelling theatre, and William Siddons wanted to marry her. But she was very young and Siddons was not at all the kind of young actor who gave much promise of rising to fame or fortune. Mr. and Mrs. Kemble reasoned with Sarah, and, after a benefit performance at Brecon where William took advantage of the occasion to recite a long and querulous poem of his own composition, deploring his manager's conduct in the affair, Mrs. Kemble boxed young Siddons's ears and Mr. Kemble dismissed him from the company. And Sarah was sent away: not *with* William, but to Guy's Cliffe in Warwickshire, where she was placed in a situation as maid to the widowed Lady Mary Bertie, daughter of the second Duke of Ancaster. William was allowed to write, and to call once or twice on his young love who received him in the servants' hall. Sally waited on her mistress and " spouted to the servants " and behaved with so much intelligence and decorum that she was soon more companion than maid to the lady who must have been at first, amused by, and then very much interested in, the beautiful young creature. These two years spent in an increasing intimacy with a cultured and aristocratic mistress, amid the well-ordered surroundings of a decent splendour, and with the occasional society of persons whose conversation and deportment must have seemed as strange as they were admirable to the observant and constitutionally imitative girl, have always been admitted by her biographers as most important in forming the manners and the mind of the future queen of the stage. They were also important to her physical well-being as providing a respite from the toil and fatigue of a strolling player's life at the moment when the still growing girl, passing through adolescence with its fervours and emotional strains, most needed the soothing influence of such a life as that of a great country-house set in one of the loveliest and most peaceful landscapes in the kingdom. In later life she was often to return, a welcomed guest, to the house she had first entered as lady's-maid. The day too was to come when a young Bertie Greatheed would bring the manuscript of a tragedy he had written for the great Mrs. Siddons, to Sheridan imploring him to persuade her to play in it, and she was at first to refuse him, because her artistic integrity was offended by the weakness of the character she was asked to take : but this turn of the wheel was far from any dream of hers or of the family she had served when, in 1773, strong in body and very much broadened in mind, she left Guy's Cliffe, married her William and set out on her travels again.

2

At first the young couple toiled round the Kemble Circuit; Worcester, Hereford, Monmouth, Brecon, Stratford, going as far north as Leeds and Sheffield, as far south as Devizes. In the last named town, by the lamplight of an inn parlour, one evening, they saw the door open to admit a little boy riding his hobby-horse, who, when he had pranced once or twice round the big table, sat down at it and drew in coloured chalks an amazing likeness of the young actress, to the delight of all who saw it, but not in the least to the surprise of the innkeeper. This was a man named Lawrence, an ex-parson and lawyer whose regular customers invariably enquired for Master Tom and chose whether the infant phenomenon should draw their portraits or recite Shakespeare and Milton for them.

Young Mrs. Siddons took particular notice of the boy. She was not, at that time, so used to sitting for her portrait as not to be flattered by the spontaneous homage of this child's drawing, and as for reciting, that was her own trade too, and Shakespeare was her text book, Milton her admiration. She took the memory of the pretty boy with her on her travels. Soon she had a boy of her own, Henry Siddons, born in 1774. But she did not settle down to the cares of motherhood. She joined Crump's and then Younger's Company and travelled a wider circuit:

Liverpool, Cheltenham, Gloucester, and attracted the attention of Tate Wilkinson the manager of the Northern Circuit who was to become one of her warmest employers and friends. At Gloucester in 1775 her eldest daughter, the tragic, gentle Sally, was born on the 5th of November, just in time to enable her mamma to recover sufficient strength to travel off to London to play Portia, at Drury Lane, not to Garrick's but to Mr. King's Shylock, on December 27th. She also walked on as Venus in a pageant that followed the play, and essayed various comedy rôles in none of which she made any mark. Finally she was allotted the part of Lady Anne when Garrick gave *Richard III* for his own farewell performance.

The poor girl was not a success in this tragic rôle any more than she had been in the comedy parts she essayed. Richard III was Garrick's part: the whole play was produced for him. The *London Magazine* reporting on this farewell performance gave all its space, as was proper, to Garrick's impersonation, ending:

> "As to most of the other characters, particularly the female ones, they were wretchedly played. Mrs. Hopkins was an ungracious Queen, Mrs. Johnston a frightful Duchess, Mrs. Siddons a lamentable Lady Anne."

So, off on her travels the young actress started once more, lucky even to be able to get provincial engagements after her failure in London. It was the same Sally as had walked under the drum who, sick with the mortification of her defeat, roused herself " for the sake of my poor children " and, aged twenty-one, with a husband and two babies to fend for, set off, not exactly on circuit this time, but to fulfil engagements of a few weeks at a time, all over the country. From London she went, first to Birmingham, then to Hull ; to York ; to Manchester ; to Hereford ; and to Liverpool, where encouraged by Wilkinson she played Hamlet, as she had played Rosalind, in a costume of the most inconvenient modesty.

The Siddons couple, though still poor, were by this time not so poor as to stroll any longer. They performed the tedious, boggy, dangerous journeys between these places by stage-coach, staying at inns by the way. It took days between one town and another when engagements could not be fitted in. And here again Mrs. Siddons's magnificent health aided her. She recovered from the strain of acting in London so soon after Sally's birth (Mrs. Clement Parsons attributes her failure with Garrick partly to the state of her health at this moment) and had a respite from child-bearing while she travelled and acted all over the kingdom. She did not at this time undergo the ordeal of the six days' travel by land and sea between London and Dublin ; but two descriptions of the hardships and distractions of this and of another journey she took, may well be quoted here. They are both taken from letters to her friends Dr. and Mrs. Whalley of Bath. The first of them relates to her journey to Ireland in 1783 in company with her husband and William Brereton who played opposite her in all Kemble's parts on this tour.

THE BACKGROUND

"We got very safe to Holyhead, and then I felt as if some great event was going to take place, having never been on the sea. I was awed, but not terrified; feeling myself in the hands of a great and powerful God 'whose mercy is over all his works.' The sea was particularly rough; we were lifted mountain high, and sank again as low in an instant. Good God! how tremendous, how wonderful! A pleasing terror took hold on me, which it is impossible to describe, and I never felt the majesty of the Divine Creator so fully before. I was dreadfully sick. . . . Mr. Siddons was pretty well.

"Here, my dear friend, let me give you a little wholesome advice: allways (you see I have forgot to spell) go to bed the instant you go on board for by lying horizontally, and keeping very quiet, you cheat the sea of half its influence.

"We arrived in Dublin at half-past twelve at night . . . and do you know, I was obliged, after being shut up in the Customs-house officer's room, to have the things examined, which room was more like a dungeon than anything else—after staying here above an hour and a half, I tell you, I was obliged, sick and weary as I was, to wander about the streets on foot (for the coaches and chairs were all gone off the stands) till almost two o'clock in the morning, raining too, as if heaven and earth were coming together."

There is an indestructible good humour visible through the storm and rain of this account of arriving at the Irish capital where every inn, hotel or lodging-house was closed to women after nightfall. Small wonder that Mrs. Siddons, normally the least self-regarding of travellers, spoke of "journeying through storm and tempest to fulfil engagements in savage wildernesses."

The next extract is famous, but it must be quoted

once more, and this time as evidence that the writer was not always solemn, and might well be excused her own not entirely unfounded conviction that at this period of her life she could play comedy. It is taken from a letter written to her friends in Bath when she had left that city for London in 1782. Travelling, clearly, had few terrors for a woman who could plan to journey from Bath to London by way of Dorchester and Weymouth!

"We were five of us in the machine, all females but one, a youth of about sixteen, and the most civilized being you can conceive, a native of Bristol too.

"One of the ladies was, I believe verily, a little insane, her dress was the most peculiar, and manner the most offensive, I ever remember to have met with; her person was taller and more thin than you can imagine, her hair raven black, drawn as tight as possible over her cushion before and behind, and at the top of her head was placed a solitary fly-cap of the last century, composed of materials of about twenty sorts, and as dirty as the ground; her neck, which was a thin scrag of a quarter of a yard long, and the colour of a walnut, she wore uncovered for the solace of all beholders; her Circassian was an olive-coloured cotton of three several sorts, about two breadths wide in the skirt, and tied up exactly in the middle in one place only. She had a black petticoat, spotted with red, and over that a very thin white muslin one, with a long black gauze apron, and without the least hoop. I never in my life saw so odd an appearance, and my opinion was not singular, for wherever we stopped, she inspired either mirth or amazement, but was quite innocent of it herself. On taking her seat amongst us at Bristol, she flew into a violent passion on seeing one of the windows down. I said I would put it up if she pleased ; ' To be sure,' said she, ' I have no ambition to catch my death.' No sooner had she done with me, but she began to scold the woman who sat opposite to her for touching her foot : ' You have not been used to riding in a *coach*, I fancy, good woman.' She met in this lady a little more spirit than she had found in me, and we were obliged to her for keeping this unhappy woman in tolerable order the remainder of the day. Bless me ! I had almost forgot to tell you that I was desired to make tea at breakfast. Vain were my endeavours to please this strange creature ; she had desired to have her tea in a basin, and I followed her directions as near as it was possible in the making of her tea, but she had no sooner tasted it than she bounced to the window and threw it out, declaring she had never met with such a set of awkward, ill-bred people ; what could be expected in a stage-coach, indeed ? She snatched the canister from me, poured a great quantity into the basin, with sugar, cream, and water, and drank it all together.

"Did you ever hear of anything so strange ? When we sat down to dinner, she seemed terrified to death lest anybody should eat but herself. The remaining part of our journey was made almost intolerable by her fretfulness ; one minute she was screaming out lest the coachman should overturn us ; she was sure he would, because she would not give him anything for neglecting to keep her trunk dry ; and, though it was immoderately hot, we were obliged very often to sit with the windows up, for she had been told that the air was pestilential after sunset, and that, however other people liked it, she did not choose to hazard her life by sitting with the windows open. All were disposed, for the sake of peace, to let her have her own way, except the person whom we were really obliged to for quieting her every now and then. She had been handsome, but was now, I suppose, sixty years old. I pity her temper, and am sorry for her situation, which I have set down as that of a disappointed old maid.

"At about seven o'clock we arrived at Dorchester."

This was a journey for pleasure as was her subsequent voyage to Calais to visit her daughters at school there some years later. But even then, and in a foreign country, the habit of travel was strong with her and she made nothing of going by *diligence* to Lille, there to witness a performance by a company of French players whose lively gestures and dramatic inflections enabled her to follow the sense of a play though she understood no word of the language in which it was spoken.

It was not until the end of her days, when she was the idol of the three capitals, that Mrs. Siddons could allow herself the luxury of her own private carriage, and even so, on returning to Ireland she had to leave it behind her and depended for her outings on the chaise and pair of Mr. P. Galindo; with what unforeseen and calamitous results the world was not to know until, in 1809, the O.P. riots made her and her brother so unpopular for a time that any malignant gossip about them was sure of a hearing.

Ireland, indeed, never was anything but a distressful country to Mrs. Siddons although she was, occasionally, entertained at the great houses in and around Dublin during her tours. When she faced the horrors of the road in order to play in Cork and Limerick after her Dublin season was over, and toiled back to Dublin again to take part in a benefit for the Irish actor Digges, she found herself involved in one of those inextricable tangles of cross-purposes, hurt feelings, real malice and complete misunderstanding that so flourish in the emotional effervescence of the Irish temper and in the queer mixture of vanity and good nature that distinguishes the atmosphere of theatrical life behind the scenes.

She did actually play for Digges, but she was said to have played badly, and the company she played with was unable to rise to the heights of *Venice Preserved*, the play chosen for the occasion. The roar of recrimination that followed the performance reached London and Mrs. Siddons was obliged to defend herself from the stage against the vociferous indignation of the pit and gallery on her reappearance at Drury Lane. Among the rather confused excuses she offered for such part of the story brought against her as was true, she, very wisely, did not include her own belief that Digges was the author of the following communication to the Press preserved for our wonder in an anthology edited by John Edwin of Dublin, and published in 1802, under the title *Pills to Purge Melancholy*.

" On Saturday Mrs. Siddons, about whom all the World has been talking, exposed her beautiful, adamantine, soft, and lovely Person for the first time at the Theatre Royal, Smock-Alley, in the bewitching, melting and all-tearful Character of Isabella. From the repeated panegyrics in the impartial London Newspapers, we were taught to expect the sight of an heavenly Angel, but how were we supernaturally surprised into the most awful joy at beholding a mortal Goddess!

" The house was crowded with hundreds more than

it could hold, with thousands of admiring spectators that went away without a sight. This extraordinary Phænomenon of Tragic excellence! this Star of Melpomene! this Comet of the Stage! this sun of the firmament of the Muses! this Moon of blank verse! this Queen and Princess of tears! this Donnellan of the poisoned bowl! this Empress *Rusty Fusty* of the pistol and dagger! this Chaos of Shakespeare! this World of weeping clouds! this Juno of commanding aspect! this Terpsichore of the curtain and scenes! This Proserpine of fire and earthquake! this Katterfelto of wonders, exceeded expectation, went beyond belief, and soared above all the powers of description! She was Nature itself!—She was the most exquisite work of art! She was the very daisy, primrose, tuberose, sweet-briar, furze-blossom, gilliflower, wall-flower, cauliflower, auricula, and rosemary; in short, she was the Bouquet of Parnassus.

"Where expectation was raised so high, it was thought she would be injured by her appearance—but it was the audience who were injured. Several fainted even before the curtain drew up!—but when she came to the scene of parting with her wedding-ring, ah! what a sight was there! The very fiddlers in the Orchestra, albeit, unused to melting mood, blubbered like hungry children crying for their bread and butter; and when the bell rang for music between the acts, the tears ran from the bassoon player's eyes in such plentiful showers, that they choaked the finger stops, and making a spout of the instrument, poured in such a torrent on the first fiddler's book, that not seeing the Overture was in two sharps, the leader of the band actually played in one flat.

"But the sobs and sighs of the groaning audience, and the noise of the corks drawn from the smelling bottles, prevented the mistake between the flats and the sharps being discovered.

"One hundred and nine ladies fainted! forty-six went into fits! and ninety-five had strong hysterics! The world will scarcely credit the truth when they are told that fourteen children, five old women, a one-handed sailor, and six common-council men, were actually drowned in the inundation of tears, that flowed from the galleries, lattices, and boxes, to encrease the briny pond in the pit. The water was three feet deep, and the people that were obliged to stand upon the benches, were in that position up to their ankles in tears!

"An Act of Parliament against her playing any more will certainly pass, for she has infected all the Volunteers, and they sit reading the Fatal Marriage, crying and roaring the whole morning, at the expectation of seeing this Giant's Causeway, this Salmon Leap of wonders at night! An address has been presented to the good Earl of Charlemont by the principal Volunteers, and backed by Doctor Quin and the Faculty of Dublin, praying him to stay at home the evening of her appearance, else they are convinced she'll tear his infirm frame in pieces with her terrific forearms, when she's dragged from the Corpse of Biron, and they'll lose the greatest General that ever headed an army. Nature, must assuredly, in one of her bountiful moments, in one of her charitable and humane leisure hours, in one of her smiling days, in one of her happy weeping months, and in one of her all-sorrowing gladsome years, have made this human lump of clayey perfection.

"Oh! happy Hibernia, blessed Ierne, sanctified land of Saints, what a hearse load, what a coffin full, what a church-yard tree of the brightest excellence of excellencies now stands on the turf of thy fruitful earth!

"From Cork, from Killarney, from Galway, from Ballinasloe, from Eyrecourt, from the East, from the West, from the North, from the South, from Island-Bridge, from Lazor's-Hill, from the banks of the Canal

Fs

to the New Road, at the back of Drumcondra, shall millions come to Smock-Alley, to see this astonishing woman!

"The streets round the Theatre shall be crowded, and the very Gabbards that carry coals to Island-Bridge shall stop at the Blind-Quay, and land their unpolished Watermen to spend thirteen-pence for a seat in the upper gallery when Isabella is performed!

"O thou universal Genius, what pity it is that thy talents are so confined to Tragedy alone! No age—nay, the Roman Theatre, the Stage at Constantinople—Nero himself never performed the scene of madness, of grief, of joy, of woe, of distress, of sorrow, and of pity, so well as Mrs. Siddons!

"May the curses of an insulted nation pursue the gentlemen of the College, the gentlemen of the Bar, and the Peers and Peeresses, whose wisdom and discernment have been so highly extolled, that hissed her on the second night. True it is, Mr. Garrick never could make any thing of her, and pronounced her below mediocrity—true it is, the London audience once did not like her; but what of that? Rise up bright Goddess of the Sock and Buskin, and soar to unknown Regions of immortal Praise, for

"'Envy will merit as its shade pursue.'"

The wonder is, after such a Press notice, not only that she did consent to play for Digges many years later, but that she ever consented to undertake the horrors of Irish travel, and the uncertainties of an Irish welcome a second time.

She fared better at Edinburgh. When she first went there in 1784 the audiences she attracted were so crowded that the General Assembly, as ever at odds with the theatre, happening to be in session at the time, there was, as Mackenzie testifies,

" great difficulty in procuring a full attendance of its members on those evenings when she was to perform." But though the clergy were in consequence prohibited from being concerned in or countenancing theatrical representations, the barristers of Edinburgh presented the actress with a silver urn and an inscribed silver tea-tray in recognition of their delight in her acting.

Her wanderings never ceased for long. In one year she covered nine hundred miles while playing on Wilkinson's Yorkshire Circuit. Once after playing three nights in Leeds she found herself obliged " to skim away to York, not knowing what was to play that night," and, when she got there, the part fixed on the playbill was not the part for which the carrier had brought the dresses and properties. On that occasion Mrs. Siddons was too tired and too desperate, or possibly too sensible, to make any fuss herself. Using that swift antithesis, that sudden drop from the lofty to the practical that so often disconcerted those unused to the accidents of her style, she described her conduct in this crisis thus :

> " I put my confidence in Almighty God and left it to Mr. Wilkinson to make such changes in the bill as were convenient to the circumstances."

Nor were the actual journeys all of the discomfort : often the inns were bad, the lodgings dirty : once she wrote to a friend :

> " I am sitting in a little dark room in a little wretched inn in a little poking village at the end of a whole day's

journey over bogs and stones in a rattling coach, with another day's journey of the same nature in front of me."

3

In 1779 after her failure as Garrick's leading lady, Mrs. Siddons accepted an engagement from John Palmer who owned the theatre at Bath, and remained with him for three years, but though she had hoped for respite, her stage-coach journeys were not entirely stopped by this comparative settling down. For Palmer owned a theatre at Bristol as well as at Bath and his leading lady had to play three nights in one town and three in the other every week, making the journey of twelve miles between the towns during the day and putting in rehearsals as well: for in those days no play was put on for a run and the change of bill was frequent and continuous.

Before the end of her first year at Bath Mrs. Siddons's third child Maria was born. In the following Spring, having painted portraits of all the notabilities of Oxford, besides attracting some degree of royal notice at Weymouth, little Tom Lawrence was brought to Bath and set about making two portraits of the lovely actress: one as Euphrasia in *The Grecian Daughter*, the other as Zara in *The Mourning Bride*, that mediocre play described by Boaden as " the only offering of Mr. Congreve to the shrine of Melpomene." Lawrence's father, who understood the whole business of being *impresario* to precocious genius, had these two portraits engraved by J. R. Smith as well as one of the

MASTER THOMAS LAWRENCE, AGED 13

young artist by himself, and published them, inscribing that of the boy painter :

> " To the Nobility and Gentry in general and the University of Oxford in Particular who have so liberally countenanced his pencil, this portrait of Master Lawrence is Inscribed by their most devoted and most grateful Servt. T. Lawrence Sen."

It is to this period of comparative tranquillity in Bath that another portrait, more lovely but less significant than little Thomas Lawrence's rather sensational and over-elaborate drawings, may be ascribed. This is the picture by Gilbert Stuart sometimes called " Mrs. Siddons at the age of twenty-one " now in the National Portrait Gallery in Trafalgar Square.

The young American painter, who had come to England to study under Benjamin West, was born in 1755 and was therefore of an age with the girl who sat to him in a turban and fichu of white muslin, worn without elegance, and folded her beautiful young hands in a rather constrained attitude above the broad ribbon of her sash. The sitter's right hand holds a book ; the index finger marks the page at which she has just closed it to turn her head towards the spectator, so that the young outline of her rounded cheek and the tip of her soft but firmly moulded chin show against the background of storm-tossed tree and cloudy sky, chosen partly to show up the whiteness of her gown and partly, it is possible, as an indication of her professional excellence in tragedy at a time when she was still playing Rosalind and Portia, Beatrice and Mrs.

Townley to satisfied audiences in Bristol and in Bath.

The girl Stuart has painted still wore powder in her auburn hair, but, escaping rather untidily from her turban, it only enhances the youthfulness of her smiling face. The eyes are dark, but they are amused as well as thoughtful, and the nose, though recognizably that feature Gainsborough five years later was to find so long, is sensitive, with nostrils that might easily quiver in mirth. Young Mrs. William Siddons was not yet a tragic actress when she sat to young Stuart: she preferred herself in certain comedy parts. She was eager, a little shy, not yet fixed in the great orbit through which presently she was to roll in majesty, filling the stage with the beauty of her gestures, the noise of her mimic rages and grief.

The Bath in which for three years Mrs. Siddons was happy as a young wife and mother and as an admired actress was then at the height of its elegant reputation. Nash and the brothers Wood had cleared away the noisome pestilences of its dirty bathing-pools and scandalous coffee-houses; the Grand Pump Room was not yet built, but the Assembly Rooms had been opened for some years, and, during Mrs. Siddons's season, Palmer was able to add an approach and a place for carriages to the attractions of his theatre. John Heath's bath-chairs were on the sidewalks; Bath Oliver Biscuits were among the dainties consumed by its visitors, and the Abbey Church, where young Mr. and Mrs. Siddons duly attended Morning Prayer on Sunday, was mellowing fast to the state in which Sir Gilbert Scott was to find it fit for his restoring hand. Ralph Allan's sham Castle had ceased to be a novelty when Mrs. Siddons became the talk of the town, but Beckford was then a boy of fifteen, and Miss Austen, still in her cradle, had not yet come to Bath. Miss Burney however came there, who sniffed a little at Mrs. Siddons, and Georgiana, Duchess of Devonshire who proclaimed her talent and beauty wherever she went, and Horace Walpole poking fun at Mrs. Thrale and "all the Johnsonhood," and Sheridan with his lovely wife, and little Walter Scott, taking baths for his lameness and being rewarded by a visit to the theatre where he may have seen Mrs. Siddons as Rosalind on the occasion when he interrupted a performance of *As You Like It* with his shout of excitement over the wrestling match. All those remembered and forgotten people who made up that London Society, which was later to go crazy over Mrs. Siddons when she returned to town, passed, at some time during these three years, through Bath and saw or heard of the new young actress. Some of them remembered her as Portia, so unbecomingly dressed in an old salmon pink sacque and coat from the Drury Lane Wardrobe a few seasons back.

But, of all the people Mrs. Siddons met in Bath, none deserves our gratitude and interest, as he certainly had hers, so much as the tall courtly divine Dr. Thomas Sedgwick Whalley who with his successive wives lived in a "winter house" in Royal Crescent and sent grapes and new-laid eggs to the young actress, noticing her frail and tired look long before anyone else in Bath began to applaud her growing success. The friendship thus begun lasted through the lifetime of Dr. Whalley himself and that of his second wife : his third quarrelled with and survived him. To it we owe those loving, affectionate, sometimes sprightly, sometimes distressed but never distressing letters, which are still among the most valuable of all the wide mass of documentary evidence now available covering those and the succeeding years of Mrs. Siddons's career. She was an indefatigable letter-writer : she wrote, besides the formal letters incidental to her business, long detailed letters to all her friends ; to Lady Harcourt at Nuneham ; to Bannister Lodge, when Mrs. FitzHugh, sister of the William Hamilton who shipped the Elgin marbles for England, spent such weeks of life as she was unable to devote to sitting in Mrs. Siddons's dressing-room at the theatre ; to Mrs. Pennington ; to Mrs. Piozzi, after that lady had overcome her first dislike of her statuesque person ; to the members of her own family, when she was separated from them while on the tours she never ceased from making.

It is, indeed, to the recurrent travels of this much driven genius that we owe the letters. When we remember the nights she had to spend at wayside inns between all the towns she visited from Weymouth to Edinburgh, her energy in letter-writing seems less ridiculous than pathetic, to us who send cables at the end of a five days' voyage across the Atlantic and picture-postcards to announce our descent from a luxury train in Rome or in Vienna.

All through her life we must picture the generous, impulsive, very human creature, sitting up by candle-light at some stage or other of her travels, writing, writing, writing, so that the solid domestic love and the real friendships she needed to retain amidst all the adulation that only bewildered her, should not fail from any lack of the fuel she herself must supply to keep those warm but distant fires glowing and alight.

II

THE TOWN

I

THE LONDON to which Mrs. Siddons came in 1782 to prove herself an actress, unrivalled in her own or any other age, and where she held the stage until 1812, possessed three fashionable theatres: Drury Lane, from which Garrick had just retired; Covent Garden; and the Theatre Royal in the Haymarket. A few years later the English Opera House was opened at the Lyceum, but before that date opera was given at all three houses in alternation with drama.

"Their Majesties," says Boaden, speaking of King George III and Queen Charlotte, "when visiting the theatres hardly ever ventured upon tragedy," showing, even in days when tragedy was still more or less fashionable, an inclination experienced by Majesty ever since. Harriette Wilson has a story of a visit to the theatre paid by the young Queen Victoria in the very early years of her reign. She was, the gossips told one another, so much taken up with Lord Melbourne and other people of her party, and so excited at the adventure of appearing in the Royal box that she did not realize King Lear had any children until the end of Act III. Her subjects may well have taken this callous attitude to the drama as a sign of grace in their pretty little Queen, seeing how much they had resented the theatrical pre-occupations of her predecessors.

This royal disposition to avoid the heavier form of entertainment offered by the theatre is the less to be wondered at when we remember that Shakespeare, as then played, had been rewritten (as well as such of the Caroline and Restoration drama as was still retained on the active list) in order to provide nothing but gloom for the tragic actors and actresses who played in classic parts. The shortened tragedies once over, a livelier note was often sounded. There were one-act farces; Interludes and Ballets to cheer the departing spectators; or two-act operettas of which, as a contemporary journalist observes " the violation of probability is generally overlooked in vehicles for music." One such oversight was conspicuous in a "*Grand Spectacle by John Fawcett with Music by Messrs. Moorhead and Davy.*" This was a ballet called *Perouse or The Desolate Island* based on quite a serious German play. In it a navigator lands on an island, so representative in its fauna, that a chimpanzee in the jaws of a bear is the first spectacle that greets his eye. The hero rescues the monkey " and thus insures the animal's attachment whose occasional returns of gratitude prove of the utmost service to the ship-wrecked navigator and his family." This piece found great favour and was put into the regular bill for some months. A natural, but unfortunate circumstance brought about its ultimate withdrawal, " Young Menange, a dancer, having outgrown his favourite character, the chimpanzee."

Another successful Interlude was called *Forecastle Fun or Saturday Night at Sea*, one of many entertainments made popular by the victories of Nelson and the general excitement occasioned by the naval campaigns of the seventeen-nineties. There was also an Interlude or Comic Piece called *Blue Devils* in which "Amusing and probable equivogues rapidly succeed each other, and form a very entertaining trifle, though founded on the melancholy intention of suicide."

This piece came from Paris, in translation, and, after running some months at Covent Garden, was transferred to the Haymarket: but the *Ballet of Joan of Arc* was an entirely British product. Its press was not good.

> "The historical fact on which this spectacle is founded, and which is not a subject fit for the English stage, underwent considerable variation. The intrepid maid, personified by Mrs. Parker, was rendered a diabolical character who sold herself to the devil and terminated her glory in hell. The dresses and decorations were magnificent."

Whether for political reasons, or because it was really a bad ballet, this piece was withdrawn, though it did not meet with the complete expunction "Not repeated or published" that follows the account of other failures, for the story and the music were both saved for print.

In the same year, four days after the King's Birthday, honoured by an interlude called *Unanimity: or War, Love, and Loyalty*, the Rank and Fashion of the town were invited to assist at a benefit for Queen

Charlotte's *General Lying-in Hospital*. The ballet rather unfeelingly selected for this occasion was called *La Vengeance D'Amour*. Such were the less important attractions against which, when Sheridan was not putting up one of his new brilliant comedies at Drury Lane, the new tragedy actress had to contend.

The time was ripe for a change in the current of public taste, and Mrs. Siddons was strong enough to change it. In 1785 a ridiculous and anonymous young man celebrated the revolt against " Continental Lightness" in a poem in blank verse, called magniloquently *The Siddoniad*. It opens with a quite candid preface, all in long ſſ.

> " The author of this Essay rather dedicates to Mrs. Siddons, that respect which is due to her, for her divine accomplishments, than the SIDDONIAD, which he publishes, more from his affection to it, as the first production of a youthful pen, than from any analogy it bears to the greatness of the Subject."

This young man's estimate of his work is correct enough. His poem bears no analogy to the greatness of his subject and contains no evidence that he ever beheld the actress whose name he has used to embellish his almost volcanic protestations of scorn for the Comic Muse :

> " *Long had the genius of the comic scene*
> *Usurp'd Britannia's stage, and sunk the mind*
> *To love of vanity ; but now again,*
> *Melpomene awakes ; and to the eye*
> *Of longing expectation raises up*
> *Her charms celestial :* Siddons *leads 'em on,*

*And ev'ry gen'rous British bosom burns
With its own native fires! from Gallia brought
The risus of depravity is scorned
Grows noisome to fair sensibility,
And feathers, fans, affected airs, and all
That pleases idiotism, are now no more."*

Presently we have a gleam of the truth. Mrs. Jordan has incurred our young gentleman's displeasure: he has also had a brush with a critic who admired that pleasant and easy-going lady.

*" No more the vain pretender to discern
The higher graces of sweet poetry
(Miss Dolly's loves and the handy-work
Of credit-yielding taylors) shall presume
To be a critic; and, with all the swell
Of impudence, and ignorance, conjoin'd,
Blaspheme the pathos of the tender scene;
Sound reason bids the noisy puppet fly,
While dress'd in grace, and majesty, the friend
Of sentimental freedom comes to meet
The Ear of Judgment, while with deepest joy
Learning itself attends; and from the lips
Of elocution such soft accents fall,
As from the magic site of ecstasy."*

Of Mrs. Siddons herself he has little to say except that she was far from being a comedy actress. He concludes with a flight of fancy about her origin:

*" From heav'n she came; and bless'd philanthropy
Scarce parted with its noblest, dearest pledge;
And when the guardian pow'rs resolv'd, at last,
Mankind should thus anticipate the joys
Futurity to virtuous souls affords,*

A new-born cherub bore her in his arms,
And kiss'd her, e'er he yielded up the prize;
Young Pathos caught her; and sweet Eloquence,
His blooming sister, nurs'd the sacred charge,
And rais'd her to adorn the tragic throne."

2

" The town in those days mostly lay
Betwixt the tavern and the play,"

and there was plenty of talk before, and still more after, the electrifying night when Mrs. Siddons, fulfilling the Duchess of Devonshire's wildest panegyrics, prostrated the entire audience of Drury Lane with the grief of her Isabella in Southerne's *Fatal Marriage*.

It was not long before Majesty was brought to see the wonder and to realize that a thoroughly good cry was, in its way, as exhilarating, as well as harder to come by in the theatre, as a hearty laugh. In a year or two, so much had the royal taste for Mrs. Siddons's acting grown upon them, the King and Queen, in one single month, saw her performances of Belvidera, Calista, Jane Shore, Euphrasia, and the still often repeated Isabella. Indeed the Royal partiality for Mrs. Siddons soon became so marked that the wits began to notice it.

" *Epigrammatic: on the King commanding the Tragedy of The Grecian Daughter on Thursday the 2nd of January* 1783.

Siddons to see, King, Lords, and Commons run,
Glad to forget that Britain is undone.

The Jesuit Shelbourne, the apostate Fox,
And Bulls and Bears together in a Box.
Thurlow neglects his promises to friends:
And scribbling Townsend no more letters sends.
Wits leave their feasts and sots desert their wine.
Each youth cries 'Charming!' and each maid 'Divine.'
See, of false tears, a copious torrent flows,
But not one real, for their country's woes.
The club of spendthrifts, the rapacious bar
Of words, not arms, support the bloodless war.
Let Spain Gibraltar get, our islands France
So Siddons acts or Vestris leads the dance . . .

. . . .

Soon foreign fleets shall rule the Western main
George fills no throne but that of Drury Lane."

There was, it will be seen, a frequent change of bill in those days. Except for ballets and interludes and for the plays that Sheridan wrote himself or had translated from the successes of the French and German theatres, there were not many first nights of any serious play in our acceptation of the word. John Philip Kemble was not alone in his opinion that all the best plays had been written and that new ones, especially new tragedies, must needs be rehashing and spoiling of old ones. People went to the theatre not so much to see the play, because as a rule they knew it more or less by heart, but to see Mrs. Jordan or Mrs. Palmer in a favourite part. When she first came to town in 1775 Mrs. Siddons, before obtaining her first engagement from Garrick, submitted her repertory for inspection. It was a large one and was made with the callous indifference to the author's responsibility for each part that all playwrights expect once their work has been seen on the stage.

Jane Shore	Marianne
Alicia	Lady Townley
Roxana	Portia
Grecian Daughter	Mrs. Belville
Matilda	Violante
Belvidera	Rosalind
Calista	Mrs. Strickland
Monimia	Clarinda
Juliet	Miss Aubrey
Cordelia	Charlotte
Horatia	Widow Brady
Imogen	

To these she was to add as many more, including Ophelia, Desdemona and Hermione and her more triumphant successes Constance and Volumnia. In non-Shakespearean plays her greatest achievements were to be Isabella in *The Fatal Marriage*, Mrs. Beverley in Moore's *Gamester*, Lady Randolph in *Douglas*, Mrs. Haller in *The Stranger* and—returning to Shakespeare—the greatest of all, Lady Macbeth.

An actress in the seventeen-eighties, like an opera-singer, repeated her successes and was judged on points very much as opera-singers are now. Indeed there was a good deal of operatic performance given and expected in the tragedies of the day. Mrs. Crawford had a shriek and a groan " that made rows of spectators start from their seats." Mrs. Siddons went further; when she shrieked the house shrieked with her; at her groan young ladies swooned in their boxes. On the days when she was to play, as on those now when a Ponselle or a Lauritz Melchior are to sing, excitement was great *before* the performance : once it began, a breathless house waited for each well-known display of virtuosity, and met again in tavern, coffee-house and drawing-room to discuss each variation from, each failure to reach, or triumph in surpassing the separate top notes of the part.

It was *acting* that drew audiences in Mrs. Siddons's day, not scenery or dresses. When she first came to London the actress brought nothing but her well-stored memory to the stage. No Kemble had ever needed a word from the prompter in any part : once indeed John Philip had been known to hesitate, but this turned out to be no more than the pause for breath inflicted on the actor by a severe cold in the head. Owing to the lack of stage-dresses of her own when she joined Garrick, the poor girl had been obliged to appear as Portia in the salmon pink sacque and coat from the wardrobe. The costume every diarist of gossip of the time had held up to ridicule did not suit her and the audience let her know it. They had probably seen that sacque and coat before—as they had seen the drops and flats, the wings and arches of the sets that served again and again for play after play, much as we used to do in the early days of the Old Vic or at Stratford-on-Avon before the fire.

A few items taken from an inventory made for the proprietor of the Theatre Royal in 1779 give some idea of the kind of scenery and properties at the disposal of the management when Mrs. Siddons came to play at Drury Lane. The whole list reads like a poem in *vers libre* : it is copied verbatim with the omission of a few repetitive lines. The italics are those of the poet himself :

> A drop wood.
> A drop palace.
> A town flat.
> Three chambers, *holes in one of them*, the doors of the door-chamber very bad.
> Prison.
> Canal garden.
> Blasted heath. *Macbeth.*
> Cut wood. *Hamlet.*
> Cave with catacombs painted on the back.
> Gothic palace.
> Long wood, a *hole* in it.
> Part of the hovel in *The Sorcerer.*
> Statue in *Merope.*
> Patty's house, *very* bad.
> Doctor's brick house in Mercury Harlequin.
> Rialto.
> The statue of Osiris.
> Aimworth's house, one *stile.*
> Battlement, *torn.*
> Tomb in *The Grecian Daughter.*
> Library.
>
> An old Patagonian chamber in *Mother Shipton.*
> Water-fall in the Dargle, very bad.
> Altar piece in *Theodosius.*
> Palace arch of Corinthian order.
> Two large wood rings, *greatly damaged.*
> One piece of clouding, very old and little worth.
> Five pairs of Gothic wings (five holes in the canvas).
> Five small tents.
> Juliet's balcony.
> Balcony in *The Suspicious Husband.*

The bridge in *King Arthur*.
Juliet's bed.
Jobson's bed.
Five sky borders.
Four Gentlemen's turbans.
Six common ditto.
Three white hats.
Bow quiver and bonnet for Douglas !
A small map for Lear.
One Shepherd's hat.
Four small paper tarts.

Seven spears.
Nine rods, one crook.
Two shapes.
An old toy fiddle.
One Goblet.
Edgar's hat.
One pediment for banquet.
Lantern in *Grecian Daughter*.
One pair of scissors.
Two pieces of scantling to hang cloathes on.
Four very small rocks.

At this point the air thickens. In its provision for storms the equipment of the Theatre Royal was richer than in that of woods or palaces or arches :

Eleven metal thunderbolts, sixty-seven wood ditto.
Five stone ditto.
Three baskets for thunder-balls.
One canopy.
The pedestal and horse in *The Sorcerer, out of repair*.
Hob's well ; two water wheels ; boat in the Dargle.
Four long barrels with multiplying wheels.
Rack in Venice Preserved.
Elephant in the Enchanted Lady, *very bad*.

Alexander's car, some of it wanting.
The star King Arthur cut across.

This lucid if fragmentary epic concludes with a little song written by one Thomas Ryder, to the title :

Left in the trunk in Mrs. Barry's Room.

A black velvet dress and train.
A yellow and silver dress.
A Spanish blue and white thread satin ditto.
A pink coloured silk ditto.
A puckered white thread satin petticoat.
A blue thread satin robe.

Ten white linen dresses.
Two stuffed petticoats and a jacket.
A red puckered dress.
A white dress covered with gauze.
Four dresses in Artaxerxes.
A pair of shepherd's breeches.

This last line moved Boaden to the annotating sigh

" For the dear woman's own Rosalind, no doubt."

There were, of course, in the larger theatres all the cars and trophies and other paraphernalia for spectacles and triumphs such as the famous one in *Coriolanus*, when Mrs. Siddons's exultation as Volumnia celebrating the victories of her son broke step in the solemn march to music as it crossed the scene and

" with head erect, and hands firmly pressed to her bosom, as if to repress by manual force its triumphant swellings, she towered above all around her, and almost rocked across the stage."

So much for the furnishing of the scene itself: the auditorium changed several times during these magnificent years: once the galleries were redecorated in blue and silver, "with elegant columns" to replace the crimson and gold more usually seen in the interior decoration of a playhouse.

When John Philip Kemble joined forces with his sister, and after years of bitter experience of Sheridan's extraordinary personal charm and unfathomable financial duplicity, managed to install himself with her in a theatre of their own, they were able to do so sumptuously enough. Here is an eye-witnesses' record of the interior of Covent Garden Theatre re-opened by Kemble playing Hamlet there on the 24th of September 1803, to be followed three days later by Mrs. Siddons as Isabella:

"The alterations and improvements which had been made in the audience part of this theatre, had been very considerable. The grand object seemed to have been the union of elegance and simplicity, so as to give to the whole the appearance of neatness and lightness, without the aid of gaudy colour or tinsel decoration. This object had been accomplished in the following manner:—The front of the boxes was uniformly painted with a beautiful dead white and gold, and the inside with party-coloured green, relieved and heightened with appropriate ornaments. The lobbies had been completely new-painted, in a style corresponding with the interior part. All the front-boxes in both tiers were enlarged, by the addition of one seat; each capable of accommodating, with ease, six persons more than it held the preceding season. The side continuation of the two-shilling gallery was now converted into boxes, called the slips. The frontispiece was raised ten feet, and sixteen private boxes were added, to which there was an entrance from Bow-street. These private boxes were soon disposed of, at £300 each, to the Duchesses of Northumberland and Devonshire, the Marchioness of Abercorn, Lady Holland, the Earl of Egremont, Lady Milner, Mrs. Vaughan, Mrs. Morton Pitt, etc.— A drop-curtain, in oil and water-colours, representing the royal arms, supported by cherubs, formed a very superb picture, and enriched the whole with an admirable effect. The piece of painting, representing the royal arms in the centre of this drop-curtain, was an exact copy of that which was used in the theatre, Lincoln's Inn Fields, during the management of Cibber, Wilks, and Booth. The ceiling was ornamented in an antique manner, without any of its heaviness."

3

Outside the theatre London, as the Kembles knew it, was still very much of a garden city; its squares open on one side to views of the river or of Hampstead; the fields opposite Sloane Street so peaceful under their elms that they inspired Sir Thomas Lawrence to that loveliest of pre-Impressionist water-colours now among the treasures of the British Museum. I know of no more charming evocation of the pleasanter aspects of the town at the close of the eighteenth and the opening of the nineteenth centuries than is given by the following prose pastel from a recent biography:

"The beauty and splendour of London, we may conclude, increased steadily from the accession of

Elizabeth, and declined, slowly but with gathering momentum, from the accession of Victoria. How beautiful the city was in the last decades of the eighteenth and the first few decades of the nineteenth centuries can be dimly understood from prints, and from the actual relics of that time. The eye fastens upon these, striving at the same time to shut out the wilderness of dreary horror which succeeding years have piled around them ; one can still distinguish the two styles of eighteenth-century domestic architecture ; the simpler, with its solid yet airy grace, its plain façades, its Grecian porticoes, and its fanlights whose woodwork suggests the filaments of a spider's web ; and the more splendid Palladian erections, with their fluted pillars and marble cornices. But it requires a strong effort of the imagination to see, as the Londoner of 1800 would have seen, these houses standing forth in their original freshness, clear of the encroachments of sham Gothic and modern concrete ; with their white and yellow plaster and pale stonework uncontaminated in the smokeless air, while the architectural triumphs of the most civilized era the world has seen were enhanced by a rural loveliness almost unspoiled from the sixteenth century."

This was the London through which Mrs. Siddons was carried in a chair or driven in a hackney coach to parties at Devonshire House, or to sit to Sir Joshua Reynolds in Leicester Square and to Mr. Thomas Gainsborough in the fine mansion he shared at Schomberg House in Pall Mall. It was in the rural shades of Soho Square Garden that Sally Siddons the younger was to walk during the first weeks of her clandestine engagement to the court painter who stole out to meet her from his rooms in Greek Street, young Tom Lawrence who was himself more beautiful than any of the beauties who sat to him and made his fortune.

That is one side of the picture : but there were narrow unwholesome streets winding about the Fleet ; there was mud and slush on the unswept sidewalks in winter ; garbage rotting in gutter and yard in the dog-days ; fogs with their accompaniment of link-boys in autumn, and drunken chairmen, and low airless shops where young apprentices slept all the year round under the counters ; and child-labour and public hangings ; and open sewers and epidemics of smallpox in London. These were the years before Jenner had dared to vaccinate little James Phipps far away in a valley in Gloucestershire, or John Nash had begun to plan those improvements and extensions of the official and aristocratic quarters the present age is so busily engaged in demolishing. Nor were open drains and foggy exhalations the only dangers to life in the London of Mrs. Siddons's prime.

Even as late as 1814, when she was established in her little country villa beyond Paddington, Mrs. Siddons was obliged to spend very quiet evenings during the winter months as the roads from the village of Westbourne into London were infested with footpads, and it was anxious work for any guest to return to town after nightfall.

It was to this beautiful, dangerous London that, in October of the year 1782, William and Sarah Siddons brought their son Henry and the two baby daughters who were to grow into lovely girlhood only to perish of consumption, brought on, partly by the almost insane treatment of pulmonary disease then in fashion, and partly by another and, in a sense, more tragic misunderstanding of the afflictions to which youth is a prey.

It was for the sake of these three children, as she had announced in an address in verse of her own composition, that the young actress left the happy security of Bath for the more precarious, more highly paid position offered her in London. The eldest of them, was, as we shall see, to contribute a by no means negligible effect to his mother's impending triumph, once the wrench had been made. She had produced him and his infant sisters from the wings at the climax of her farewell to Bath, when in words of her own composition she declaimed:

> "*Stand forth, ye elves! and plead a mother's cause,*
> *Ye little magnets, whose soft influence draws*
> *Me from a point where every gentle breeze*
> *Wafted my bark to happiness and ease—*
> *Sends me adventurous on a larger main*
> *In hopes that you may profit by my gain.*"

Then the children had only clung to their mother's wide and flowing skirts, peeping from among its folds with rehearsed and bewitching shyness: a few weeks later she was to lead her eight-year-old Henry across the stage, dressed for the part he had learned, as Biron's son, the infant source of, and partial consolation for, the introductory woes of Southerne's Isabella.

PART III

Cloudy Symbols

"The enthusiasm she excited had something idolatrous about it; we can conceive nothing grander. She embodied to our imaginations the fables of mythology of the heroic and deified mortals of elder time. She was not less than a goddess or a prophetess inspired by the gods. Power was seated on her brow; passion radiated from her breast as from a shrine; she was Tragedy personified."—HAZLITT.

MRS. SIDDONS AND HER SON AS ISABELLA WITH BIRON'S CHILD

I

THREE PLAYS

I

IT IS DOUBTFUL if any actress presenting herself for the first time at Drury Lane in 1782 would have ventured to do so in an unknown play : Mrs. Siddons, returning to that theatre seven years after the defeat she had suffered there under Garrick's direction, was far too experienced a woman of the stage to attempt to do more than succeed in a well established and popular tragedy.

The play chosen for what was in truth her second début was Garrick's version of Southerne's *The Fatal Marriage : or the Innocent Adultery*. This quasi-Shakespearean drama had held the boards for the best part of a century and the part of Isabella had, ever since 1694, been in the repertoire of every famous actress. Originally written for the great Mrs. Barry and for Mrs. Bracegirdle it contained one tragic and one comic lead. Of Mrs. Barry's performance as the tragic Isabella, Southerne himself wrote :

> " I made the play for her part, and her part has made the play for me ; it was a helpless Infant in the Arms of the Father, but has grown under her care ; I gave it just Motion enough to crawl into the World,

but by her power, and Spirit of playing, she has breathed a soul into it, that may keep it alive."

This was a high legend to follow, and if possible, surpass, and Mrs. Siddons, who was not usually at her best in love-scenes, would have preferred to make her new appearance in town in *The Grecian Daughter*. The part of Euphrasia in that play, though it now seems, to use the slang of the day before yesterday, rather shy-making, was one in which filial piety is displayed to an extent unparalleled in any other tale. And Mrs. Siddons knew herself capable of a moving performance in this character. Isabella on the other hand made enormous demands on the actress who undertook it. The part was one long and almost uninterrupted series of love-scenes leading up to a terrific suicide *on* the stage and *by* a raving lunatic. Southerne's play had been purged by Garrick of the comic scenes. In this the actor showed a double wisdom for, not only are these scenes extremely tiresome in themselves, but they carry a second plot of no value and worse still, they provide a part for a second star. Garrick knew that Mrs. Cibber or Mrs. Crawford could carry the play, with him as Villeroy, without the introduction of any comedy queen, with her consequent handsome young lover to share the honours of the piece. And the handsome Irishwoman Mrs. Crawford was still very much alive in Dublin. Young Mrs. Siddons was in no mind to dispute the part with her in London.

But Sheridan was wiser than his new leading lady. She had played Isabella in Bath : she should open with it in town. She had moreover an eight-year-old son, Henry, who could be taught to run on and off the stage chirruping the tiny part of Biron's child. Two rehearsals of the play, well-known by all the rest of the company, were all that were necessary. At the second of these little Henry Siddons, watching Isabella's death-struggle, was so terrified by its realism that he made a small scene of his own, crying and protesting that he could not bear to see his mamma about to die. This testimony to the force and realism of the new leading lady's acting encouraged everybody to the greatest good spirits and, in spite of the attack of stage-fright which, in common with the least talented player, she always had severely before a first performance, the evening opened well. Mrs. Siddons passed through one of her desperate tranquillities in her dressing-room and before she had been three minutes on the stage " her fair admirers were in tears as she questioned her son."

From that moment there was no respite for the audience : by the time the last curtain fell, as Boaden who was present in the house records, " literally the greater part of the spectators were too ill themselves to use their hands in applause."

Sheridan, knowing that in every audience there is a percentage of those who must have laughter in the bill, followed up the shortened tragedy with William Whitehead's farce *A Trip to Scarborough*, and Mrs. Siddons went home to her lodgings, in thankful silence, and sat down with her old father and her husband, who had not been well enough to come to the theatre " to a frugal, neat supper " at the conclusion of which the triumphant actress went to bed and "fell into a sweet and profound sleep, which lasted into the middle of the next day."

With the exception of Belvidera in *Venice Preserved* (played now and again by our more intelligent private societies) and of the heroines of Shakespeare, none of the parts in which Mrs. Siddons rose to be the idol of the theatre-going world has been seen on the stage during the lifetime of any but the most venerable theatre-goers. As the plays in which they occur are, for the most part, of very slight literary merit, a good deal of interest may be found to-day in the attempt to recover from the musty pages of a seventeenth century prompt-book the part in which so stupendous a dramatic triumph was achieved.

Southerne's play opened originally with a prologue written for Mrs. Bracegirdle. This cannot have been spoken in Drury Lane in front of Mrs. Siddons's appearance as Isabella, because the part of Victoria, a most pert and on-coming young woman, had been excised from the tragedy; but its earlier lines are worth quoting here as proof that, though the production of a new tragedy in blank verse is now unthinkable, the professional critic's attitude towards such a play was much the same two hundred and forty years ago as it would be to-day.

> *"When once a Poet settles an ill Name,*
> *Let him Write well, or ill, 'tis all the same :*
> *For Criticks now-a-days, like Flocks of Sheep,*
> *All follow, when the first has made the Leap.*

> *And, do you justice, most are well inclin'd*
> *To censure Faults you know not how to find :*
> *Some cavil at the Stile, and some the Actors ;*
> *For, right or wrong, we pass for Malefactors.*
> *Some well-bred Persons carp at the Decorum,*
> *As if they bore the Drawing-Room before 'em.*
> *Sometimes your soft respectful Spark discovers,*
> *Our Ladies are too coming to their Lovers ;*
> *For they who still pursue, but ne'er enjoy,*
> *In every case expect a Siege of Troy."*

The scene is "*A Street*," in a town (on the seaboard of Bohemia for all we know), in any case, a cosmopolitan sort of place. It is inhabited by a Count Baldwin whose two sons are named Carlos and Biron ; by a nobleman called Villeroy ; by four gentlemen known severally as Frederick, Fernando, Fabian and Bellford. Their various servants, all male, answer to the names of Jacqueline, Sampson and Pedro and the cast is completed by the Baldwin family Nurse, once in charge of the elder Biron's welfare and now devoted to his son and his supposed widow.

It is to this conventionally garrulous lady that the exposition of the main plot is entrusted. Encountering the servant Sampson she indulges in a heart-satisfying gossip with him, and informs the audience of much that must have puzzled it, up to this comic interlude. For Isabella has preceded this small fry on the stage.

Robed in the sable of her seven years' widowhood the tragic heroine, in the presence of her little son, receives not for the first time the honourable proposals of the wealthy and attractive Villeroy, and,

Hs

yet once more rejects them. She does this because the exigencies of virtuous tragedy demand that she shall remain faithful to a shade although herself extremely poor, the nunnery from which she fled to marry having retained the whole of her dowry and her father-in-law remaining obdurate. As we do not know these circumstances at the moment, her refusal of Villeroy seems less unreasonable than it really is. Indeed Villeroy seems such a good as well as determined young man that we begin to hope his suit may presently succeed.

> "*Those pious Tears you hourly throw away*
> *Upon the Grave, have all their quick'ning Charms,*
> *And more engage my Love, to make you mine.*
> *When yet a Virgin, free, and indisposed,*
> *I lov'd, but saw you only with my Eyes;*
> *I could not reach the Beauties of your Soul;*
> *I have since liv'd in Contemplation,*
> *And long Experience of your growing Goodness:*
> *What then was Passion, is my Judgment now.*"

This scene, once we have allowed for the tiresome convention that makes a virtue of tears, is good enough for any opening, and is rendered charming in itself and admirable as an actress's opportunity by the child whose one speech is natural and moving. Isabella has, rather rhetorically, asked her son if he can forgive her for even listening to Villeroy, thus displaying more than a gleam of that coquetry which makes far more cheerful women encourage a lover's admiration and envy by lavishing on an infant graces and attentions he cannot fail to desire for himself. The boy replies in a prose, simple in itself, and very effective as denoting childish simplicity after the rhetorical verse his elders have been exchanging above his head :

" Why, have you done a Fault? You cry as if you had : Indeed now, I have done nothing to offend you : But if you kiss me, and look so very sad upon me, I shall cry too."

After some parleying Isabella and her child obtain entrance to Count Baldwin's house, thus giving the Nurse and Sampson their opportunity. The audience, having gathered that the lady means to ask her father-in-law to pay some of her debts, cannot have been surprised when, after a pause, he appears ejecting her and his grandson from the door with a great deal of verbal violence.

"Would my Ruin please you?" asks poor Isabella, and Count Baldwin, as snappily as any Noel Coward parent, gives his repartee :

" Beyond all other Pleasures."

Count Baldwin, for a seventeenth century tragic character, is uncommonly modern both in temper and in diction.

Half-way through a long and quite period speech, pointing out that, bad though it was to lose her husband, being disinherited by his father is worse, Isabella calls upon her child to join with her in trying to make his grandfather see reason, and uses Portia's argument :

*" O, if you ever hope to be forgiven,
   As you will need to be forgiven too,
   Forgive our Faults, that Heaven may pardon yours."*

This is too much for the Count.

> "*How dare you mention Heaven?*"

he snaps back and then goes on to point out, in more flowing phrases, that a nun who breaks her vow is not the person to exhort a father-in-law to righteousness. "Can you think," he growls,

> "*The sacrilegious Wretch that robs the Shrine*
> *Is Thunder-proof?*"

After several long speeches in the same vein Count Baldwin offers to keep the child, now threatened with starvation, on condition that his mother undertakes not to see him again. Isabella, being not only a mother but a heroine, decides to beg "*from Door to Door rather than lose him*" and the first act is over.

ACT II

Isabella is at home talking to the Nurse while "*her little son plays upon the floor.*" She has pawned her jewels and thinks she may possibly raise a little more money on them. But the pawnbroker has a heart of stone.

No sooner has Isabella delivered herself of twenty-five lines of blank verse comment on this news than the Nurse comes back, all in a fluster, to tell her that her creditors are marching in "A regiment of rogues" to seize her goods and plunder the house. "What will you do, Madam?" she cries. And Isabella, who has already said more than enough, contents herself with a single and singularly obstructive line :

"*Do ! Nothing, no, for I am born to suffer.*"

This contains the whole philosophy of every tragic heroine since Cleopatra and Lady Macbeth exhausted the dynamic possibilities of calamitous women : it was considered one of the top notes of the play by audiences accustomed to wait for it at Drury Lane and to commend its adequate delivery by their applause.

So the creditors rage together and presently Carlos, Isabella's brother-in-law, now his father's heir, comes along to plead Villeroy's cause. Villeroy is able and willing to pay Isabella's debts if she will give him the right to do so. Seeing that no heroine can accept money from any hand but that of a husband Isabella finally yields. She is, indeed, so touched by the beauty of her suitor's person and character that she admits, in giving him her hand, she hopes she may one day be able to give her heart as well.

Villeroy is enchanted.

"*Send for the Priest*," he cries, "*This night you must be mine.*"

The Nurse bustles off to arrange for an immediate wedding, and Isabella proceeds to qualify her consent. She has a condition to impose.

"*On your Word*
Never to press me to put off these Weeds,
You shall command me."

As Isabella's Weeds had seen her through seven years of increasing poverty as well as almost continual weeping, they must have grown a little rusty: still, as worn by Mrs. Siddons at Drury Lane, they were undoubtedly becoming, and Villeroy is much too excited to make a fuss over a scruple he can trust Time to remedy.

ACT III

The wedding preparations are well under way to the tune of Villeroy's note of almost giddy rapture—

" I have joy sure ;
All that this Life can give me ; he must be
More than a Man who can be happier.
I am so much transported with the Thoughts
Of what I am, I know not what to do "—

when Isabella enters.

She has changed her dress!

" This," cries the enraptured Villeroy, *" is a welcome Gallantry indeed,"*

and Isabella answers:

" Black might be ominous."

Here follows a scene of congratulation and junketing in the midst of which, in Southerne's day, a perfectly enchanting thing happened.

" An Entertainment of Dancing : after which a Song sent by an unknown Hand, set by Mr. Henry Purcel, and Sung by Mrs. Ayliff," sounds a note of lyric beauty and peace in the midst of the hectic rejoicings :

I

" I Sigh'd and own'd my Love :
Nor did the Fair my Passion disapprove :
　　A soft engaging Air,
　　Not often apt to cause Despair,
Declar'd she gave Attention to my Pray'r.
　　She seem'd to pity my Distress,
　　And I expected nothing less,
Than what her every Look did then confess.

II

　　But, oh, her Change distroys
The charming Prospect of my Promis'd Joys
　　She's robb'd of every Grace
　　That argu'd Pity in her face,
And cold, forbidding Frowns, supply their Place.
　　But while she strives to chill Desire,
　　Her Brighter Eyes such Warmth inspire,
She checks the Flame, but cannot quench the Fire."

Isabella almost forgets her grief. She is really sorry to hear that Villeroy must leave her on business the following day. They go into dinner in a very pleasant state of mind.

ACT IV

We are now admitted to Isabella's bed-chamber. Villeroy has left her and a woman servant is spreading a table for a late breakfast. The lady has found herself by no means unhappy in her second nuptials and, now, a messenger has come bearing a ring and announcing that its owner waits below. This, as we already know, is the token she has given to her first husband on the morning of her first marriage. Biron has returned from the grave, after the usual shipwrecks and coincidences that in all travellers' tales prevent the missing from sending any news of themselves to parents and wives for seven whole years.

Biron is in a very good temper.

"*I have a Father here. . . . You know my story*," he says to his friend Bellford, an Englishman, and then, with that abrupt change of subject so often noticeable in the conversation of beauties of both sexes on or off the stage, asks : "*How does my beard become me ?*"

This is no mere indication of our hero's vanity. Action, rather than the development of character, was still the business of the stage in 1694. Biron has, in fact, disguised himself in order to increase the sensation his return is bound to make. With his return the tragedy takes on an excitement and an increasing grandeur of language and characterization that explains the hold it still had on London playgoers a hundred years and more after its author's death.

Biron's first thought, naturally, is to make himself known to his wife. Isabella, with a callousness her previous sensibility has not prepared us to accept, has taken Villeroy home to the very house in which her married life with Biron had been spent. She cannot help feeling her situation now, but, in spite of the constraint of her welcome to him, Biron notices nothing amiss : he is happy to be home at last and too tired to think of anything but going to bed.

> "*I know the way, my Love. I shall sleep sound.
> You'll make haste after....*"

From this moment to the end of the play the interest of the action depends increasingly on the successive stages through which Isabella's distraction passes to genuine madness. This is developed in three soliloquies including the dying speech with its famous couplet:

> "*The Waves and Winds will dash and Tempests roar,
> But Wrecks are tossed at last upon the Shore*"—

which, in delivery, left Mrs. Siddons's audience helpless with grief. Of these three soliloquies however the finest is the second. Isabella, having had a further scene with him, Biron, unable to understand her growing frenzy, goes out and elicits the truth from the Nurse. Angry with his father, and with his usurping brother Carlos, rather than with his unhappy wife, Biron returns and falls asleep exhausted. The curtain falls. When it rises once more our mind's eye shows us one of those small inset almost secret pictures the imagination of William Poel has reset for us when reviving plays of this or a slightly earlier period.

Southerne's own stage direction runs:

> *Scene drawn, shews Biron asleep on a Couch. Isabella comes in to him.*

Even a reading of this scene from the yellowed pages of the little volume in which it is printed, with the long ſ and the plentiful besprinkling of capital letters of the seventeenth century is enough to conjure up the dim-lit stage, the heavy looping of curtains, the little inset space holding the couch and its sleeper and the chair into which Isabella is presently to fall, and to bring, with these imaginary adjuncts, the thrill of expectation. How in Drury Lane on that impassioned first night must the spectators have waited for the actress who had held them enthralled all evening, to begin her most poignant declamation! Even in the imagination it is almost unbearable to think of the voice of Mrs. Siddons, in the most dulcet notes of its tremendous range, half whispering, half cooing to her unconscious lover:

> "*Asleep so soon! O happy! happy thou!*
> *Who thus can'st sleep: I never shall sleep more.*
> *If then to sleep be to be happy, he*
> *Who sleeps the longest, is the happiest;*
> *Death is the longest Sleep. O! have a Care,*
> *Mischief will thrive apace. Never wake more;*
> *If thou didst ever love thy Isabella,*
> *To-morrow must be Dooms-day to thy Peace.*
> *—The sight of him disarms ev'n Death it self.*
> *—The starting Transport of new quick'ning Life*
> *Gives just such Hopes; and Pleasure grows again*
> *With looking on him—Let me look my last—*
> *But is a Look enough for parting Love!*
> *Sure I may take a Kiss—where am I going!*
> *Help, help me, Villeroy!—Mountains, and Seas*
> *Divide your Love never to meet my Shame.*"

The stage direction here is "*Throws herself upon the Floor*," and we may imagine with what convulsive sobs she filled the pause until, as directed, "*She raises her self upon her Elbow.*"

And, now, it is Fear, rather than Love or Self-pity, that seizes upon Isabella.

> "*What will this Battel of the Brain do with me !*
> *This little Ball, this ravag'd Province, long*
> *Cannot maintain—The Globe of Earth wants room*
> *And food for such a War—I find I'm going—*
> *Famine, Plagues, and Flames,*
> *Wide Waste and Desolation, do your Work*
> *Upon the World, and then devour your selves.*
> *—The Scene shifts fast—*"

At this point the actress is directed to rise to her feet. The lull in the storm has begun: the tumult is dying down. With the approach of madness there is a sense of release from responsibility, a silencing of the voices of Duty and Remorse.

> "*. . . 'tis better with me,*
> *Conflicting Passions have at last unhing'd*
> *The great Machine ; the Soul itself seem'd chang'd :*
> *O, 'tis a happy Revolution here !*
> *The reas'ning Faculties are all depos'd,*
> *Judgment, and Understanding, common Sense,*
> *Driv'n out, as Traitors to the publick Peace*
> *Now I'm reveng'd upon my Memory,*
> *Her Seat dug up, where all the images*
> *Of a long mis-spent Life, were rising still,*
> *To glare a sad Reflection of my Crimes,*
> *And stab a Conscience thro' 'em : You are safe,*
> *You Monitors of Mischief ! What a Change !*
> *Better and better still !*"

Then follow lines so lovely, so perfectly calculated in their broken rhythms and falling cadences to express the exhaustion of a pure spirit, overburdened and sinking to a momentary oblivion, that many a lesser actress than Mrs. Siddons might draw tears, even from us, even to-day, delivering their murmuring words :

> " *This is the Infant State*
> *Of Innocence, before the Birth of Care.*
> *My Thoughts are smooth as the Elysian Plains*
> *Without a Rub : The drowsie falling Streams*
> *Invite me to their Slumbers.*
> *Would I were landed there—*"

We must go back to the Potion Scene and to Shakespeare for anything to match this particular interlude in the driving action of the piece. To-day a poetic dramatist having reached such a lulling close would be content to let his play end here.

But, in those robuster days, a great deal more violence was looked for from the leading actress, and a good squaring of all accounts before an audience would disperse satisfied and the critics go home to find fault with a play. So Biron is set upon in a street brawl by the treacherous Carlos, and rescued, though mortally wounded, by Villeroy. There is a general meeting of all characters on the stage ; Biron to die in Isabella's arms ; Villeroy to fail, in spite of the sweetness of his nature, to comfort her, and Isabella to terrify all hearts by her ravings before she stabs herself and recovers sufficient sanity to bless her weeping son. A little justice is done by the obdurate Count Baldwin, repenting too late of his hardness, and the tragedy is over.

Sheridan, as we have seen, gave his audience an opportunity to recover from the exhaustion of the emotions consequent on Mrs. Siddons's terrific portrayal of her part by putting on the farce *A Trip to Scarborough* to finish the evening's entertainment.

In the days when Betterton played Villeroy to the first great Mrs. Barry's[1] Isabella, Mrs. Bracegirdle spoke the Prologue against critics. Another comedy actress, Mrs. Verbruggen, was allowed to restore the spirits of the audience with the spice of an Epilogue that began:

> "*Now tell me, when you saw the Lady die,*
> *Were you not puzzled for a Reason why?*
> *A buxom Damsel, and of Play-house Race,*
> *Not to out-live th' injoyment of a Brace!*
> *Were that the only Marriage-curse in Store,*
> *How many would compound to suffer more,*
> *And yet live on, with Comfort, to threescore?*
> *But on our Exits there is no relying:*
> *We Women are so whimsical in Dying.*
> *Some pine away for loss of ogling Fellows:*
> *Nay some have dy'd for Love, as Stories tell us:*
> *Some, say our Histories, though long ago,*
> *For having undergone a Rape, or so,*
> *Plung'd the fell Dagger, without more ado.*
> *But Time has laugh'd those Follies out of Fashion.*"

But cynicism had gone out of fashion with the Hanoverian Advent and the plays of the Restoration had been bowdlerized into pure tragedies, all their post-Shakesperean salt left out of them, in order that the audiences of the eighteenth *fin de siècle* could cry without hindrance through the first half of their evening, and, if they wanted to, enjoy

---

[1] The second Mrs. Barry was known later as Mrs. Crawford, Mrs. Siddons's immediate predecessor as leading tragedy actress.

a good laugh on other provocation before going home.

The next day Mrs. Siddons was the talk of the town. She had come, said Quin, to found a new religion. The dress she wore immediately set a fashion, and not her dress only—" It was no delusion," says Boaden, " which led me to notice in the loveliest faces in the world a strongly marked *sensibility* derived from the enjoyment of this fascinating actress." Madame de Staël devoted two rich pages of *Corinne* to an eulogium of Mrs. Siddons's utterance of Isabella's screams, and a description of the nobility of her manners throughout the play. " *Madame Siddons ne perd rien de sa dignité quand elle se prosterne contre terre*," she pronounced— and we can well believe her correct in her judgment.

It was perhaps carrying adulation a little far to attribute the success of a certain Mr. William Pitt, in rebuking the levity of Mr. Fox's and Mr. Burke's remarks on the Address from the Throne, to the effect Mrs. Siddons's performance of Isabella had made on the mind of the daring young orator: but Boaden does not shrink from assuring the world that " the severer muse aided the youthful debater " at this moment.

2

With the exception of Lady Macbeth, Isabella was possibly Mrs. Siddons's greatest tragic rôle. She certainly never had another outside Shakespeare that retains its affecting qualities so unaltered to this day: in her own time she was unrivalled in this part as she was in the character of Mrs. Haller, one of the very few she created herself.

The play, known to the English stage as *The Stranger*, is a translation by Benjamin Thompson from Friedrich Ferdinand von Kotzebue's drama *Menschenhass und Reue*. Thompson's book was polished by Sheridan who had previously rejected a version of it by a Mr. Schinck. This gentleman, in order to avoid the criticism he foresaw, had modified the central situation and had made Eulalié von Waldburg, alias Frau Haller, less guilty in English than she was in German.

" She had eloped, a frightful crime ! but saw the error just before the purpose of her seducer was accomplished," and Thompson thinking rightly, that " the distress must be less as the crime was lowered," left her story as he found it. Boaden, who cannot contain his alarm at the inroads of continental immorality, so likely to follow the breach in decorum made by this German play, flutters between admiration of the acting and dismay at the perversity of the author. To him however the main thing is that, at the first performance, the acting honours went mainly to Kemble, and Mrs. Siddons " certainly sank under her brother " that night.

Kemble, his dignity a little ruffled from having had to climb in and out of Gothic windows while playing in Monk Lewis's drama *The Castle Spectre*, took this new part with a solemnity he had never before displayed.

While he was studying Kotzebue's lines, Boaden popped in on him several times.

> "His head and his heart experienced a very serious call indeed. . . . Although I had many times perceived, upon entering his library, pretty strong indications of the present study, yet I certainly never knew any other take such severe hold upon his countenance and general manner. He relapsed from his usual kindness into gloomy abstraction; and admirably neat as he was in general, I saw for some days a carelessness about his person."

It is, of course, possible that this lapse from kindness into gloom may have been the tragedian's way of indicating to Mr. Boaden that, while an actor is learning a new part, a chatty and inquisitive visitor is, like Charles Lamb's skylark in a counting-house, out of place and in the way. Boaden seems to feel his comment a little severe—for, soaring off into one of his exuberant parentheses, this time relegated to a learned note, he babbles on:

> "In his cloathes and dress Mr. Kemble preserved the Ciceronian medium; a perpetual cleanliness, without the appearance of pains; free from the affectation of singularity; and avoiding the extremes of a rustic negligence and foppish delicacy."

Kemble's temporary neglect of his toilet was not in vain:

> "On the ninth of March," chirrups Boaden, "the results astonished the town."

The play, however, fell more and more into Mrs. Siddons's hands as time went on, and soon became a vehicle for every woman star, as well as a rich mine for the satiric passages in many a novel and squib. It is one of the plays that figure in *Rejected Addresses* where James and Horace Smith, having tried and failed to cram *Macbeth* into a gallop of mockery, get well away with Kotzebue:

> "*Who has e'er been at Drury must needs know the Stranger,*
> *A wailing old Methodist, gloomy and wan,*
> *A husband suspicious—his wife acted Ranger,*
> *She took to her heels, and left poor Hypocon.*
> *Her martial gallant swore that truth was a libel,*
> *That marriage was thraldom, elopement no sin:*
> *Quoth she, I remember the words of my Bible,*
> *My spouse is a Stranger, and I'll take him in.*
>   *With my sentimentalibus lachrymae roar 'em,*
>   *And pathos and bathos delightful to see;*
>   *And chop and change ribs, à-la-mode Germanorum,*
>   *And high-diddle-ho-diddle, pop-tweedle-dee.*"

The success of *The Stranger*, the pother its subject and treatment roused among critics and playgoers, are interesting to the students of English literature and morals as marking the first onset of Romanticism and that rather belated recognition of Rousseau which was to come to its flower a few years later in the works of Scott and Byron. The influence of Rousseau, already welcomed in Germany, is noticeable here in various sentimental outbreaks and in symptoms of Nature-worship, and modern Drawing-room comedy has sometimes been traced to its source in "*The Drawing-Room of Wintersen Castle, with a Piano Forte, Harp, Music, Bookstand, Sofas, Chairs, Tables, etc.*" The author, at last, has begun to be fussy about his play, and by his stage directions to evoke that present-day power behind the curtain, the then non-existent producer.

The book of Mrs. Inchbald's edition of this play is indeed remarkable for the increase of stage directions over those given for earlier works, though Thompson did not by any means transcribe them in his version with the profusion of Kotzebue who accompanied his original dialogue with a constant rubric.

It is not for these reasons however that it is interesting at this point to examine the play in which Mrs. Siddons in 1789 created and sustained the most famous of her later parts. Troubles professional and private were gathering around her: the first flush of her theatrical triumphs was over, and she had good reason for being more than ready to play, almost in support of her brother.

Act I. opens out of doors. "*The scene is: the Skirts of Count Wintersen's Park. The Park Gates in the Centre—on one side a Low Lodge among trees—on the other—in the Background a Peasant's Hut.*"

Peter, a servant, is talking to himself and his discourse is of Mrs. Haller the housekeeper up at the great house, who has sent him to deliver "a green purse" to the poor old yokel who inhabits the Hut in the Background. Mrs. Haller is evidently not so depressed a character as Isabella: "When she laughs," says Peter, "one can bear it well enough: there is a sweetness even in her reproof. . . ." But Peter has not told us more than this of the lady when:

"*Enter, from the Lodge, the Stranger followed by Francis his servant. At sight of Peter the Stranger stops and looks suspiciously at him. Peter stands opposite to him with his mouth wide open. At length he takes off his hat, scrapes a bow and goes into the Hut."*

Here we have the effective entrance given its proper seriousness. It can be imagined with what a lofty bearing Kemble stood to receive the plaudits of the crowd before booming out the first of the many monosyllabic speeches in which the part is rich. *The Stranger*, though full of tragic emotion, is, by virtue of its happy ending, a comedy, and is written in what passed at the time for colloquial prose.

" Who is that ? " says the Stranger and sets wide the flood-gates of information. Peter is one of Count Wintersen's servants ; Mrs. Haller is Count Wintersen's housekeeper and lavishes her benefactions on the poor : one of them lives in the Hut : he is called Tobias. As the Stranger's Lodge is on one side of the Castle Gate while Tobias lives on the other, it seems odd that the gentleman, who has been in constant if mysterious residence for some weeks, should not know the old man. Having put the audience in possession of a good many facts the author further develops the Stranger's character. He is generous by nature but inclined to melancholy and to attacks of crossness. The stranger, it appears, has to-day some cause for ill-temper. He had wanted to give alms to Tobias himself but Mrs. Haller has been before him.

"Who is this Mrs. Haller ? " he asks. " Why do I always follow her path ? Go where I will, whenever I try to do good, she has always been before me."

A good deal of moral talk then ensues in the course of which Francis having observed : "*Hope is the nurse of life,*" is snubbed by the reply : "*And her cradle is the grave.*" Old Tobias arrives and, having announced that Mrs. Haller's purse is green, an important point, and that it contains money enough to see him through the winter, is given a much larger sum by the Stranger who has already formed the worst opinion of the lady, and has showed himself abominably suspicious of Francis as well. Left in solitude the Stranger "*Throws himself on a seat ; takes from his pocket Zimmerman ' On Solitude' and reads.*"

How the audience identified this work when it was drawn from the Stranger's pocket on the German stage we do not know. When Pendennis saw the play no such niceties troubled the producer. Then Bingley, as the Stranger, uttering his lines with " the moan of a bassoon in agony " . . .

> "was reading out of the stage-book—that wonderful stage-book, which is not bound like any other book in the world, but is rouged and tawdry like the hero or heroine who holds it ; and who holds it as people never do hold books, and points with his finger to a passage, and wags his head ominously at the audience, and then lifts up eyes and finger to the ceiling professing to derive some intense consolation from the work between which and heaven there is a strong affinity."

Thackeray, who was only six years old when Kemble retired from the stage, can hardly have seen the original solemnities of the part the tragedian created : but the performance he describes is so evidently based on one in the Kemble tradition that to read the fourth chapter of *Pendennis* is probably to get nearer than anything Boaden has to say of it to the effect Kemble's acting would have on us to-day. In the rest of the chapter too, young Arthur Pendennis, falling in love with the magnificent creature who played the part created by Mrs. Siddons, feels much as we might feel if that daughter of the Muses could return to act Mrs. Haller for us, as Miss Winifred Emery did for our fathers, when she played it opposite Wilson Barrett at the Olympic Theatre in 1891.

The Mrs. Haller Pendennis saw cannot have been very much unlike, though she was a year or two younger than, Mrs. Siddons at the time she played the part.

> " . . . She was of the tallest of women. . . . Her eyes, when she lifted them up to gaze on you, and ere she dropped their purple deep-fringed lids, shone with tenderness and mystery unfathomable. Love and Genius seemed to look out from them, and then retire coyly, as if ashamed to have been seen at the lattice. Who could have had such a commanding brow but a woman of high intellect ? She never laughed, but a smile of endless tenderness and sweetness played round her beautiful lips, and in the dimples of her cheeks and her lovely chin. Her nose defied description in those days. Her ears were like two little pearl shells, which the earrings she wore (though the handsomest properties in the theatre) only insulted. She was dressed in long flowing robes of black, which she managed and swept to and fro with wonderful grace, and out of the folds of which you only saw her sandals occasionally. . . . But it was her hand and arm that this magnificent creature most excelled

in, and somehow you could never see her but through them. They surrounded her. When she folded them over her bosom in resignation ; when she dropped them in mute agony, or raised them in superb command ; when in sportive gaiety her hands fluttered and waved before her . . .

"With what smothered sorrow, with what gushing pathos, Mrs. Haller delivered her part ! At first, when as Count Wintersen's housekeeper, and preparing for his Excellency's arrival, she has to give orders about the beds and furniture, and the dinner, etc., to be got ready, she did so with the calm agony of despair. But when she could get rid of the stupid servants, and give vent to her feelings to the pit and the house, she overflowed to each individual as if he were her particular confidant, and she was crying out her griefs on his shoulder."

This heroine appears for the first time in the second scene of Act I., "an Antechamber in Wintersen Park." All is bustle and confusion on account of the impending arrival of " His Right Honourable Excellency Count Wintersen, and Her Right Honourable Excellency the Countess Wintersen, and His Honourable Lordship Baron Steinfort "—and " Lord have mercy," as the steward, a comic character, says, " Nothing in proper order." This scene so reminiscent of the day before the wedding in *Romeo and Juliet*, is given its note of solemnity with the appearance of Mrs. Haller who, once she is left alone, observes :

"Alas ! Alas ! How wretched is the being who fears the sight of any one fellow-creature ! But, oh ! superior misery ! to dread still more the presence of a former friend ! "

Horses are heard without. A member of the party has arrived before the others. Mrs. Haller is thus faced with Countess Wintersen's brother, the young Baron Steinfort, who " more and more struck as her understanding opens upon him " asks her " What are your employments for a day ? "

As a question to his sister's housekeeper, this does not seem quite necessary : but the young man is by this time dazzled by the presence of one whom he has already described to her face as " Retirement's lovely advocate."

Even in the throes of love at first sight the Baron must have been a little astonished by the housekeeper's reply :

"Oh, my lord ! you cannot imagine how quickly time passes when a certain uniformity guides the minutes of our life. How often do I ask, ' Is Saturday come again so soon ? ' On a bright cheerful morning my books and breakfast are carried out upon the grass plot. Then is the sweet picture of reviving industry, and eager innocence, always new to me. The birds' notes so often heard, still waken new ideas : the herds are led into the fields : the peasant bends his eye upon his plough. Every thing lives and moves ; and in every creature's mind it seems as it were morning. Towards evening I begin to roam abroad : from the park into the meadows. And sometimes, returning, I pause to look at the village boys and girls as they play. Then do I bless their innocence, and pray to Heaven those laughing thoughtless hours, could be their lot for ever.

Baron : This is excellent !—But these are summer amusements.—The winter ! the winter !

Mrs. Haller : Why for ever picture winter like old age, torpid, tedious, and uncheerful ? Winter has its own delights: this is the time to instruct and mend the mind by reading and reflection. At this season, too, I often take my harp, and amuse myself by playing or singing the little favourite airs that remind me of the past, or solicit hope for the future."

Presently they are interrupted by Tobias who insists on thanking Mrs. Haller in the Baron's presence for the green purse. The rubric here surpasses itself.

> "*Mrs. Haller casts her eyes upon the ground, and contends against the confusion of an exalted soul, when surprised in a good action. The Baron stands opposite to her, and from time to time casts a glance at her, in which his heart is swimming.*"

After this, the Baron, supposing Mrs. Haller to be a widow, is only restrained from declaring his passion by "Rural music without" and Mrs. Haller's exclamation:

> "I hear the happy tenantry announce the Count's arrival."

The scene now shifts to "The Lawn. Solomon and Peter are discovered arranging the Tenantry and, to more Rural Music, enter Count and Countess Wintersen, the latter leading her child: the Baron, Mrs. Haller and others following."

In spite of the cordiality of Countess Wintersen "who has in the meantime embraced Mrs. Haller" and drawn her attention to the little William's growth, "deep melancholy overshadows Mrs. Haller's countenance": its cause is revealed in soliloquy:

"I have a William too ... if he be still alive ... his little sister too...."

The audience is thus prepared for the news, disclosed some scenes later, that Mrs. Haller is no widow but a faithless wife who has fled from a noble spouse and lovely infants in the society of Another. This conduct is the more regrettable as it took place at a time when her husband, having lost money without telling his wife of his misfortune, has asked her to be a little more careful with the housekeeping money. We already know how much such a request must have galled the lady's generous nature: for the steward has been obliged to inform Count Wintersen that Mrs. Haller has been giving away his "Siventy-six Hock" to the villagers. The Count passes over this lack of common sense in a housekeeper, his attention being distracted by the news that his little William has fallen into a pond and has been rescued by the Stranger now in occupation of the Lodge outside the gates.

Anxious to return this courtesy Countess Wintersen sends her maid to invite the Stranger to dinner.

Act III. opens as Act I. has done in the Skirts of the Park and the Stranger is discovered reading. The title of his book is not given this time but we may presume that its theme was *Menschenhass*. The following dialogue ensues:

"*Francis*: Sir, sir, dinner is ready.
Stranger: I want no dinner.
Francis: I've got something good.

Stranger : Eat it yourself.
Francis : You are not hungry?
Stranger : No. (*Rises.*)
Francis : Nor I. The heat takes away all appetite.
Stranger : Yes.
Francis : I'll put it by ; perhaps at night——
Stranger : Perhaps.
Francis : Dear sir, dare I speak?
Stranger : Speak.
Francis : You have done a noble action.
Stranger : What?
Francis : You have saved a fellow creature's life.
Stranger : Peace.
Francis : Do you know who he was?
Stranger : No.
Francis : The only son of Count Wintersen.
Stranger : Immaterial.
Francis : A gentleman, by report, worthy and benevolent as yourself.
Stranger (*angry*) *:* Silence ! Dare you flatter me? "

Presently Countess Wintersen's very pert maid Charlotte arrives and delivers her mistress's invitation to Francis who passes it on to his master. The Stranger's answer to this politeness does no credit either to his intelligence or to his manners.

" I am not a wild beast, to be stared at, and sent for as a show," he growls. " I will not be invited to any house."

Here we see, and on the stage, that inaccessible but attractive because misogynistic hero who is, fifty years later, to come to his full stature in Heathcliff and Mr. Rochester.

No one has ever been ruder to his valet than the

Stranger is to poor Francis : their intercourse is dotted with apologies such as no really nice man should ever find himself in the position of having to make. Stung to the quick by the Wintersens' quite excusable desire to offer him hospitality the Stranger decides he must leave the Lodge at once and speaks very unkindly to Francis in the course of giving his orders. For the second or third time on the stage (presumably that kind of thing has often occurred " off "), Francis protests :

"*Francis :* This is too much.
Stranger : Am I in the wrong ?
Francis : You are indeed !
Stranger : Francis, my servant, you are my only friend.
Francis : That title makes amends for all."

So, for the moment all is well. But the Stranger sees

" uniforms and gay dresses in the walk again. . . .
They come this way ! . . . Francis I shall lock my door."

Into the Lodge the Stranger accordingly stalks, just in time to avoid Countess Wintersen and Baron Steinfort who have, as he surmised, undaunted by his previous refusal of their attention, come to call on him. Francis explains that, though rude, the Stranger is secretly quite noble.

" I mean his real self—His heart ! His soul ! His worth ! His honour ! "

Baulked of their object the Countess and her brother discuss Mrs. Haller, and the young Baron persuades his sister to be his friend in the matter of getting Mrs. Haller to marry him. The Countess protests that Baron Steinfort cannot seriously purpose to introduce the lowly menial " to the circle we live in." Here the voice of a translated Rousseau breaks through—Germany is let loose on the London stage. The Baron is not merely a man who wants a wife ; he is a man

> "who has deliberately poised advantage against disadvantage ; domestic ease and comfort against the false gaities of fashion. I can withdraw into the country. I need no honours to make my tenants happy ; and my heart will teach me to make their happiness my own. With such a wife as this, children who resemble her, and fortune enough to spread comfort around me, what would the soul of man have more ? "

Presently the entrance of Count Wintersen with Mrs. Haller leaning on his arm, breaks up the conference. It is clear that the housekeeper is already treated as one of the family.

The scene shifts to " A close Walk in the Garden " and here the actresses' first really great opportunity occurs. In answer to the Countess's disclosure that the Baron loves the housekeeper, the torrents of confession are let loose. Eulalié (in English, Adelaide) discloses herself as the guilty Countess Waldbourg who, three years before the play opens, has made herself the talk of a neighbouring Court. " The creature plunged an honourable husband into misery. She ran away with a villain——"

At first the Countess is shocked at this confession which, as it is made in the third person, she finds it difficult to believe : but Mrs. Haller weeps so freely, throws herself on the ground with so much energy, and declares so firmly that " the serpent tongue of my seducer " did not charm for long (" in a few weeks the delirium was at an end ") that the Countess, who has enjoyed the luxury of being shocked and then of melting into pity almost as much as the housekeeper has enjoyed that of confession, announces that they are to be friends for life.

" Embracing her " is the stage direction that precedes the Countess's speech :

> " Here, here, on this bosom only shall your falling tears be shed ; and may I, dear sufferer, make you again familiar with hope."

It was at this point that the British public awoke to the astonishing novelty of a situation such as had never before sullied their stage. The indecencies of Restoration comedy were still with them. Congreve and Wycherley, though out of fashion, might be tolerated, as they were often followed. But that, in a serious play, a virtuous wife and mother could be represented as offering affection and a home to an escaped adulteress was, as one fervid protestant declared, a sign of the approaching day " when not a child in England will have its head patted by its legitimate father." Mrs. Haller was, in short, the precursor of Paula Tanqueray. But Pinero knew that the great heart of the public does not change, and that to satisfy it the sinner who is found out must perish. So his Paula killed herself. Morality was appeased. So were the critics, and the only actress of our time who might have kept Eulalié alive on the stage for another decade had a triumph as great in its way as Mrs. Siddons made in the first forgiven sinner of the stage.

The Stranger—having conveniently sent Francis for little William von Waldbourg and his sister—does consent to dine at the Castle. He arrives. The Count, all innocent of the story his lady has kept secret from him, advances to meet his guest.

"My dear Sir—Lady Wintersen—Mrs. Haller," he coos urbanely. Then—

"*Mrs. Haller, as soon as she sees the Stranger, shrieks, and swoons in the arms of the Baron. The Stranger casts a look at her, and, struck with astonishment and horror, rushes out of the room. The Baron and Countess bear Mrs. Haller off; Count following, in great surprise.*

CURTAIN."

Act V. finds the Baron, disappointed in his own love, simply bursting with magnanimity.

"I cannot myself be happy; but I may, perhaps, be able to reunite two lovely souls whom cruel fate has severed."

It was not only kind but extremely penetrating of the young man to have kept his faith in the Stranger's loveliness of soul in spite of the rudeness of his behaviour; but they had been boys together and have had a scene of explanatory recognition in Act IV.

But, as even a Fifth Act must run at least ten minutes, the Baron does not find it too easy to accomplish his amiable purpose. He approaches the lady first, announcing that her husband still loves her and might be persuaded to take her back. Far from being pleased at this news Mrs. Haller rebukes the young man first for calling her Countess ("Not that title I beseech you") and then for suggesting that either she or the Stranger can ever be happy again.

> "No," she says, "he must purify his heart of a weakness which would degrade him."

It is perhaps as well that the reformed housekeeper should take up this attitude, as the Baron has only interpreted the Stranger's feelings by the light of his own indulgent and bachelor heart. When he proposes reconciliation the Stranger—whom we may now call Charles—replies "with extreme asperity":

> "Sir! A wife, once induced to forfeit her honour, must be capable of a second crime . . . oh! what a feast it would be for the painted dolls and vermin of the world, when I appeared among them with my runaway wife upon my arm! Never! Never! Never!"

Mr. Kemble at this point, we may well believe it, was terrific.

However, Mrs. Haller has expressed a wish that she may look upon her Charles for a last, agonizing moment, and if possible on her little William as well, so Charles, granting this almost dying wish, approaches her "with averted countenance and in extreme agitation."

The lady has prepared a document, containing

evidence of her guilt sufficient to enable her lord to obtain his divorce and so, if he wishes to, " to chuse another wife ; in whose chaste arms may Heaven protect your hours in bliss."

The ensuing moment was Kemble's. Boaden describes it as only a keen and well-versed critic of drama can :

> " But there was a beauty of action in the scene with his wife, that showed how happily he evinced the most refined delicacy : and how his very *hands* spoke, what could in no way be conveyed by language. When the Countess has put into his possession the details of her infamy, that he may divorce himself from her polluted person,—the *pause* for a few seconds ; the *deliberate tearing* of the papers ; and the way in which he let them *escape* rather than strew them from his hands ; were so consummate a proof of his feelings and judgment, that it remains before me with no parallel in any other's performance."

From that moment to the end of the play the spectator has little to do but cry, or fidget, according to his nature. Charles and Eulalié are firm they will *not* be reconciled.

> " *Mrs. Haller :* Forget a wretch who never will forget you.—And when my penance shall have broken my heart—when we again meet in a better world——
>
> *Stranger :* There, Adelaide, you may be mine again.
>
> (*They part, weeping.*)
>
> (*But, as they are going, she encounters the Boy, and he the Girl.*)
>
> *Children :* Dear father ! Dear mother !
>
> (*They press the Children in their arms with speechless affection;*

then tear themselves away—gaze at each other—spread their arms, and rush into an embrace. The Children run, and cling round their Parents.)

THE CURTAIN FALLS."

This most natural ending, proper to the common-sense and *Gemüthlichkeit* which gleams all through the clouds of Romanticism and Sensibility in Kotzebue's drama, was heartily disapproved of by everyone who could dissociate a critical faculty from the hypnotic effect of the two great Kembles deploying their tear-raising strength together. Perhaps no one has expressed the verdict of the thoroughly *bourgeois* mind of the day, face to face with a new morality, better than Mrs. Inchbald in her note on what she plainly calls the " catastrophe of the conclusion." Even allowing for the classical sense in which the word was then employed, its significance is still critical:

" Notwithstanding all these distressful and repentant testimonies, preparatory to the reunion of this husband and wife, a delicate spectator feels a certain shudder when the catastrophe takes place,—but there is another spectator more delicate still, who never conceives, that from an agonizing, though an affectionate embrace, (the only proof of reconciliation given, for the play ends here,) any farther endearments will ensure than those of participated sadness, mutual care of their joint offspring, and to smooth each other's passage to the grave."

Then, drawing another breath and admitting that there may be yet another interpretation to this climax, she adds a word of warning:

"What woman of common understanding and common cowardice, would dare to dishonour and forsake her husband, if she foresaw she was ever likely to live with him again?"

In spite of all this protest, and naturally to some extent because of it, *The Stranger* succeeded so well in London that, at the close of the season, Palmer, the actor who had played Baron Steinfort at Drury Lane, went on tour with the play, taking Kemble's part. The event was tragic. Depressed by the news of his own brother's death in Dublin; tired after a long season in town, and also very probably over-exerting himself in an effort to rival the gloom and thunder of the creator of the part, poor Palmer fell dead on the stage after being "energetic and loud in the description of his false friends" in Act IV.

At a benefit given for his wife and children the Epilogue was spoken by a fellow actor. Its opening lines with their sidelong reference to the Muse of Tragedy, still retain the nobility of feeling the eighteenth century could express so crisply and so well in the couplets of its chosen and dignified verse form:

> "*Ye airy sprites, who, oft as Fancy calls,*
> *Sport 'midst the precincts of these haunted walls!*
> *Light forms, that float in Mirth's tumultuous throng,*
> *And frolic Dance, and Revelry, and Song,*
> *Fold your gay wings, repress your wonted fire,*
> *And from your fav'rite seat awhile retire!*
> *And Thou, whose power sublimer thoughts impart,*
> *Queen of the springs that move the human heart*
> *With change alternate; at whose magic call*
> *The swelling tides of passion rise or fall—*

Thou, too, withdraw ; for 'midst thy lov'd abode,
With step more stern, a mightier power has trod :
Here, on this spot, to every eye confest,
Enrob'd in terrors, stood the kingly guest ;
Here, on this spot, DEATH *wav'd th'unerring dart,*
*And struck—his noblest prize—*AN HONEST HEART ! "

So Kemble created *The Stranger*, and Palmer, following him, died in the part, and presently all we hear is that Mamma, or Mrs. Siddons, or the Tragick Muse is playing Mrs. Haller, and that, whenever and wherever she plays it, the house is packed and the audiences cry tear for tear with her. And it is the first play in which she has lent the full force of her genius to the portrayal of a woman who, consciously and wilfully sinning, has redeemed her sin, not only by her tears, but by the consistent nobility of her character and conduct before her expiation was complete.

3

The play, however, around which more discussion raged than was raised by any other dramatic work of its time was Home's *Douglas : A Tragedy*.

The part of Lady Randolph in this piece had, for years, belonged to Mrs. Crawford whom Mrs. Siddons succeeded, not, at first, without divided honours, as the tragedy queen of the English stage. A pamphlet by a certain Mr. Milliken, sold in Dublin for the price of one British shilling, set forth in prose and verse its author's conviction, even so late as 1802, that Mrs. Crawford had been the better actress. This publication was timed to coincide with Mrs. Siddons's final appearance in Dublin in all her famous parts.

Its title sets the tune to which the stanzas that follow are to march:

> Funereal Stanzas/inscribed to the/Revered Memory/of Mrs. Anne Crawford/with/A Comparative Dissertation.between/Her Theatrical Merits/and those of/Mrs. Siddons./

A long introduction then displays some variety in antithesis. Mrs. Siddons, we read, was, like Ben Jonson, "critically correct and judicially just" whereas Mrs. Crawford, like Shakespeare, had always appeared to be "sporting with every rule but the rule of the heart" ... Mrs. Siddons "whose great and acknowledged talents have justly been the theme of popular admiration ... is the Perfection of Art": Mrs. Crawford "was the living image of Nature" ... "Mrs. Siddons rouses our admiration: Mrs. Crawford arrested our *Feelings*."

The author, breaking out more and more into italics, then proceeds to verse, glancing continually sideways at Mrs. Siddons as he celebrates the acting of Mrs. Crawford.

> "*The studied glance, the deep sepulchral tone,*
>   *The preconcerted mechanism of woe,*
> *As artists from mock gems produced from stone,*
>   *May strike some minds as nature's genuine glow....*"

But Mr. Milliken had other tastes:

> "*Through five long acts Sicilia's Princess see.*
>   *What! not one rant! Not one terrific stare?*
> *No! Crawford! No!*"

Mrs. Crawford it appears, though quiet in herself was, when on the stage, the cause of violence in others :

> "*Divine Enthusiast! art thou then no more,*
> *Who oft on Death's domain hast Virtue's temple built——*
> *From his dread brow the Fates' tiara tore——*
> *And launch'd his horrid dart to pierce the mind of guilt?*
>
> '*Ah Burleigh!* Bloody Murd'rer!—*Where's my lord?*'
> *Forlorn with woe, the madd'ning Rutland cries.*
> *The conscious murd'rer shudders at the word;*
> *And* 'I committed MURDER!' *raving loud replies.*"

This rather turgid passage is illuminated by a footnote :

> "Those who remember Mrs. Crawford will recollect that she possessed a peculiarly impressive manner of pronouncing the words 'bloody' and 'murderer'—a manner which no one has hitherto imitated without absurdity, and from which few could deviate with success.—Once, in Mr. Barry's days, she was performing the Countess of Essex in her first style of excellence. In that scene where Essex is dragged to execution leaving the Countess fainting on the stage, a remarkable circumstance occurred, to which these lines allude. Mrs. Crawford's usual management of this affecting situation was, half-raising herself from the stage, and looking round with wistful anxiety, she suddenly sprang from the floor, and seizing the arm of Burleigh, exclaimed in accents that were truly terrific—'Burleigh! *bloody Murd'rer!* Where's my husband?' A well-dressed man in the pit jumped up from his seat, and with the most violent emotions of agony clapped both his hands to his face, and making his way to the door, ran out of the house, crying aloud, '*Oh! God! I committed a Murder!*' He had been remarkably attentive

during the play; and such was the universal consternation at the circumstance, that no one attempted to prevent his escape.—What a forcible instance of the awful operation of conscience acting through the moral power of the drama!"

So far it is possible to agree with Mr. Milliken, but his final conclusion—

"Need it be added, that it was a greater proof of Mrs. Crawford's excellence as an actress than all the applause she received during her whole theatrical career."

seems open to question.

But Mrs. Crawford's celebrant erred in stating that Mrs. Siddons was all sound and fury and Mrs. Crawford invariably self-contained and gentle. When, at the close of the year 1783, Mrs. Siddons followed up her success as Isabella by attempting Mrs. Crawford's most famous part and appeared at Drury Lane as Lady Randolph, she was careful to whisper the great moments in which Mrs. Crawford's shrieks had brought the pit to its feet in excitement, and to use her power of shedding real tears to the full extent allowed for by the text.

The part of Lady Randolph, indeed, made possibly the greatest demand of any known to the serious stage on the portrayer's lachrymosity. Mrs. Siddons must have required as much beer before attempting it as she did years later when playing Mrs. Haller in *The Stranger*, during which performance, as her children boasted, "Our mother weeps most dreadfully."

It was, however, not only the dispute as to

whether Mrs. Crawford's scream or Mrs. Siddons's whisper were the truer to Nature and to Art that made this play the centre for discussion. It had been cradled in debate : in debate it continued to hold the stage.

Douglas : A Tragedy had been played for nearly thirty years when Mrs. Siddons first appeared in it. It had begun its career as a storm centre of great violence in Scotland where, after its first performance, with a Mrs. Ward as Lady Randolph, " the town was in an uproar of exultation that a Scottish clergyman should write a tragedy of the first rate, and that its merits were first submitted to them." The Presbytery, learning that more people went to see Home's play than came to church, began fulminating against anyone who entered any theatre. Home was invited to resign the living of Athelstaneford bestowed on him after he had fought for the Pretender ; a Mr. White the minister of Libberton was suspended for a month, a mitigated sentence, in consideration of his apology " that he attended the appearance only *once*, and endeavoured to conceal himself in a corner, to avoid giving offence." The quarrel took on an international importance. The Church of England permitted its members to attend the performance of so highly moral a work as *Douglas* : The Church of Scotland replied that the pit of a theatre had ever been the entrance to the Bottomless Pit itself. There was schism in Scotland ; the Presbytery of Dunse wrote to the Presbytery of Edinburgh, " We cannot allow ourselves to think that a thing, really criminal in itself, can be innocent or indifferent on the other side of the Tweed." One faction in the Presbytery then decided to have a copy of the play burned by the Common Hangman. This most useful publicity was so good for the box office that *Douglas* was played to crowded houses at a moment when normally its run might have begun to flag a little.

The success of *Douglas* seemed the more grievous that its author was a minister and, until this outburst of prosperity, had indeed written plays, but no one would stage them, and was mainly occupied in preparing a history of the rebellion of '45 and in angling, ever the sport of godly men.

Home's biographer Henry Mackenzie gives a spirited and detailed account of these controversies and contributes his own view of them in well measured terms. Much as Mackenzie admired *Douglas* and its author, some plays and some theatres were, he was bound to admit, indubitably morally injurious.

> "Something, however, must be allowed to custom, in considering the lesser moralities of manners and deportment. The nakedness of an American or a Hindoo, is no breach of modesty or decorum, but that of an inhabitant of London or Edinburgh, would be a flagrant offence against both."

Once started however nothing could stop the success of the Scottish Shakespeare as he was almost universally called. Home went to London and became tutor to the Prince of Wales. *Douglas* was produced at Covent Garden. Mrs. Litchfield followed Mrs. Ward and preceded Mrs. Crawford as

Lady Randolph. Garrick became uneasy. He had a few years earlier refused *Douglas* as well as another and much worse tragedy called *Agis*. The then unknown and dejected author, repairing from Drury Lane to Westminster Abbey, had soothed his wounded ambition by writing in pencil on what he mistakenly called " Shakespeare's tomb " the following request :

> " *Image of Shakespeare ! To this place I come*
> *To ease my bursting bosom at thy tomb ;*
> *For neither Greek nor Roman poet fired*
> *My fancy first, thee chiefly I admired ;*
> *And day and night revolving still thy page,*
> *I hoped, like thee, to shake the British stage ;*
> *But cold neglect is now my only meed,*
> *And heavy falls it on so proud a head.*
> *If powers above now listen to thy lyre,*
> *Charm them to grant, indulgent, my desire ;*
> *Let petrefaction stop this falling tear,*
> *And fix my form for ever marble here.*"

The authorities removed the scrawl from the monument, but the aspirant to petrefaction had made a copy of the verses and thus preserved them for our enjoyment.

When the tide turned it turned indeed. Garrick, having let *Douglas* slip between his fingers, bethought him of *Agis* and, as nothing succeeds like success, was able to write to his dear friend Mr. Home on the morning after he had played Lysander to Mrs. Cibber's Euanthe :

" My dear Friend,

" Joy, joy, joy to you !

" My anxiety yesterday gave me a small touch of the

gravel, which, with a purging, weakened me prodigiously; but our success has stopped the one and cured the other. I am very happy, because I think you are so. The Ode, as I foretold, is certainly too long. There were other little mistakes, but all shall be set right to-morrow.

Ever most affectionately,
"My genius
"D. GARRICK.
" Pray, let me see you at twelve to-morrow."

Home then wrote another tragedy specially for Garrick: it was called *The Siege of Aquileia* and was a failure. But, as he had the script of three blank verse plays in his desk, the time seemed ripe for publication. Home printed all three together, and dedicated his book to his royal pupil. The Prince of Wales becoming King of England later in that same year rewarded his dramatist tutor with a pension of £300 a year from the privy purse.

This was in 1760. Twenty-three years were to elapse before the play was to reach its utmost extension through the gifts of Mrs. Siddons. Mrs. Inchbald, who had seen both actresses as Lady Randolph, had, in spite of Mr. Milliken, the final word:

"To Mrs. Siddons," she wrote, "it is given to unite the same bursts of pathetic tenderness, so wonderful in Mrs. Crawford, to that matronly beauty of person, and dignity of action wherein it was denied Mrs. Crawford to paint this exquisite drawing in faithful colours."

Douglas: A Tragedy was played in the provinces up to the last decade of the nineteenth century and I can remember my father telling the story of a young actor in Manchester who, acting the part of Norval against the surging impediment of a cold in the head, began the famous speech:

"*By dame is Dorval od the Grabpiad Hills*"

only to be interrupted from the gallery by the injunction

"Blow tha' dose, Dorval."

The same Mancunian spirit had wrecked Mrs. Siddons's performance of Juliet in the same theatre a hundred years earlier by shouting to the girl in the hesitations of the potion scene:

"Soop it oop lass. Soop it oop."

But *Romeo and Juliet* is still a living tragedy, and *Douglas* is so dead and so irrecoverable as provocation of any emotion but a little laughter and a little astonishment, that it is worth while to reconstruct its action and to attempt to describe the performance of the one actress it is possible to imagine as capable of freezing up our blood were she to return to weep and rave through it for us to-day.

Home lived to see and be moved by the acting of Mrs. Siddons who, as we read in contemporary records, "in her interview with the Old Shepherd has so called forth and exhausted the feelings as to leave only their languid remains to the future scenes of the play." It is also true that languid remains are almost all the author has left of his subject by the time Act IV. begins.

4

It took the Scottish clergyman five years to write the five short acts of his masterpiece, and, even so, the fair octavo pages on which its blank verse is offered to the reader are barren of those stage directions so fussily occupying the better part of the space devoted to printing a play in these times. It is a relief to begin at once with the terse, Shakespearean " SCENE—The Court of a Castle surrounded with Woods " and to find, instead of the now only too common stage direction, " John exits with Philip," " Exeunt Lady Randolph and Anna—Manet Glenalvon " to help us to recreate the action of the piece.

" It is," wrote David Hume when criticizing *Douglas* at its author's request, " it is reserved to you, you alone, to redeem our stage from the reproach of barbarism." But it was of the dialogue rather than of the stage directions that he was thinking. This, as we shall see, was anything but barbaric, anything too, in spite of contemporary opinion, but Shakespearean.

The scene opens with Lady Randolph in soliloquy addressing the woods that overshadow her husband's castle:

> *" and draw forth*
> *The voice of sorrow from my bursting heart."*

A few lines later she discloses her Christian name alliteratively when speaking of " *Matilda's moan,*" and ends her speech with two lines from which the poet's five years of labour might have sufficed to remove a cacophony and make it the closing snap of a Shakespearean couplet :

> " But Randolph comes, whom fate has made my lord
> To chide my anguish, and defraud the dead."

By this the lady means that she was a widow when Randolph married her, eleven years after the death of her first husband, and not altogether against her will.

Randolph is a difficult character : " He hovers," says David Hume, the historian and the author's cousin and critic, " between vice and virtue, which, though it be not unnatural, is not sufficiently theatrical nor tragic."

The Baron's not unnatural vice appears to have consisted in marrying a widow for her money in order to protect her from less respectable suitors, and his punishment for this is already heavy enough when the play opens, though it grows heavier as the acts roll on.

> " *Seven long years*
> *Are passed, since we were joined by sacred ties :*
> *Clouds all the while have hung upon thy brow*
> *Nor broke, nor parted by one gleam of joy.*"

The occasion is not a happy one for this rebuke as it happens to be the eighteenth anniversary of Lady Randolph's first husband's death as well as that of her own brother who perished in the same battle. As Mr. Home puts it, in one of the finer, though rather more hissing, lines of his verse :

> " *This fatal day stirs my time-settled sorrow.*"

They begin to argue about this, as wives and husbands will, and, as husbands will, Lord Randolph utters a few home-truths about his father-in-law. Sympathy then passes to the lady.

"*Oh! rake not up the ashes of my fathers,*"

she exclaims and follows this cry with the peculiar comment:

"*Had they not been so stern
I had not been the last of all my race.*"

A modern, if prurient, curiosity might desire to explore this statement but Lord Randolph passes it by and returns to his own grievance:

"*Decent affection and complacent kindness
Were all I wished for; but I wished in vain.*"

Lady Randolph, we gather, has inherited at least one trait from her forefathers and has not given any younger Randolphs to the world.

Changing the subject Lord Randolph then remarks that he has been feeling in the mood for a little warfare for some time past and now the glad news of an imminent Danish invasion seems to promise well. Instead of rejoicing with her lord that opportunity for the indulgence of his favourite pastime is at hand, the lady shows herself to be a regular spoil-sport:

"*O! may adverse winds
Far from the coast of Scotland drive their fleet!
And every soldier of both hosts return
In peace and safety to his pleasant home.*"

This speech is interesting both dramatically as constructing character (none but the most obtuse of women could suppose that Lord Randolph's return would be to a *pleasant* home) and grammatically as showing how a Scottish clergyman and poet of the eighteenth century handled one of the most inelegant knobs on English syntax.

It is now Lord Randolph's turn to be cross.

" *May the wind blow, till every keel is fix'd
Immoveable in Caledonia's strand,*"

he counters. This marital opposition has the not altogether unnatural effect of calming the lady, and, the moment being now dramatically ripe for a set speech, she lets him have the Danes and turns her invective on to the stupidity of war between England and Scotland. The theme is reasonable, and some of the lines are quite charming.

" *A river here, there an ideal line,
By fancy drawn, divides the sister kingdoms.
. . . They go forth
Gay in the morning, as to summer sport:
When evening comes, the glory of the morn,
The youthful warrior is a clod of clay.*"

It is quite possible to imagine a good actress delivering the nineteen lines of the passage in which these phrases occur with considerable effect, but only a very great one could persuade an audience that, coming from a wife who had not smiled once at her husband in seven years, the discourse made him answer :

> "*I'll hear no more : this melody would make*
> *A soldier drop his sword, and doff his arms*
> *Sit down and weep the conquests he has made ;*
> *Yea ; (like a monk) sing rest and peace in heaven*
> *To souls of warriors in his battles slain.*"

Lord Randolph goes off at this point to see if the Danes have yet landed and the lady is joined by her friend and confidante Anna. It becomes clear, after the first interchange of dialogue between them, that Anna knows nothing either about the lady's first husband or of the mysterious child she has spoken of in her opening soliloquy. Anna supposes her mistress to be mourning the death of her brother only, and we begin to wonder whether Lord Randolph, like Orsino, believes that it is time all these tears for a brother should be dried away. However the moment seems ripe for disclosure and the lady discloses :

> "*In the cold bosom of the earth is lodged,*
> *Mangled with wounds, the husband of my youth*
> *And in some cavern of the ocean lies*
> *My child and his.*"

Matilda, in short, eighteen years before our story opens, had been guilty of a secret marriage with the son of the then Lord Douglas, her father's plighted foe, who, as sons will, had made Matilda's brother his closest friend, and finally, his best man at an irregular, but valid, wedding.

> "*Three weeks, three little weeks, with wings of down,*"

marked the extent of Matilda's married life and then her husband and her brother went off together to the local war and were killed, leaving her nominally a maid, actually an expectant mother. The priest who had married Douglas and Matilda, having fallen in the same inconvenient battle, there was no one she could turn to for help but her nurse. This faithful creature had managed to keep Matilda's secret until the child (a boy) was born and had then hurried out with him into the darkness of a December night and, with him, had perished in the storm.

The delivery of this news, though rather complicating, is new, and good enough for any audience, but it puts Anna in a queer position. Hume pointed this out to the author and made a very good suggestion which Mr. Home was either too conceited, or too busy teaching the Prince of Wales, to take :

"After Anna had lived eighteen years with Lady Randolph, and yet had been kept out of the secret, there seems to be no sufficient reason why, at that very time, she should have been let into it. The spectator is apt to suspect that it was in order to instruct him ; a very good end indeed, but which might have been attained by a careful and artificial conduct of the dialogue . . . Might not Anna be supposed to have returned to her mistress after a long absense ? This might account for a greater flow of confidence."

Anna, though suitably astonished at these disclosures, is not too overwhelmed by the flow of confidence to remark the approach of a new character. She, like her mistress, falls at critical moments into hissing alliteration.

"*Glenalvon comes*
And hitherward he slowly stalks his way."

Glenalvon, though not apparently Lord Randolph's son by an earlier marriage, is nevertheless his heir: he is also in love with Lord Randolph's wife and has therefore a double motive for plotting to come into his inheritance at once. He is altogether an ignoble character. Hume considered Glenalvon to be among " the more considerable objections to the play ":

> " Glenalvon's character is too abandoned. Such a man is scarce in nature: at least it is inartificial in a poet to suppose such a one, as if he could not conduct his fable by the ordinary passions, infirmities and vices of human nature."

Another more ingenuous critic has wondered that any actor could be found " willing to pourtray such a monster." This shows an engaging ignorance of the actor's appreciation of a part. Glenalvon as an acting part, is one of the plums of the piece. Not only has he the three first curtains (he would undoubtedly have had the fifth but that he has been slain earlier in the act, after a magnificent exit with drawn sword, exclaiming " Now is the time!") but he is the moving spirit of the plot which begins with his entrance. Glenalvon also has more soliloquies than any other character in the play, thus proving himself a villain in the tradition of Crookback and Iago, and his lines are frequent in such effectiveness as:

> " *Darkly a project peers upon my mind,*
> *Like the red moon when rising in the east*
> *Cross'd and divided by strange coloured clouds.*"

or, more viciously :
> "*He seldom errs
> Who thinks the worst he can of woman-kind.*"

Garrick however, when *Douglas* was offered to him thought even less of Glenalvon's part than he did of the rest of the play, which he read and rejected in 1756. His criticism is considerably embittered by a feeling that Lady Randolph was too old, at the time of the action of the play, for all three male characters in it to be, or to be supposed to be, in love with her.

He expatiates to Lord Bute :

> "Glenalvon's Suspicions and Jealousy upon it (without saying anything of *his* violent Love for y[e] Lady, who cannot be of a Love-inspiring Age) are premature and unnatural ... *Glenalvon* is a villain without plan or Force ; He raises our Expectation in a Soliloquy at y[e] first, but sinks Ever after—L[d] Randolph is unaccountably work'd upon by *Glenalv*[n] to believe his Lady fond of *Douglas*, and the Youth is as unaccountably attack'd by Ld. Randolph, and looses his Life for a suppos'd Injury which he has done to him, whose Life he just before preserv'd—and what is this Injury ? Why Love for a Lady, who is old Enough to be his Mother, Whom he has scarcely seen, and wth whom it was impossible to *indulge* any Passion, there not being Time, from his Entrance to his Death, ev'n to *conceive* one."

The introduction of Glenalvon at the end of the First Act is, in spite of Garrick, a good piece of theatre. Lady Randolph, refusing to meet her enemy, retires, not before she has observed to Anna with that increase of sibilance we have already had occasion to remark in the poet's diction as the tide of emotion rises :

> "*Self denied*
> *And master of his appetites he seems :*
> *But his fierce nature, like a fox chained up,*
> *Watches to seize unseen the wished-for prey.*"

Then, leaving the stage for the first time since the raising of the curtain, Lady Randolph goes out on the rather weak line :

> "*Stay and detain him till I reach the castle.*"

Glenalvon, possibly through nervousness, is even more alliterative than his relatives have been. His first line when left alone with Anna runs :

> "*What doest thou muse on, meditative maid ?*"

Anna does not discourage him too harshly and after a little dalliance (" Thy youth, thy beauty, cannot be questioned ") she leaves him. Glenalvon then takes the centre of the stage and informs the audience that, so far as Lady Randolph is concerned, his intention is to " woo her as a lion woos his bride " and further that Lord Randolph " has lived too long." He announces that the lady has no relatives to interfere with his intentions and that " the deed's a-doing now " that will dispose of her husband that same afternoon. As for the neighbours :

> "*I know no chief that will defy Glenalvon.*"

With this effective line a good expository First Act is over and the curtain descends.

CLOUDY SYMBOLS

So far, except for a few stray lines such as

"*This fatal day stirs my time-settled sorrow—*
Troubles afresh the fountain of my heart"

those given to Lady Randolph have yielded nothing to make the twentieth century playgoer wish to have seen Mrs. Siddons in the part. In fact it is quite easy to imagine all the faults contemporary critics allowed themselves to find in her, displayed here to their highest degree. Lugubrious, humorless, sepulchral, lachrymose, the actress is forced by the part into being. That Mrs. Siddons brought personal beauty and great majesty of bearing to Lady Randolph we know, but we still must suspect her of having been almost funny at moments, even to an audience inured to tragedies in blank verse and in contemporary modern dress.

Act II. opens with exposition over and done: the play quickens into action and begins to justify its fame. The scene is unchanged. As the curtain rises Lady Randolph enters followed by Anna and meets a clamour of servants surrounding a stranger. They are quickly joined by Lord Randolph " and a Young Man with their swords drawn and bloody." At first it seems that Lord Randolph has obtained his wish and has been out fighting: but it soon transpires that he has done nothing more dangerous than go for a walk by himself and get into trouble at the crossroads with some robbers from whom the Young Man—a person of great nobility and beauty of aspect—has saved him. Soon we are in the midst of discoveries. The Young Man makes a speech beginning with the well-known declaration:

> "*My name is Norval : on the Grampian Hills*
> *My father feeds his flock.*"

The rest of the speech has worn better than its now too hackneyed opening. Lord Randolph is quite pleased with his modest and beautiful young rescuer until, having decided to present the youth to the King of Scotland as a reward for his valour, he hears a well-known sob, and enquires, rather tartly,

> "*Ha, my Matilda! wherefore starts that tear?*"

to which Lady Randolph makes the irritating and bodeful answer :

> "*I cannot say : for various affections,*
> *And strangely mingled, in my bosom swell*
> *And each of them may well command a tear.*"

The Young Man, now become Norval in the rubric, goes off with Lord Randolph to take a look at the still inactive army, the Baron announcing his intention to get home in time for dinner, in the following periphrasis :

> "*About the time that the declining sun*
> *Shall his broad orb o'er yonder hills suspend*
> *Expect us to return.*"

A scene between Lady Randolph and Anna now follows and here, at last, we get a taste of the stuff from which great acting springs. The lady's tears flow still, but not from her eyes : they form the

CLOUDY SYMBOLS 167

unseen undercurrent of a memory that is quivering with unreasonable yet persistent hope . . .

> "*How blest the mother of yon gallant Norval!*
> *She for a living husband bore her pains,*
> *And heard him bless her when a man was born:*
> *She nursed her smiling infant on her breast;*
> *Tended the child, and reared the pleasing boy.*
> *She, with affection's triumph, saw the youth*
> *In grace and comeliness surpass his peers:*
> *Whilst I to a dead husband bore a son,*
> *And to the roaring waters gave my child.*"

The boy she has seen must be of an age with the child she has lost.

> "*Whilst thus I mused, a spark from fancy fell*
> *On my sad heart, and kindled up a fondness.*"

Little by little instinct gropes nearer to the truth.

> "*I'll be the artist of young Norval's fortunes.*
> *'Tis pleasing to admire! most apt was I*
> *To this affection in my better days . . .*
> *Have you not sometimes seen an early flower*
> *Open its bud, and spread its silken leaves*
> *To catch sweet airs, and odours to bestow . . .*"

Her spirit, half healed now, drifts on in a happy melancholy until Glenalvon enters and we realize that the attack on Lord Randolph has been engineered by him and that his feelings about young Norval are positively viperish. Glenalvon is true to type. Like all stage villains he is better at making plots than at bringing them off. His reflections on his career, made after Lady Randolph has trounced him roundly and left him to think over his position, are frankly bitter. The oath that intensifies them, though violent in intention, has something of the weakness of real villainy about its spoken utterance.

> " *Why, rape and murder are not simple means !*
> *Th' imperfect rape to Randolph gave a spouse ;*
> *And the intended murder introduced*
> *A favourite to hide the sun from me ;*
> *And, worst of all, a rival. Burning hell !* "

He elaborates a plan, sneak that he is, for suborning Norval's servant and extracting from him " venom most fatal to his heedless lord." Having worked the situation up to danger point he brings down the curtain.

With Act III. we reach the climax of the acting opportunities of the play. In a long and most skilfully suspended scene a peasant, whom Lord Randolph's servants have seized because he has been found with a great deal of handsome jewellery in his possession, reveals to Lady Randolph that her son is still living and that the jewels, which she recognizes as the property of her dead husband Douglas, were found on the infant rescued from the sea who has grown up to be known as Norval. This is Lord Randolph's rescuer.

We have the written testimony of persons who attended the first performance of Mrs. Siddons in this part, to the shiver that crept through the house when, instead of interrupting the peasant's account of how he rescued the unknown male child from the sea by shrieking, as Mrs. Crawford had done, she whispered in a dry hoarse voice :

"*Was he alive?*"

Once again, in her own words, "the awful consciousness that one is the sole object of attention to that immense space, lined, as it were with human intellect from top to bottom and all around" passed, and she was lost in the miracle of being not Sarah Siddons attempting to rival Mrs. Crawford, but Lady Randolph—another Lady Randolph— as real as, and, as she must in some triumphant song of her heart have then known, greater than any before her.

From that moment the act proceeds through a crescendo of confirmation and excitement, held up for a moment only by a narrative interlude at the point where the shepherd announces that he and his wife, deciding to bring up the foundling with their own children, began to use to the family's advantage the gold and jewels with which its cradle had been lined. Here the eighteenth century breaks in to remind us how much the mechanism of drama has lost by the disappearance of Calvinistic doctrine. The spirit that inspired Mr. Home at this point became so consciously virtuous that he broke, for a couplet, into a never to be corrected rhyme.

"*We left the country, travelled to the north*
Bought flocks and herds and gradually brought forth
Our secret wealth. But God's all-seeing eye
Beheld our avarice, and smote us sore :
For one by one all our own children died
And he, the stranger, sole remained the heir
Of what indeed was his."

No stage directions indicate Lady Randolph's behaviour during the recital, but Anna has a speech that gives us some idea of what Mrs. Siddons did with her part at this crisis :

> "*Just are your transports—High fated dame!*
> *But yet remember that you are beheld*
> *By servile eyes ; your gestures may be seen*
> *Impassioned, strange . . .*"

Lady Randolph, accordingly, puts a curb on her emotion and calling the servants together gives the shepherd a safe conduct through the countryside and sends him to search for young Norval, in order that, wearing his father's bracelets, he may claim his inheritance, now held by an uncle. It is at this point that Lady Randolph begins to refer to Lord Randolph as "the baron" and Norval who has already changed his name in the rubric from "A Young Man" to "Stranger" before becoming Norval is hereafter given both in text and rubric the title of Douglas.

Lady Randolph is now all afire with maternal affection.

> "*Most of all I long to clasp his neck,*"

she exclaims, and the prudent Anna again warns her :

> "*In public lest your tenderness break forth,*"

adding the only too true generalization :

> "*For, if a cherub in the shape of woman*
> *Should walk this world, yet defamation would*
> *Like a vile cur, bark at the angel's train.*"

CLOUDY SYMBOLS 171

While they are yet devising means to recognize young Douglas with proper caution Glenalvon comes to announce that the Danes are here at last, not on a mere pleasure excursion for a taste of battle, but with serious agricultural designs.

"*They come to settle.*"

This means real warfare and Lady Randolph, anticipating Shakespeare, has an apostrophe on the news, beginning :

"*How many mothers shall bewail their sons !
How many widows weep their husbands slain.*"

In her excitement at the imminent reunion with her son, a little flustered too, by Glenalvon's news, the lady treats the villain with a gentleness to which he, having a nasty masochistic strain in his psychologically improbable make-up, does not respond, though, hypocrite that he is, he pretends that to please her he will cease from assailing her virtue and take her new protégé under his wing during the forthcoming battle.

Once alone on the stage however he unmasks his change of purpose. After observing that "*flattery direct rarely disgusts*" he announces that the lady as well as her lord stands in the way : both must perish, and since it is unlikely that a noble and virtuous matron can be slain on the battlefield, he will arrange for Lord Randolph himself to make away with his wife by cooking up a story that the lady has fallen in love with Norval. The situation is delicate :

> "*Fate o'er my head suspends disgrace and death
> By that weak hair, a peevish female's will,*"

but, at the same time,

> "*Norval, I'm told, has that alluring look,
> 'Twixt man and woman, which I have observed
> To charm the nicer and fantastic dames.*"

It will be easy enough to rouse the baron's jealousy. As for the lady—the curtain falls on his already quoted epigram:

> "*He seldom errs
> Who thinks the worst he can of womankind.*"

With Act IV. the interest definitely passes to the eponymous hero of the play who is, as, indeed, is only fair, given the curtain with a threat to Glenalvon.

> "*When we contend again our strife is mortal.*"

Before this has happened there has been a further disclosure, explaining the hero's proficiency in arms and general culture. These he has acquired from a hermit who was once both a nobleman and a crusader and had had the misfortune to slay, quite by accident, his own long-lost brother. Interrupted by fits of insanity this retired hero has conducted the young man's education in the secret recesses of his cavern. The narration of this rather superfluous tale holds up the action, and bores Lord Randolph who, impatient to be off fighting again, observes coldly, at the close of the story:

> "*Hard is his fate for he was not to blame.*
> *There is a destiny in this strange world*
> *Which oft decrees an undeserved doom.*
> *Let schoolmen tell us why.*"

Fortunately for the baron an officer enters to announce :

> "*My Lord, the trumpets of the troops of Lorn*"—

a line that must have enchanted Sir Walter Scott when he went to see Mrs. Siddons in the part at Edinburgh.

There follows what should be, in spite of commentators, the most moving scene in the piece. Lady Randolph, once more anticipating Shakespeare, remarks to her son :

> "*The soldier's loftiness, the pride and pomp*
> *Investing awful war, Norval, I see*
> *Transport thy youthful mind.*"

Then leading him to the shade of " yon spreading beech " instead of taking him up to her boudoir as a less agitated woman would have done, she discloses to him gradually that she is his mother. Moving though the scene by its nature must be, it is a little marred by the lady's callousness in one important respect. The baron, who has been, in the words of a nineteenth century widow, " more like a friend than a husband by reason of his kindness " to her for over seven years is now to be deprived of

> "*Yonder castle and the wide domain*
> *Which now Lord Randolph, as my husband, holds.*"

The young man, with the pride and generosity of youth, protests that his father's lands and money are quite enough for the present:

" And in the field I'll seek for fame and fortune."

Putting aside for the moment the project of impoverishing her kind husband for this by no means needy son, Lady Randolph breaks into a lament to which the dove's voice and the smiling tenderness Mrs. Siddons had at her command must have given an overwhelming beauty:

" O, my son,
The noblest blood of all the land's abashed,
Having no lackey but pale poverty.
Too long hast thou been thus attended, Douglas."

The lyric strain is not kept up and the speech concludes with a long passage, probably the very one referred to by Horace Walpole when he declared he had read nothing but Mr. Home's *proses*, announcing Lady Randolph's almost idiotic intention of sending her son " a billet by thy rustic follower's hand " appointing a future meeting place.

It then appears that Old Norval is concealed behind a tree " as useful witness " and, having apprised her son of this the lady warns him to beware of Glenalvon. Norval departs, vowing to avenge his mother's outraged feelings. After this piece of irritating silliness is over the dramatist once more mounts to the height of his argument;

Manet Lady Randolph.

"*There burst the smother'd flame!—*
O! thou all righteous and eternal King!
Who father of the fatherless art call'd,
Protect my son! Thy inspiration, Lord!
Hath fill'd his bosom with that sacred fire,
Which in the breast of his forefathers burn'd:
Set him on high, like them, that he may shine
The star and glory of his native land!
Then let the minister of death descend,
And bear my willing spirit to its place."

These ten lines of dramatic writing are good enough to inflame imagination still with some vision of the fire and the pathos that vibrated in the delivery of them by the greatest actress of all time. But the enjoyment of supposing what effect she must have achieved in them is soon ruined for us, by a descent into bathos as sudden as it is smug. The baron is seen approaching with Glenalvon. Instead of expressing some regret for the material losses she is about to inflict on her husband, the lady enquires:

"*How do bad women find*
Unchanging aspects to conceal their guilt?
When I, by reason and by justice urged,
Full hardly can dissemble with these men
In nature's pious cause?"

The case against Family Ties, so loudly urged by our youngest reformers to-day, could hardly find in English literature a stronger instance of the criminal potentialities of maternal affection than this once admired Matilda, who, instead of going frankly to her husband and introducing his stepson and the heir of his estates, thus settling the whole business on a sensible basis, is determined to oust the baron and, like the successful business man, to do it now.

The whole tragedy turns, not on the wickedness of Glenalvon, but on the propensity of Lady Randolph, when not in floods of tears and eloquence, to behave like a perfect goose.

She seems to have written her billet to Norval before the interview under the spreading beech: otherwise how could it have come into Glenalvon's hand so that he can show it to the baron as soon as she has left the courtyard? Randolph is only mildly upset by this proof of his Matilda's giddiness. His feelings can be expressed briefly:

"*She never loved me. What can I expect?*"

He has his hands full, what with the general business of the estate and this war that is going on on the other side of the castle. He would prefer to let well alone. But Glenalvon like Iago, or Polonius, is not to be done out of one of the villain's most popular stock-tricks:

"*This billet must to blooming Norval go,*"

he declares. Then, at midnight, Lord Randolph shall hide him in a thicket and watch his lady's dalliance with the stranger. Not content with this, Glenalvon pushes Lord Randolph behind a convenient bush at once, because he has caught sight of our hero "off." When Norval enters "in a proper mood to chide the thunder" Glenalvon thunders and is chidden. The young men are about to draw their swords when Lord Randolph appearing from his bush forbids two such valuable soldiers to waste their lives in a private quarrel, and a servant appearing with the unexpected announcement :

> " *The banquet waits,*"

the scene comes to an end.

The Fifth Act brings a change of scene. THE WOOD, a simple but adequate stage direction, is amplified immediately by the hero's remark :

> " *This is the place, the centre of the grove ;*
> *Here stands the oak, the monarch of the wood.*"

After some lines of Nature-study Douglas is joined, not by his mother, although he has received her billet by now, but by Old Norval. For some time they recapitulate their several tales, amplified by assurances that the bond between them is far from severed by recent events. Old Norval then begins to explain that while he " fondly trod in each accustom'd path, that to the castle leads," he overheard the baron and Glenalvon plotting the young man's death. Douglas finds it hard to believe that the baron could be so unkind, though he holds Glenalvon capable of anything. A good deal of deeply boring conversation and soliloquy follows. Old Norval repairs to his cottage. Douglas after a little recurrence of Nature-study plans to be the David to some Danish Goliath, on the grounds that his " soul's unaltered wish " still is :

> " *Dead or alive, let me but be renowned !* "

Presently Lady Randolph appears to keep her foolish and unnecessary tryst. After a series of whispered but affectionate passages between mother and son, the baron and Glenalvon duly emerge from their thicket. Revenge is on their brows but as Lord Randolph very properly remarks :

"*Not in her presence.*"

After this the scene positively whirls with the exits and entrances of all four characters. At one moment Glenalvon, left alone, prays :

"*Demons of death come settle on my sword !*" —

at another Lady Randolph " appears at the opposite side of the stage, faint and breathless." As she has only had about thirty seconds in which to run round the backcloth this effect cannot be numbered among the major triumphs of any actress who achieved it. When the other three are, once more and all at once, on the stage " Enter Douglas with a sword in each hand."

Glenalvon is killed off ; Douglas dies from a wound in the back. While he is dying the lady explains to the baron that Douglas is her son and then faints beside the body. Anna, who has this long while been forgotten, enters and says rather superfluously to Lord Randolph :

"*Look there, my lord.*"

After some repetitive dialogue the lady recovers consciousness and breathes the last of her famous speeches :

> *" My son, my son !*
> *My beautiful ! My brave ! how proud I was*
> *Of thee and of thy valour."*

When this is over and Anna has followed her distraught mistress from the stage, Old Norval appears and, solely for the purpose of giving Lady Randolph time to commit suicide, begins a series of remarks the first of which is :

> *" I hear the voice of woe ! "*

Presently, having come to the end of his vocal resources, the actor tears out bunches of his hair and strews the dead body with them. This excess unnerves Lord Randolph who promises the old man a reward if he will only stop doing it.

To them comes Anna with the news that Lady Randolph, while seeming by her gestures to ask : *" Why am I forced to this ? "* has jumped into a waterfall and is no more.

The news is evidently a relief to the baron. His wife, his stepson and his heir are all dead. He is at last free to devote himself to his favourite pastime. A perfectly good war is still on and there are three funerals to arrange for. Rather than face the fuss of these he will repair straight to battle.

Bidding Anna to see that

> *" Cost and pomp upon their funerals wait,"*

he expresses a half-hearted wish that he may fall fighting, and on this rather lame conclusion the curtain falls.

Contemporary opinion was unanimous on the failure of Act V. to sustain the flight which had carried the Acts I., II., and III. to such a pitch of favour with audiences for over fifty years ; but, weak and ridiculous as it now seems to an age that finds the last acts of *Hamlet* and *King Lear* rather too heavily strewn with corpses to be taken seriously, Home's tragedy is full of indestructibly good acting stuff and it is easy to see why Mrs. Siddons made so great a personal triumph in it.

She was a very careful reader of any part offered to her.

" When a part is first put before me for studying," she once said, " I look it over in a general way, to see if it is in Nature, and if it is, I am sure it can be played." To Mrs. Siddons, who had lost several children, a part in which a mother is inconsolable for the loss of an only son would appear to be quite in nature. There was also another, more secret, reason, as we shall see later, why she should excel, as the still beautiful, still desired Matilda : but of this she was probably only dimly conscious at the time.

What she did know was that *Douglas* was a good commercial proposition. It had never failed with any audience yet, and she herself was aware of the extent to which she could now electrify the house in any part she had accepted whole-heartedly. Besides there really was a demand from the public for an exhibition of her power in this real test of a tragedy queen's quality. Her attitude towards a play was far from being wholly, or even in any large measure, commercial. The strength of her greatness lay in her artistic integrity. One of the reasons that made her as a player more impressive than her brother was that, unlike him, she did not believe that all the great plays were already written and that new plays by new authors were bound to be nothing but rehashing, and rubbish at that. After her success as Lady Randolph, when gratitude and self-interest combined to urge her to play the leading lady in Mr. Samuel Greatheed's tragedy *The Regent*, she did her best to refuse the part, and for reasons expressed forcibly enough in a letter to Dr. Whalley:

"It strikes me that the plot is very lame, and the characters very, very ill-sustained in general, but more so the lady for whom the author has me in his eye. This woman is one of those monsters of perfection, who is an angel before her time, and is so entirely resigned to the will of Heaven that (to a very mortal like myself) she appears to be the most provoking piece of still life one has ever had the misfortune to meet. Her struggles and conflicts are so worthily expressed, that we conclude they do not cost her much pain, and she is so pious that we are satisfied she looks upon her afflictions as so many convoys to Heaven, and wish her there, or anywhere else but in the tragedy."

We must therefore suppose that she found Lady Randolph "in Nature." At all events she played the part so convincingly as to eclipse the memory of all other actresses in it, excepting Mrs. Crawford, although the *Encyclopædia Britannica*, with a lightheartedness which distinguishes the attitude to the drama of that otherwise accurate and informing compilation, mentions Peg Woffington alone among her predecessors in the part.

It is interesting too, in this connection, to remember that Lady Randolph was still in popular demand by the time Henry Siddons had grown up and was able to play the part of Norval, and also, on one occasion when Kemble's accomplished fellow-actor the tragedian Cooke was too drunk to play opposite her Elvira in *Pizarro*, to read his part so well that the audience gave him a very special round of applause. He died in 1815.

5

In these three plays, none of them of the first order of excellence, Mrs. Siddons had accomplished three distinct and varying triumphs. In Isabella she had revived an old part of her own and, fresh from the provinces, had taken London by a particularly violent storm : in Lady Randolph she had essayed to vanquish a great reputation already established in this more or less contemporary work, and had left even Mrs. Crawford in a second place : in Mrs. Haller she had herself created a new part, in an entirely new form of drama.

By the time she appeared in *The Stranger* she was established both on the boards and in Society as the queen of the hour.

As varnish to the pictures of Mrs. Siddons in these three parts it is not without interest to consider the tone of a highly moral pamphlet published anonymously in 1783. The author calls his tribute *The Theatrical Portrait* and gives an account in verse of " the celebrated Actress " in four of her parts ; Calista in *The Fair Penitent* ; Jane Shore ; Belvidera in *Venice Preserved* and Isabella. His verse merits little attention, being flat and uncritical. But in his Advertisement to a not very interesting poem the author strikes that note of moral sublimity associated for ever with the name of Kemble and sounded every time the words " Mrs. Siddons " occur on the lips of posterity.

" This little Piece is presented to the Public with a View of drawing the Attention to reflect on the Morals and Sentiments contained in the different Plays alluded to—as well as portraying the inimitable Performances of Mrs. Siddons ; to keep awake in the Mind the various Virtues and Vices of each Character, that the One may be pursued with more Alacrity, and the Other shunned with the greater Detestation.
" It need not be told to any but the plain and unlearned Reader, that the first Plays acted on the English Stage, were collected either from the Scriptures or historical Events recorded in Sacred History, at a Period when the Dawnings of Christianity began to spread over the Land, and disperse the gloomy Clouds of Heathenism and Idolatry. At this early Area, the Theatre was resorted to as a Place of Divine Exercise, and peculiarly devoted to Virtue and the Muses. In every Place where Theatres have been erected on this Plan, they have not only reformed the Manners, but refined the Ideas of the People. It was from those of this kind, that ancient Rome owed all her Glory ! They inspired her Sons with such Ideas of Heroism and Virtue, that they sacrificed even Life itself to excel in either—and thus became the Masters of the World ! And may I not add, that Plays have in a great Measure infus'd that intrepid and daring Spirit into the Breasts of Englishmen which is unknown to all Nations but ourselves ! Our Poets never failing to introduce in their

Pieces, Warriors of gallant Bearing, and Statesmen whose piercing Eyes can see beyond the Clouds! In short, the Theatres are Places of Vice and Dissipation to none but those who makes them such. Many go there to have their Passions warmed, but few their Hearts; some for Fashion's Sake, and some to pass away an idle Hour; and of Course Depart as Simple as they went.

"If the Theatres were shut because they are frequented by the Disorderly and Profane, on the same Grounds, we may close the Church Doors, and at once deprive the rising Generation of knowing Good from Evil, and let the World revolt back again to Ignorance and Superstition. No, rather throw the Doors wider open to admit base Characters than otherwise, for at the Worst they are Beasts of Reason, and have Souls as capable to rise in Virtue as sink in Vice.

"Doubtless there are some Persons (more Pious than Wise) who look upon the Stage as unhallowed Ground, and dare not intrust themselves there; by which absurd Notion, they are more subject to become the Dupes of designing Villains and flattering Sycophants, than the rest of Mankind. For there we read Menkind and know the World: there being not a Virtue or a Vice that ever entered the Human Mind but is at Times hinted at and shewed in its proper Light and Colour.

"The Theatres as they are at present governed, are the Glories of the Nation, the Fountains of our Liberties, the Encourages of every fine Art, patronizing Merit in every Line of Life, refine the Manners, improve the Taste, and are Enemies to nothing but Vice and Folly."

Soon after the publication of this eulogium Mrs. Siddons received the Royal command to present herself at the Palace—then called Buckingham House—there to give readings to the King and

Queen and their children. At the same time she had been asked to sit to the three great English artists, who happened to be the most fashionable of contemporary portrait painters. It will be interesting to see what the giants, Gainsborough and Reynolds, made of their beautiful young sitter, and how the brilliant young Lawrence treated her, first and last, during the period of her glory.

II

FOUR PORTRAITS

I

On the 24th day of April 1784 Mrs. Siddons and her brother appeared in Thomson's *Tragedy of Tancred and Sigismunda*. This had been one of Garrick's successes with Mrs. Cibber and, as Boaden points out,

> "Mrs. Cibber is said to have been extremely like Mr. Garrick, below the middle stature like him . . . they might have been thought brother and sister—a sort of advantage, which Kemble and Siddons *fully* enjoyed, with the greatest elegance of figure."

The part of Sigismunda in the early scenes is mostly a thinking one.

> "In the whole second act, Sigismunda only *once* appears; and that is oppressed with grief and passing *silently* through the back scene."

But in the protracted death of Sigismunda which closes the play Mrs. Siddons carried off the four long speeches given by the heroine *after* the fatal wound with so much power that the audience regretted the management's decision to omit the Epilogue given to the character of the Tragic Muse and always spoken in Mrs. Cibber's day after the final curtain.

This regret is said to have inspired Reynolds with the idea of painting the magnificent Portrait of Mrs. Siddons as the Tragick Muse, a picture acclaimed, not only as a masterpiece in itself but also as the greatest portrait ever painted of a woman. Reynolds, who saw her in Thomson's play, may possibly have conceived his picture when the curtain rising on Act III. " discloses Sigismunda seated in melancholy rumination." We know how majestic her poses, how soft her melancholy could be, and we can understand how, moved by the communal emotion of the whole house after the death scene, the pictorial effect of that earlier vision may well have returned to the painter's visual memory and so fired his genius.

Sir Joshua had made an exhaustive study of the compositions of Michael Angelo and the figure of the Prophet Joel from the Vatican frescoes was, we are told, in his mind when he conceived his version of the Tragick Muse. In the fresco the prophet is seen seated and bending over an unrolled scroll; the right foot thrust forward beneath his heavy draperies, the left knee bent backwards: two attendant figures stand behind his chair. The composition of the Tragick Muse follows this arrangement in all but one detail.

Sir Joshua conceived of the actress as a figure— fully lit, her footstool on the clouds that roll above Olympus, studying her part, seated, in the attitude of Joel, while behind her chair, Terror bearing the bowl of purgation, and Pity bending her head sideways in grief—stand, in the shadow, against a cloudy background. Robed in a reddish brown velvet underdress bordered with gold, with a skirt and over-sleeves of yellow satin against which a thickly twisted rope of pearls fell knotted to her waist, the lady is said to have assumed the required pose. As the painter began to make the first outlines of the model on his canvas a bird, on a branch outside the open window, burst into song. The actress, mobile in her response to any emotion expected or surprising, dropped her scroll and raised her head to listen and the painter, seeing his own more definitely conceived pose of the actress studying her part thus broken, bade her stay as she was and painted Mrs. Siddons listening to the voice of nature. Mrs. Siddons herself, many years later, gave a different version of the tale, saying that she took up her pose of her own accord, and that Sir Joshua was enraptured with it, seeing it as a fine inspiration. In one way or another, the pose was obtained, and the picture remains a masterpiece of collaboration between a great painter and a sitter as great in her own art. The effect is so spontaneous and so grand, the composition so balanced in its magnificence, that the mixture of the allegorical with the actual does not disturb the spectator's mind. He does not feel it ridiculous that a solid footstool should rest on clouds nor that two spirits in Greco-Roman attire should wait on a goddess dressed, and head-dressed in the height of fashion for the year 1784.

The first version of this enthralling picture, once in the possession of the Grosvenor family, has now gone to America bearing still the signature of the master who painted it on the hem of the underdress worn by the goddess he painted, to be seen more clearly in the Californian sunshine than it could be in our more misted sunlight : but a replica, made for a Mr. Desenfans, is still in the possession of the Dulwich Gallery. Unfortunately the bitumen used by Sir Joshua to the fatal detriment of much of his work, is eating its way through the pigment, and all now to be seen in England of the masterpiece is a dark and shadowy blistering of brown paint from which the noble pose and exquisite face of the sitter are seen with a trace of the softness of pearls against the perfect skin of her neck and bosom painted as softly as the lovely and expressive hand emerging from the billows of lawn used for the undersleeves, their rounded folds balancing the cloud below the footstool of the Muse.

The usual effect on the lay mind made by this impressive composition, is the one aimed at by the painter : but anyone who has come upon an enlargement of the head made from a photograph or has had the rare opportunity of isolating the head from the rest of the picture and studying it at close quarters, will observe that the genius of the artist has succeeded in depicting, not merely the great actress whom it was no flattery to call the Tragick Muse, but a woman of singularly tender and expressive beauty as well. The famous Kemble nose, large as it is, is fine, with sensitive nostrils ; the eyes are liquid and expressive, the lips are sensitive and mobile.

The Tragick Muse of Sir Joshua is the same dewy and passionate creature as Lawrence painted in the "toothache bandage" picture. We can almost speak to her and hear her speaking in reply from her frame on the wall in the National Gallery to-day.

But Lawrence's sitter was a woman disarmed by the occasion, while the actress who sat for Reynolds came to him trailing the clouds of her fame and safe in the control that must always lie behind the display of any assumed and dramatic emotion.

The genius of Reynolds, the infatuation of Lawrence, these have given us Mrs. Siddons as she breathed and looked, the tragic actress, the impulsive and loving woman; with Gainsborough we come to a different but no less illuminating aspect of her triumph. It was to Georgiana, Duchess of Devonshire, that Gainsborough owed his two masterpieces in female portraiture: first he painted the lady herself with her beautiful sister. Years later, when, largely owing to the enthusiasm of the Duchess, Mrs. Siddons returned to conquer London —Gainsborough—two years before his death, made the stately portrait of a fashionable woman, a picture more widely known, possibly because it is better preserved and has been for so long accessible to the general public, than the flowing and now half-perished splendours of Reynolds.

Gainsborough was at the height of his fame when Mrs. Siddons, young, successful but still a little shy and solemn off the stage, came every morning from her lodging in the Strand to Schomberg House, the mansion in Pall Mall in which the fashionable painter was installed. Whether because whom Gainsborough painted he painted in the hat that still bears his name, or because it was still fashionable to wear black velvet and ostrich plumes with powdered hair in London in 1782, and Mrs. Siddons naturally wore them then (though she was almost the first Englishwoman to wear her hair unpowdered), it is in powder and black velvet that her head is dressed in this, almost the only portrait that shows her thus.

The silky gleam of her blue striped dress, the painting of the fur muff from which her hands have slipped, have made this picture a model for the art students of a century, and, as such, it still holds its own with any other picture now in the National Gallery. But, as a portrait of Mrs. Siddons, it tells us little but that she was lovely, even with that nose the painter could not make an end of, and young in spirit; a little timid even, in spite of her thirty years and her growing success in the fashionable world. Isolate the long, calm face from its fan of hair and its commanding hat, and you are left with the delicate features of a woman, still hardly more than a girl, rather anxiously trying to keep her pose; looking, almost too steadily, at that point outside the picture the artist has told her to keep her eyes on; pleased by the honour of being painted by him, but quite ready to sweep downstairs to her hackney carriage and go home to take off the blue silk gown and the gauze scarves and the huge top-heavy hat, and to shake the powder out of her auburn hair.

Gainsborough was too fine a portrait-painter to treat any sitter merely as a lay figure, but his was not the genius of a Sir Joshua recognizing genius in another guise, and a different art from his own, nor had his interest in this quite newly risen star of the theatre grown with him since childhood, as we are presently to consider that of the young Lawrence growing, till in the full strength of his power he painted the portrait we have already considered for a moment in connection or rather in contrast with the Tragick Muse.

The National Gallery Catalogue describes No. 785 as

> "MRS. SIDDONS : in a white dress, a blue sash, and a green cloak which hangs loosely over her shoulders,"

adding a note to the effect that this picture was exhibited at the Royal Academy in 1797.

It was known in the Siddons-Kemble circle as the toothache-bandage picture. The portrait was painted some time before its exhibition and remained in the possession of Mrs. Siddons's daughter Cecilia until her death in 1868. It does not represent the actress in any of her parts, nor is it a personification, much less an ambitious and conventional portrait of a fashionable beauty. Painted a dozen years later than Gainsborough's masterpiece, it shows a woman no less beautiful but far more approachable than the stately wearer of powder and plumes who sat for the great canvas now hanging a few yards away from it in the adjoining room. No photograph begins to do justice to the liquid melancholy, the almost smiling tenderness of the eyes that look out under the soft clustering of brown curls confined by the famous " toothache bandage " said to have been invented for her by the painter when they discussed together her costume for the sleep-walking scene in *Macbeth*.

The dignity of the Muse who sat to Reynolds; the slight tension of the woman who knew she was, after all, only posing as a lady of quality to Gainsborough; the stiffness of the girl who sat to the painter of her own age in Stuart's delightful picture already referred to in Part II, are all gone here. Lawrence has painted Sarah Siddons at home; disarmed; herself. There is a slight disarray, an unassumed negligence about her dress, as though he had caught her relaxing her efforts after a successful night, or indulging in one of her displays of comic singing to her children, and, interrupting the laughter or the doze, had said " Stay as you are! I will paint you so."

Go and stand before the small canvas, it is little more than two feet square, and you will be faced by a woman off her guard; a woman happy and bemused by her happiness; a woman who was almost as enchanted by what she saw, or by the shimmering pleasure of her silent thoughts, as the lover of beauty who stood and set that beauty down in so eloquent a statement. The painter must have been subjugated by the subject of his brush, and by the mood he must have shared or he could never have thus captured it and so made himself and his sitter immortal. I know of no other portrait in which the harmony between the two people concerned in its making is so absolutely conveyed as it is in this picture of a woman half smiling, wholly tender in her response to the flattery and affection we see reflected from the painter's eyes and shining in her own.

Another and a very different picture of the same woman was to find a place in that same exhibition of 1797. The significance of this will be best observed at a later stage of the present narrative. For the moment we are concerned in following Mrs. Siddons through the days of her success, and so come chronologically to the year 1804 when a full length portrait of Mrs. Siddons was also exhibited in the Royal Academy.

As by that time Lawrence was supposed not to be on speaking terms with any member of the family it has been assumed that Mrs. Siddons either sat (or rather stood) for this unpleasant picture some years earlier, or it might be fancied that it was painted from memory and from those other portraits, drawings, sketches, pastels he had never ceased making of her since the days when as a child his pencil had noted every detail of her ridiculous over-elaborate stage toilettes in her two earliest tragic parts. But the portrait was painted for Mrs. Fitz-Hugh—the actress's intimate friend, and bears every sign of coming straight to the artist from the sitter herself. The woman who stands, enormous in black velvet, facing the spectator is past the beauty of her prime. Her figure is full; her arms hang heavily from the white satin lining of the short bunched sleeves of her dress. The magnificent features are still well cut and regular and the hair, parted in the middle and drawn down in bandeaux on either side of the forehead, has lost its curls and its auburn tints though it is still thick and glossy. A Spanish comb gives height to a figure already tall enough, and a brooch and ring of cornelian with a necklace and earrings, either to match or of a corresponding shade of red coral, relieve the sombreness of the velvet dress; this opens over a petticoat of white satin against which the tassels of her girdle—as large as hearth-brushes and as sooty in texture—hang down below the knee. The wall behind her is an angry red; she stands by a table, far too low for its purpose: on this a folio volume is propped by a smaller book from which a red book-marker hangs, repeating the colour of the brooch and ring she wears. The canvas is large: the figure full length, full face, full size, the ugliest way to paint any human portrait. The painting is heavy and deliberate, the work of a man in a deliberate rage. No need here to put a frame around the face to reach its full significance. It is the same face as looks out of the toothache bandage and of all the other portraits we have considered. Mrs. Siddons had features too regular and too marked for any competent artist to make a bad portrait of her. Here, though the picture as a picture is worse than bad, the likeness is still speaking. Mrs. Siddons is now a favourite at Court: she gives readings to the Royal family; and elsewhere; she is asked to more parties than she can attend and has close friends in the highest circles. And Lawrence, who has adored her for twenty years and more, is angry and jealous. His frivolity has brought unhappiness into the family life he was so glad to share; his uncontrolled and fluctuating ardours have broken two young hearts and wrecked a mother's peace. And now, banished from her presence he puts on to canvas the smouldering resentment of his own vanity and gives to the tragic eyes he can never forget a look of suffering, and to the still beautiful face a flush of anger, as if this were her answer to the prayers for forgiveness he had so often and so wildly made.

In all Lawrence's portraits but this one—whether it were man, woman or child he was painting—we can see the pleased response of the sitter to the captivating charm of the artist whose business it was to please as well as to paint his model. In both senses of the word this portrait-painter flattered. But in these two portraits of the woman he painted more than any other there is no flattery ; here, if anywhere, Lawrence was sincere.

Hanging in the same room of the National Gallery as the small enchanting head and shoulders of Mrs. Siddons when she was his friend, is the larger portrait of Queen Charlotte painted at Windsor and exhibited in 1790. It is interesting to turn from one picture to the other and to see with what ease the volatile genius of the artist selected the material on which to focus his own enjoyment of his work. Compared with the Queen's picture that of Mrs. Siddons is a mere sketch from which the lovely, ardent face looks out, enchanted and enchanting as he made and saw it. When as a youth of barely twenty-one he went to paint the plain, dull, kindly rather stupid German lady who was wife to George III, Lawrence solaced himself by lavishing all the brilliance of his consummate technique on the white lace, the silver galloon, the royal rope of pearls, the delicate royal hands against the blue of the Queen's shimmering silken skirts. The likeness is there, but, because there must be excitement as well, it goes into each fine accessory to this portrait of a self-effacing woman sitting by an open window through which a view of Eton College Chapel gleams, white against a blue sky and the green and gold of massed trees painted almost as Giorgione might have seen them. This royal portrait, the work of a boy of twenty-one, is among the glories of the National collection. The same artist's last portrait of Mrs. Siddons is so little worthy of his fame that we hide it in a dark corner of the basement under the side-walks of Trafalgar Square. And yet he was at the height of his powers when he painted it. His failure to give it any of the superficial beauty, he of all painters was so easily able to evoke, is a sign of something outside the province of an observer looking at the painting only to interpret. We shall presently see, in what circumstances, and for what cause he allowed himself to make the glowering record of so heavy a change.

PART IV

The Sitter

I

HER PRIVATE STYLE

I

WHEN AS a girl of sixteen, thwarted in her love for young William Siddons, Sarah Kemble left the stage and went into her pleasant exile at Guy's Cliffe, she addressed a farewell poem to her lover, breathing a vow to which she remained technically faithful to the end of her days :

> " *Say not, Strephon, I'm untrue*
> *When I only think of you ;*
> *If you do but think of me*
> *As I of you, then shall you be*
> *Without a rival in my heart,*
> *Which ne'er can play a tyrant's part.*
>
> *Trust me, Strephon, with thy love—*
> *I swear by Cupid's bow above,*
> *Naught shall make me e'er betray*
> *Thy passion till my dying day :*
> *If I live, or if I die,*
> *Upon my constancy rely.*"

These girlish verses with their commonplace rhymes and innocent unnecessary change from the plural to singular personal pronoun probably caused more tears to flow from the writer's eyes than she shed over any later page of her own composition. The young are readily moved by their own intrinsically imitative efforts at self-expression and, as one of the wisest of men has observed, "*les lettres d'amour vraiment passionées sont souvent plus dangereuses pour celle qui les écrit que pour celui qui les reçoit.*"

Sarah Kemble had a long lesson to get by heart both as a woman and as a writer, before, having returned to and retired from the stage where she had, and has never been, excelled, she wrote the poem which sums up the lifetime's experience of her warm and impulsive heart:

> "*Say, what's the brightest wreath of fame*
>   *But canker'd buds, that opening close;*
> *Ah! What's the world's most pleasing dream*
>   *But broken fragments of repose?*
>
> *Lead me where Peace with steady hand*
>   *The mingled Cup of Life shall hold,*
> *Where Time shall smoothly pour his sand,*
>   *And Wisdom turn that sand to gold.*
>
> *Then haply at Religion's shrine*
>   *This weary heart its load shall lay,*
> *Each wish my fatal love resign,*
>   *And Passion melt in tears away.*"

These verses mark, not only the great distances that separate a girl's dream of constancy from a woman's knowledge of her own heart, but they display a command of language, a literary skill and judgment sufficient in themselves to prove that the writer of both pieces had such gifts for assimilation and self-improvement, such elasticity of mind as always distinguish the really great artist.

These two poems may be taken, the first as an introduction to, the second as an epitome of, her private life, written for and to herself. We also possess another and a differently revealing piece of Mrs. Siddons's literary work, accomplished earlier, but not given to the world till 1822, when John Murray published a little book called:

" *The story of our First Parents :* /selected from Milton's Paradise Lost,/for the use of Young Persons/by Mrs. Siddons."

Mrs. Siddons had, from childhood, preferred Milton to any other poet: it was from his works that she gave her celebrated readings, quite as often as from the plays of Shakespeare. There is a story of a certain party at which, in one of her solemn replies to a question put to her by a stranger, she declared that not only was Milton her favourite poet but that she was never without a copy of his works. Her interlocutor, not knowing his opponent, challenged this statement, whereupon Mrs. Siddons, diving into the commodious reticule she carried, produced a volume of *Paradise Lost*.

It has been suggested that the dignity and refinement of mind so often observed in peasants of the Scottish Highlands and in the shepherds and slate-quarriers of North Wales is due in a great measure to their familiarity with the text of the Authorized Version. And indeed, the constant and almost exclusive study of the complete literature of any race, especially of such a race as the Hebrew and in such a language as early seventeenth century English, is capable of providing, if not a liberal, at any rate an education at once liberating and disciplined. Mrs. Siddons, whose business was Shakespeare and whose pleasure was Milton, could not fail to grow in richness of mind, feeding as she did on such literary pastures, and, when she came to write herself, in the power of felicitous and graphic expression. We have seen how various and lucid in style her letters to her friends were. When she dealt with more formal business she was able to write a quite admirably cadenced prose. This is how she introduces her little book to the world :

> "The following Abridgement of Paradise Lost was made several years ago for the purpose of being read to my children. A taste for the sublime and beautiful is an approach to virtue ; and I was naturally desirous that their minds should be inspired with an early admiration of Milton. The perfection of his immortal Poem is seldom appreciated by the young ; and its perusal is, perhaps, very generally regarded rather as a duty than a pleasure. This has been attributed by Dr. Johnson to *the want of human interest*. In those passages, therefore, which I selected for our evening readings, my purpose was to obviate this objection, by bringing before my family, in uninterrupted connection, those parts which relate to the fate of our first parents ; and by omitting everything, however exquisite in its kind, which did not immediately bear upon their affecting and important story. Such was the origin of the present volume. Without wearying the young attention of my auditors, it was calculated to afford occupation and amusement for four evenings. Some friends lately suggested to me, that the Abstract, which had been found interesting and instructive to my own children,

might not be wholly unprofitable to those of others; and in that hope, I have been persuaded to the present publication."

A study of her selection, and more enlightening still, of her omissions from the text, throws light on the educational values of the time. Many of the excisions are such as any editor preparing reading for the young might make. Very little of Books II. and III., for instance, was left for the little Siddonses to hear; the long and one-sided conversation between Adam and the Archangel Michael which occupies most of Books XI. and XII. was also, mercifully, spared them, as was that dialogue between Father and Son into which so strong a flavour of contemporary Royalist and Roundhead controversy enters. Also, as we might expect from almost any but the most Russian-minded of our present-day mothers proposing to entertain her nursery, Mrs. Siddons has excised the more luscious descriptions of " the rites mysterious of connubial love," though she has allowed " He for God only, she for God in him," and " sweet, reluctant, amorous delay " to introduce

" *The savoury pulp they chew, and in the rind,*
Still as they thirsted, scoop the brimming stream."

But there are other smaller and less obvious omissions. Those familiar with the unrelenting curiosity and the watchful logic of the infant mind will sympathize with our author when she left in as shortened an account as possible of the banquet served by Eve to Adam and their six-winged guest, and cut out the controversial statements as to what happens to the food consumed by an Angel after it has been eaten

> "*with keen dispatch
> Of real hunger and concoctive heat.*"

But it seems hard, to those of us who remember discovering in *Paradise Lost* images and attitudes that made research in its pages as rewarding as a study of the bound brown volumes of *Punch* (never a completely comic business to the grave innocence of childhood) to find that the Siddons children were deprived of " smooth Adonis from his native rock " running purple to the sea ; of " sporting the lion ramped and in his paw dandled the kid " ; of the unwieldy elephant wreathing his lithe proboscis just to amuse the pair ; and of Satan's remarkable quick change from cormorant to lion, and from lion to tiger, waiting to seize Adam and Eve, one in each paw.

Some of her smaller cuts are not easy to follow. Why for instance did Mrs. Siddons allow her children to be frightened by " Moloch horrid King besmeared with blood " and leave out Charlemain at Fontarabbia ? Why too could she not have curtailed some further passages of angelic but repetitive discourse for the sake of such lovely images as the evening mist that—at the very close

> "*Risen from the river, o'er the marish glides,
> And gathers ground fast at the labourer's heel
> Homeward returning.*"

Possibly Mrs. Siddons, in spite of summer holidays

at Weymouth and although she called her rural retreat at Westbourne Grove a Farm, did not put any great literary or poetic value on fishermen and farm-labourers : perhaps she was rather pressed for space. Certainly she held that the narrative rather than the language was what young readers of *Paradise Lost* needed to be made to hear.

On the other hand it may not have been altogether without guile that she excised some of the more recondite passages from the text as it now appears. Sally and Maria and little George Siddons might have sat quietly enough in the drawing-room in Great Marlborough Street or at Weymouth, for the four evenings it took to get through their mamma's revised version of her favourite poem. But, before the day of publication came, Mrs. Siddons had to take on her knee that bright sprig of the Kemble stock, young Fanny Kemble. A child who at the age of four, could meet the threat of a whipping with the comment " Good for the circulation," was quite equal to putting awkward questions to " Great-Aunt Melpomene." " Blind Thamyris and blind Mæonides " might not have been past the aged Muse's wit to explain, but they have been banished with Mulciber and many another sounding name from the pages where it was also deemed wise to find no room for

" *the three maritime kings,*
Mombaza, and Quiloa and Malind."

Mrs. Siddons, then, valued Milton's poetry less for the more lyric strains of its organ music than for the emphasis laid by it on an uncompromising morality. This is far from being the only evidence that the great actress believed in the delusion, proper to the age in which she lived, that Right and Wrong and Virtue and Vice are easily and clearly distinguishable from one another. That, in practice she was, at one important period of her life, to indulge in a casuistry that might remind some people of the Church in which her father was born and her brothers were brought up, is a matter we shall investigate presently.

For the moment it is useful to a consideration of what kind of woman this was who housed so overwhelming a genius in so expressive and beautiful a body, to weigh the accusation brought against her by every biographer to the effect that, when in company, she varied periods of silence by the utterance of remarks so commonplace that it was difficult to meet them with an instant reply, and couched these speeches in an iambic pentameter that, by its heavy roll, actually made reply impossible.

The two most familiar examples of this habit are:

"*You've brought me water, boy : I asked for beer,*"

and

"*Beef cannot be too salt for me, my lord.*"

A third

"*I wish to God that I had seen the Marquis,*"

may be considered with them.

The first thing that occurs to the critic confronted with the first and second of these lines is that they are Miltonic rather than Shakespearean in structure, and secondly, that they were both spoken at table. History tells us that they belong to the period of her visits to Edinburgh and were uttered on more or less ceremonial occasions, when a large company heard, marked and subsequently made jest of them. There are many other stories of her solemnity and slowness, to illustrate Mrs. Piozzi's exclamation carefully preserved by the patronizing malice of Miss Burney:

> "Why, this is a leaden goddess we are all worshipping! However we shall soon gild it."

But Mrs. Siddons, the woman, was never gilded. To the end, when out of her immediate circle, she retained that "steadiness in her manner and deportment" little Miss Burney found "by no means engaging." This steadiness, coupled with a simplicity and literalness of manner in replying to the giddier sallies of the wits and quizzes who took her appearance in Society much as they would have taken that of a talking horse or a performing elephant, has given rise to the generally accepted verdict that the poor lady was deficient in that strange and never properly defined quality called a sense of humour. Before we agree with this verdict, or accept it as unfavourable, it is well to reflect that the people who are most given to denying this gift in their estimation of others, usually claim it for themselves. To say "Thank God! I, at least have a sense of humour" has come to be one of the most definitely conclusive evidences of a second-rate mind.

It is difficult to understand how cultured and sympathetic persons, having read Mrs. Siddons's letters to her real friends, can maintain the idea that she was a heavy and humourless woman. We find, on the contrary, in those letters written in the midst of the most painful experiences of her life, flashes of wit and discernment, a mingling of shrewdness with real good humour and sound judgment such as could only come from the workings of that so much misunderstood quality. In the abyss of her misery over her daughter Maria's last terrible illness she finds time to write from Brighton to Mrs. Pennington of Lady Jersey, whom she was obliged to meet at supper, being commanded thither by the Prince Regent:

> "She is really wonderful in her appearance. Her hair was about an inch long all over her head, and she had ty'd round her head one single row of white beads: this I thought was ill-judged."

Later, when impressing the need for the utmost discretion on her kind but far too expansive friend, she flashes a light on the character of her sister-in-law:

> "Mrs. Kemble with a thousand good qualities is so fond of talking over other people's concerns—that it is no exaggeration to say this affair would be known in every Milliner's shop in the Town, had she the least intimation of it."

If Horace Walpole had written this paragraph it would not have been counted unto him for humorlessness. Nor is the story of the bore who would persist he had seen Mrs. Siddons as Millamant, thirty years before meeting her in a drawing-room, to be taken as evidence that the lady herself was a bore as well. After meeting the gentleman's insistence with a steady and dignified denial that she had ever played in *The Way of the World*, Mrs. Siddons rose from her seat and observing " I perceive it is time I changed my place," took leave of the gentleman who had committed the unpardonable clumsiness of failing to distinguish a famous tragic actress from a lesser, and a comic star. Other times, other standards of the funny ! Had she lived to grow stout and impressive in 1930 Mrs. Siddons would very probably be enjoying a reputation as a wit in two continents, and we might all be rushing about saying, " My dear ! Have you heard what that divine Mrs. Siddons said to a Hollywood manager last week ? "

There were, at times, pompous thunderings in her written as well as in her spoken intercourse with her fellows : but these sounded only on formal or embarrassing occasions, as when she wrote to a patron of her son Henry whom she was helping to start on a theatrical career in Edinburgh :

> " His abilities as an Actor need not my eulogium and his private respectability is so universally acknowledged as to spare his mother the pain of boasting."

Under embarrassment she was capable of an involved turgidity it would be hard to rival. There is her letter to Sir Thomas Lawrence, acknowledging his reference to herself in his Presidential Address to the Royal Academy in 1824. The painter had spoken of Sir Joshua Reynolds's Tragick Muse in terms of the most complete and enthusiastic acceptance of it both as a portrait and as a masterpiece of painting. Mrs. Siddons, ill and away from London, hearing this echo of her own glory, wrote to the man she no longer knew:

> "Situated as I am, with respect to the glorious Picture so finely eulogized, and with its illustrious Panegyrist, what can I say, where should I find words for the various and thronging ideas that fill my mind? It will be enough, however, to say (and I will not doubt it will be true to say) that could we change persons, I would not exchange the Gratification in bestowing this *sublime* tribute of praise, for all the fame it must accumulate on the Memory of the Tragick Muse.
> "Yours most truly,
> "S. SIDDONS."

There *is* a clue to this maze of phrases, but it has nothing to do with the infirmities of age. Mrs. Siddons, though she was close on seventy when she penned her letter, was in full possession of her normal powers of expression: but she was profoundly embarrassed, as well as touched, by the occasion, and here, as elsewhere when ill at ease, fell a victim to the confusions of her own heart.

This is only another way of stating the conclusion to which a sustained comparison of her letters and of her reported speech seems to lead: Mrs. Siddons, in spite of her profession, and to a great extent because of it, was an incurably shy woman.

2

The border line between genius and talent is, like that between genius and madness, anything but straight. The exercise of great and well disciplined talent has often produced masterpieces of perfection: the manifestations of genius are, as often, imperfect and faulty. Great talent must be accompanied by that infinite capacity for taking pains so mistakenly said to be the whole business of genius, whereas it is only one of the activities genius can, but does not invariably, betray. In considering Literature the distinction can be drawn more easily than in any other art, as those students of contemporary letters who bring a critical attention to bear on two such masterpieces as *The Brook Kerith* and *The Plumed Serpent* have often been known to maintain. With acting, quite apart from the necessarily ephemeral nature of those performances by which the artist of the stage has to be judged, the distinction is harder to make because the momentary responses of several human beings to the voice and presence of a player are far more delicate and more subject to variation than are those existing between a book and its readers. It is possible to sit in a theatre and be moved to rapture by a performance that leaves the critical intelligence in the next stall cold, or even scornful. But when we are faced, either to-day or in the records of the past, by a display of the extraordinary power of welding an audience into a single entity that is the first effect of a great artist's appearance upon the scene, and when we possess the detailed analysis of the visible means by which, at certain electrifying moments, the player's induced emotions have been communicated to the collective understanding of the public, we shall generally find certain concomitant elements in that player's life and characteristics that are always associated with the supernormal endowments we recognize in the constitution of genius. It is only necessary, at this point, to examine two of these characteristics, since it is not the art but the life of Mrs. Siddons that is here under consideration.

The first of them is that the genius, in common with the saint, invents or adopts a well-defined, if sometimes idiosyncratic routine for the purpose of achieving the release of supernormal power that produces a miracle or an ecstasy. This is as true of religious experience as it is of such acting as that of Mrs. Siddons, according to those who saw it, must have been, and as that of Sarah Bernhardt so triumphantly was when she convulsed, electrified and bewitched those of us who are fortunate in being old enough to have seen her Phèdre, her Roxane, or her Marguerite Gautier.

Mrs. Siddons's method, as we know, was first a critical reading to see " if the part be in Nature " ; secondly a silent learning of the words ; thirdly an almost inaudible rehearsal on the stage for cues and positions, and finally a passing through the trance-like form of stage-fright she called her " desperate tranquillity " before the release came in such performances as her Isabella, her Lady Randolph, and most powerfully of all in her Lady Macbeth. This process, instinctive in its nature, was fortified by any amount of painstaking and intelligent thought.

Mrs. Siddons was no silly amateur to depend on a so-called inspiration. She did not depend on inspiration for the interpretation of her part: she made it her business to understand her part and then waited for the almost agonizing process by which an uncontrollable power took possession of her strongly controlled faculties and swept her through into an experience as great and as thrilling for the actress as it was for the audience who wept and trembled at her will. The reaction was inevitably exhausting. Mrs. Siddons, as an opera-singer still must, acted only on three, or at most four, evenings a week. Once, on tour, she played every night in one town and this was noted as an excess and a hardship. But then she was playing parts so well known, and to provincial audiences so hypnotized by her fame, that she did not need to pour forth the whole of her creative power in any part as she was forced to do when creating one or playing one for the first time before a new public.

Side by side with this supernormal faculty, Mrs. Siddons had a degree of common sense never possessed before or since by any actress who has made a lasting name for herself. She made no particular fuss about her exertions and was careful to rest and also to eat well after each of these manifestations, taking the effort, the exhaustion and the recuperation in a natural sequence. But her self-protective instinct worked on the mind as well as the body: the retiring flood of induced emotion left a vacuum behind it: it was that salutary emptiness she, unconsciously perhaps, protected from invasion. When the foolish drawing-rooms set about her with questions as to *how* she did it ; when an impertinent young lady of fashion burst into her dressing-room saying that, as she had not time to see the performance, she must at any rate see the goddess who was the chief topic of conversation among her friends, Mrs. Siddons was dry, and short and uncommunicative as only the fundamentally shy and self-protective can be. The members of Brooks's collected a purse for her as a sign of homage : but Lord Carlisle who was deputed to present the offering was disappointed in her reception of it. " She was not *maniérée* enough," he said to Horace Walpole. This was still the leaden goddess, and Walpole, it was one of his crosser days, added on his own account a description of her acting leading up to the final condemnation " When without motion, her arms are not genteel."

3

She also fell into blank verse. Of course she did ! The iambic five-foot beat of English verse is an extremely difficult rhythm to avoid using once it has been fixed in the mind. All writers know the snare, and almost every writer has at times to reset a verse line back to its prose form. We all know the Death of Little Nell, and most of us can cite modern instances of prose writers whose emotion carries them into verse. One of Mrs. Siddons's great successes was Mrs. Beverley in Edward Moore's play *The Gamester*, a work its author thought he had written in prose, whereas the merest flicker of emotion is sufficient to drive him into lines such as his villain breathes when he has mentioned (quite inaccurately) to Mrs. Beverley that Mr. Beverley has a mistress :

> "*The seeds of jealousy are sown already.*
> *If I mistake not they have taken root.*
> *Now is the time to ripen them and reap*
> *The harvest* . . ."

In Mr. Beverley's dying speeches (neither he nor his wife seems to have had a Christian name) the verse flow is almost continuous :

> "*Down restless flames* . . . *down to your Native Hell.*
> *There you shall rack me. Oh for a pause from pain.*
> *Where is my wife ? Can you forgive me, love ?* . . .
>
> *But even now, thus dying as I am,*
> *Dubious and fearful of hereafter,*
> *My bosom pang is for your miseries.* . . .
>
> *Some ministering angel bring her peace.*"

Nor is this liability to lapse into iambics peculiar to the late eighteenth century : or to writers. A young woman of my acquaintance, having spent a day lately in reading that now forgotten achievement *Aurora Leigh*, went to a dinner party on that same evening and created a most unfavourable impression by delivering herself of the customary platitudes cut up into verse lengths :

> "*I fear I did not care for Cavalcade*"
>
> "*The fashions for the autumn rule out fur*"

and many other equally undistinguished but pompous sounding lines.

But it may not only have been because blank verse came naturally to her that Mrs. Siddons took refuge in it so often. The terrifying experience of finding herself, *as* herself, the object of a not altogether friendly curiosity, when she went or rather was dragged into Society, was certainly intensified in her case, because she had to make these excursions shorn of all the accessories which surround the actress when she is at work. The very greatness of her dramatic triumphs unfitted her to shine in Society. When she entered on the stage she knew that beyond the fourth wall was a mass of emotion, attentive to the least flicker of her eyelashes, following her every gesture, swayed and thrilled by each word she spoke. It was only in the spasms of stage fright *before* she faced that swimming, responsive, light-shielded blackness that she thought of the auditorium as " lined with human intellect." Once she had assumed her part and had imposed it on the house she thought of it no more, accepting it subconsciously as the necessary adjunct to, a component of, the whole performance. While she was in the theatre she kept in her part throughout, differing in this from Garrick who could crack jokes in the wings after his most savage efforts. During a performance of *Douglas*, Mrs. Siddons was Lady Randolph from the rise of the curtain until long after it had fallen for the last time. Her children knew what part she had been playing by her demeanour at supper on the nights when she was fortunate enough to do what suited her best and drive straight from the theatre to her home, there to recover from the trance her part had wrapped about her. She had never stopped crying, they tell us, after playing Mrs. Haller by the time she reached home ; and it is interesting to note that she seems to have recovered more quickly from the parts ending with the death of the heroine on the stage.

It was the hopelessly frivolous Sheridan who forced his way into her dressing-room on the first night of *Macbeth*, and in the interval before the sleep-walking scene, tried to persuade her to do it without setting down her candlestick in order to go through the motion of washing her hands. Sheridan failed. The scene as she played it was the high-water mark of her career and of the stage-history of *Macbeth*. If Sheridan had succeeded in breaking through the trance in which the considered judgments of her actively conscious hours were held inviolate and unchangeable, there might have been no such an overwhelming release of power—there might have been no sleep-walking scene that night, or ever again from her.

She was too old—twenty-eight is too old—and too little used to mere parties, when success in the fashionable world came to her, to take her entry into Society lightly or easily. As a girl at Guy's Cliffe she had needed merely to be respectful and obedient : on tour with her husband there was no question of social amenities : playing at Bath, with performances at Bristol three nights a week, there could only be occasional appearances at routs. The pleasant and comfortable friendship of the Whalleys who began by being sorry for the beautiful girl whose eyes were too large for her frail lovely face, and sent her wine and fruit and eggs, was not a demand on her for any formal return. The Whalleys established their relationship with the delicate mother of two babies rather than with the promising young actress. All through her letters to them we see her gay, simple, quite at her ease, completely forgetful of the blank verse line. But carry her to an assembly and she became at once Mrs. Piozzi's leaden goddess. Entering a crowded and critical reception-room she instinctively took refuge in those grandeurs and nobilities that could carry Queen Katharine to the height of her power in the trial scene in *Henry VIII*, and remembered the furious majesty of the captive Zara in *The Mourning Bride*. Off the stage these same attitudes and intonations not only failed of their effect, but produced another, and a differently alarming one, on an audience standing on the same level and under the same lights as the goddess. Some of them found her a little ridiculous at close quarters : Horace Walpole never succumbed to her beauty either on or off the stage : in Ireland she was never completely accepted : but that was because the Irish vanity never forgets, and Mrs. Crawford had married an Irish actor. When she went to Court her first impulsive movement towards the baby Princess Charlotte was quelled by the royal infant putting out its hand to be kissed, a gesture that would have been accepted as proper and even charming by anyone less nervous than the poor great actress who, in addition to her nervousness, had to endure the fatigue of standing for hours in the Presence or while giving one of those powerful readings from Milton.

The chilling effect of her own demeanour on others had its repercussion back to herself again. The player exists *by* not *for* applause. It is quite as much by the response of the audience as by his own calculated efforts that his genius is liberated. Mrs. Siddons herself has given valuable testimony to this necessity for response felt by her the more intensely as her output was great. In one of those bursts of candour and lucidity that seem humorless to some people she wrote

> "Acting out of London is double fatigue ; there the loud and long applause at the great points and striking situations invigorated the system, and the time it occupied recreated the *health* and nerve."

Going into Society, where applause failed and she did not know the cues, was bound to have a depressing effect on " health and nerve." Small wonder that, lacking the isolation and familiar trappings of the stage, her clutching spirit seized on the most potent rhythm it had exercised and drew her utterance into verse !

> "*Beef cannot be too salt for me, my lord.*"

It is to be remarked that Mrs. Siddons never fell into verse, as so many second-rate writers do, in the more pompous or emotional passages of her letters. In these, as we have already seen, she could write confusedly enough : but, when verse came, it was real rhymed verse of her own, and if not her own, then it was the best verse always. She begins a letter from Cheltenham where she was making a three night stand in 1798:

> *" One woe doth tread upon another's heel,*
> *So fast they follow . . ."*

but her own sentences, completing her comment on the news she has received from, and the news she is about to give to, her correspondent are all in good, clear, if slightly agitated prose.

Mrs. Siddons, in short, is an example, and a magnificent one, of that dual personality observable in all creative artists, intensified in her case by the nature of her art. At home and with her relatives and closest friends she was a kind, capable, affectionate, industrious and most virtuous woman who would have been more than a little indignant if anyone had told her she was not really a religious one. On the stage, even when no longer young, she exhibited a charm equal to her beauty, and, as her powers ripened, a demoniac power that could raise a mediocre play to the status of tragedy and illuminated the greatest of tragedies with a light which, though we have never seen it blaze, still leaves an indelible afterglow in history to make us wonder if it can ever be equalled again.

We have considered some instances of the way in which her greatness as an actress affected Mrs. Siddons's behaviour when off the stage. A more interesting enquiry can be made into the effect her private life had on her artistic performance. In order to do this it will be necessary briefly to recapitulate the story of her young womanhood, and to pay more detailed attention to the singular domestic tragedy that occupied her early middle age and was definitely responsible for her withdrawal from the stage some years before, in the normal course of her career, she should have left it.

4

Married at eighteen ; the mother of two children soon after she was twenty ; dragged from childbed at Gloucester to be presented on the London stage with every attendant discomfort jealousy and mismanagement could devise, before she was twenty-one ; driven, half crazy with mortification and physical weakness, back to the road a few weeks later ; finding herself at twenty-three the wage-earner for a husband and two young children, with a third baby imminent ; working every night, either at Bath or Bristol, and bearing a fourth child which did not survive its inevitably difficult infancy in 1781 ; Mrs. Siddons, when she reached Drury Lane for the second time, at the age of twenty-seven, had known pain, fatigue, anxiety and disillusionment, but she had suffered no particular frustration either physical or of the spirit. She had married her first love while they were both still adolescent ; she had borne him lovely and beloved children ; she had found him fond, faithful and a good accountant, which in some ways was better than being a good actor and outshining her. Year by year, she had felt within herself the steady growth of her own powers and had had her own inner knowledge confirmed by the increasing reputation each fresh season at Bath brought her. She came to London in radiant health, with dazzling beauty and the exhilaration of her own genius to give excitement to her conquests, and with the steadying weight of a satisfactory marriage, safe at last in the financial security she herself could obtain for her home by the exercise of her adored and most rewarding art. There were no repressions and no bitterness in her private life. Even the knowledge that every penny she earned was, by law, the property of William Siddons, whose own earnings as an actor had always been meagre, gave her no prophetic pang. Siddons (she generally referred to him as " Sid ") became her business manager and agent, and accumulated in his own bosom such bitterness as the union distilled. Every now and again she grew a little impatient with his slowness and with a certain obstructiveness that seems, not altogether unnaturally, to have developed in his attitude towards his famous and almost terrifyingly energetic wife. Her phrase, when writing of him, " that want of an agreeing mind (my misfortune, though not *his fault*) " sums up her side of the irritation caused by the inertia through which an otherwise not very powerful man could and did make himself felt at certain crises of the family life. His attitude to her was once epitomized by him when, in conversation with Mrs. Piozzi, he quoted :

> "*Merab with spacious beauty fills the sight,*
> *But too much awe chastised the bold delight ;*
> *Like a calm sea, which to the enlarged view*
> *Gives pleasure, but gives fear and reverence too.*"

This was all very well as an ornament to drawing-room conversation but, even when he was not being cross and obstructive, Sid gave other signs of anything but a chastened attitude towards his lady. By the time his two daughters Sally and Maria returned from their finishing school at Calais, the Siddons home was run on the assumption that Mamma was a beautiful angel, often sadly overworked, but full of sympathy for and admiration of her girls, and Papa, though useful as a chaperon and a figurehead at times, was a difficult, when not an almost negligible, factor. Besides he had gout (or was it rheumatism ? no one seems to have bothered to make sure)—and spent an increasingly great part of his time at Bath.

The birth of Cecilia Siddons in 1794, when Mrs. Siddons was in her fortieth year, possibly marks the termination of conjugal relations between the pair : it certainly coincides with the opening stages of a drama which placed the goddess in a relation to all her three daughters, the grave lovely Sally ; the brilliant wilful Maria ; the happy baby Cecilia, none the less remarkable that she herself was, at any rate for some years, quite unaware of her own true attitude in, and feelings towards, the other player in the drama.

Thinking of herself, quite justly, as a woman of unperturbed chastity, in whom the upheavals of sex had had their full expression and had died away through twenty years of reasonably happy and almost too fruitful marriage ; believing that the exercise of her art gave full outlet to her emotional nature (as well it might have done) ; behaving in

Ps

private as though her one thought were to earn sufficient money to retire on while leaving her husband and children well provided for, Mrs. Siddons found herself caught in a net so fine, so strong and so woven of the incredible and the preposterous that she did not know it was about her and supposed herself to be struggling for everybody's freedom but her own.

THOMAS LAWRENCE AS A YOUNG MAN

II

LOTHARIO

I

ON THE 21st day of May in the year 1793 Mrs. Piozzi and her friend Mrs. Greatheed took a party of young people to Ranelagh where, the night being fine, they stayed amusing themselves until dawn. Sally Siddons, then aged eighteen, and her younger sister Maria, fresh from her boarding-school at Calais, were there and Sally was evidently the sensation of the evening. "She quite outlooked her sister" says Mrs. Piozzi "and was very finely dressed." Three weeks later the kind but critical lady reports on the sisters again, this time with the rather cryptic explanation : " Sally . . . is prettier than Maria, because her face looks cleaner." There is also some talk of a diet of asses' milk for Sally, who had been suffering from attacks of spasmodic asthma, and a general air of preferring the character as well as the appearance of the elder sister. Maria Siddons was a little bit of a romp at fifteen, just the kind of tomboy who would occasionally forget to wash her face in the tiny hand basin in the little dark closet opening out of a panelled bedroom where such ablutions could be performed, by those who considered them necessary, in England in 1792.

But it was not long before Maria began to pay as

much attention to her appearance as any young lady should. She ripened quickly into a hectic loveliness, a bloom so soft and brilliant that, for a time, it was mistaken for the bloom of health. There is one portrait of her, a swift water-colour sketch made when she was nearly eighteen by Thomas Lawrence, and reproduced by Lord Ronald Sutherland Gower to whom it once belonged. This shows an oval and peach-like face, with cloudy brown hair and an almost gold and rosy skin; a girl with sidelong mischievous eyes and a lovely wilful mouth, still half asleep in the dream of adolescence and yet more than half aware of the power of her young beauty. There is something almost sultry in the flush of consciousness with which the young Maria seems to answer the ardour of the painter's eyes— of his words too, as he set this transient, exquisite bloom on the paper that still holds it and makes it live again. No photograph or engraving, and I have seen three or four, makes anything but a heaviness of this soft and tender sketch which has all the freshness of impulse that distinguishes the work of Sir Thomas Lawrence at such moments as this one clearly must have been. One of his critics has put it down to the vanity of all sitters, which Lawrence was too urbane to resist, that almost all the master's portraits smile out of the canvas; but other portrait-painters have allowed their sitters to smile out of their own vanity; it is only in the Siddons' pictures that we see the painter's smile answered in each sitter's eyes and on her pouting lips.

Maria was a spoilt young beauty. Four years younger than Sally and six years older than George,

Mrs. Siddons's next surviving child, she had been baby to her sister and to her elder brother Henry, as well as to her father who had a special fondness for her, long enough to learn how to take full advantage of that indulged position. She was sent to school in France with Sally while little George was in his infancy. She came back to a London that had made her mamma the fashion and to the group of young pleasure-loving companions already gathered round Sally and Henry and their extraordinarily handsome and attractive uncle Charles Kemble, barely one year older than Sally herself and, like the sisters, educated abroad, though he went to college at Douai and was a Roman Catholic. This difference in religion, very lightly, if at all, noticed by any of the elder Kembles, was no sort of barrier between Charles and his two pretty and amusing nieces. Charles Kemble had a friend, also called Charles, the younger brother of General Moore, who was reading for the Bar, and these two young sparks often spent evenings at Great Marlborough Street where the Siddons girls and their friends Miss Sarah Bird and Miss Amelia Locke played and sang to them, songs composed by Sally herself. They were all very young and very merry and just a little silly with their jokes about the two Charleses and about birds being flown, and their severe young criticism of new plays and specially of Grétry's comic opera *Blue Beard* which, although real live horses came on the stage, Maria found tiresome and ill told.

To Great Marlborough Street there also came, from time to time, an older man, still under thirty, but of such mercurial spirits and such clear-eyed seraphic beauty as to seem almost as boyish as the two Charleses themselves. This was Tom Lawrence who, for some years now, had had a secret understanding with Sally Siddons. The brilliant young painter, who owed so much of his phenomenal success in society and at Court to the introductions his friendship with Mrs. Siddons had procured him when he first came to town as a boy of eighteen, had been made an A.R.A. in 1791, and, the following year, at the age of twenty-three, had succeeded Sir Joshua Reynolds as Principal Painter to King George III. He was therefore a more than eligible suitor for the hand of the actress's pretty daughter, and her biographers have been at some pains to explain why this so natural and charming engagement met with enough opposition to cause it to be kept secret. Some have surmised that Lawrence was not merely extravagant but over-generous as well, and that he spent so much on keeping his parents and sister in comfort that little was left to settle on a wife, and that Mrs. Siddons dared not ask her husband to make Sally an allowance. Others, with more justice, suggest that Mrs. Siddons wished the young couple to wait a year or two to allow Sally's health to establish itself. Later on she expressed herself very clearly on the obstacle to marriage ill-health in a woman must inevitably present.

> "Will a husband's tenderness keep pace with and compensate for the loss of a mother's, her unremitting cares and soothings? Will he not grow sick of these

repeated attacks, and think it vastly inconvenient to have his domestic comforts, his pleasures, or his business interfered with by the necessary and habitual attentions which they will call for from himself and from his servants ? . . . To say the truth a sick wife *must* be a *great misfortune*."

Whether these or other considerations moved her in those first days of the young painter's attraction towards Sally is immaterial. Whatever their nature Mrs. Siddons's reasons were strong enough to make her insist that the engagement should remain a secret. She told neither her husband nor her brother of the business, but went about, believing herself to be the sole confidante of an affair she half hoped, by keeping secret, to stifle. It is however improbable that Maria, after her return from Paris, should not have shared, or at all events guessed, her sister's secret.

Lawrence, young, capricious, successful and attractive, was not the man from whom a dogged fidelity was to be expected. Mrs. Siddons who, in her own youth, had been made to wait two years for her William, could easily persuade herself that she was inflicting no hardship on Sally in putting her to a like test, even, perhaps, that she was saving her child from the humiliation of having a published engagement broken by inconstancy on the lover's side.

And here the first suspicions of half ignorant, half wilful mismanagement begin to thrust themselves between the lines of the story. Sally's illness was asthma : its paroxysms came on after fatigue or anxiety : during the months of her uninterrupted hope of ultimate marriage she seems to have been free from attacks.

But, some time in 1797, when Sally was twenty-two; Maria nineteen; Lawrence twenty-eight and Mrs. Siddons not quite forty-three, Sally fell ill again and this time seriously. She was laid up for a long time and, when her convalescence began, it was slow. No connection is made between this painful recurrence of Sally's asthma and the emergence of Maria's clandestine meetings with Lawrence. Their friend Sally Bird was staying with Lawrence and his sister at Greek Street at the time and connived at a secret correspondence. Maria would go out on some innocent pretext and return, hours later, to dress for dinner in the dark, for fear her late-lit candle should betray the length of her absence. Once she pretended to have been to the play and had to patch up an account of the evening from Miss Bird's impression of it; once when her father asked her for an explanation she told him a story " and there was an end of it." Altogether Maria behaved in a thoroughly naughty and selfish way. She had entangled her sister's lover in an affair with herself, almost it would seem on purpose and out of mischief. And Sally, ill and unhappy, was still so sweet and yielding that she broke off her own engagement without a murmur and did her best to further her sister's happiness.

Running out to Greek Street, and waiting under the trees of Soho Square Garden to meet a lover whose many social and professional engagements must inevitably have caused him to be late as often as not, was no sort of occupation for a delicate girl in a London winter. We may be sure that Maria, being young and lovely, and in love, went out in ridiculous little sandals and the thinnest of thin silk dresses under her coat and waited about in the fog, or walked home, because she dared not risk the noise of a sedan or a hackney coach arriving at the door, even if she had the money to pay the fare. Hot with excitement; cold with suspense on the occasions when she was almost found out; troubled a little with remorse at her sister's sufferings, and sometimes with jealousy because Lawrence had to spend so much time with such lovely sitters; fretted and impatient with her mamma who, after being angry at first, was now half complacent, half afraid of telling Papa, Maria caught cold after cold; concealed a cough; neglected a temperature, and, by the beginning of January, had made herself so ill, that her mother, in despair, broke the news to Mr. Siddons, whose favourite child Maria had always been. Yielding to the assertion that, if she can just be allowed to think she may one day marry Lawrence Maria will get well again, Mr. Siddons, rather grumpily, made arrangements to provide Maria with a dowry out of her mother's earnings of which, being her husband, he had full control, and the young Court painter was allowed to see his betrothed in the drawing-room at Great Marlborough Street every evening. This acknowledgment of her claim on Tom Lawrence was looked to as a cure for Maria's ailment, and Sally, watching the smoothness of the path lying before her quondam lover and her wilful sister, asked Miss Bird—" But what will our friend do without some obstacle to overcome?"

No one who reads the letters of Sally and Maria Siddons to their friend Sarah Bird at this period will have much difficulty in seeing what was bound to happen. Sally's letters are those of a sweet but highly intelligent and well-educated girl, musical, amusing, unselfish, good-tempered: Maria's are impulsive, self-assertive, egotistic, vain and silly. To meet the lovely, excited, ardent little creature for a few stolen moments; to witness the delicious confusion his own perfections had stirred in her; to share a romantic and self-deceiving belief, that they two were lovers persecuted by grim and tyrannical parents, was one thing: but to sit by a feverish, little, empty-headed chatterer, in licensed courtship, under the chandeliers of a well-furnished drawing-room for an hour or two every evening of the week was quite another, especially when a grave and lovely girl to whom he could now only pay the distant and limited attention of a prospective brother-in-law sat quietly at her tambour-frame in another corner of the drawing-room, or, worse still, entertained Charles Kemble and Charles Moore and other young men of their acquaintance with smiles and conversation in which Maria would not allow him to take any part. Sally was well again for the moment. She composed a song " When summer's burning heats arise " and copied it out many times for her friends. It is more than possible that Sally was asked to sing during these evening visits of Maria's thrilling and splendid betrothed: it would have been more than human in her to decline such a request.

Lawrence seems after a time to have taken to

looking in at other times than the evenings appointed for his visits to his betrothed. Maria, once she was out of bed at midday, occupied the drawing-room where a thermometer hung so that the temperature might not be allowed to fall below a certain point, but, before she came in, Sally might be caught there alone, writing letters, and so one morning Lawrence caught her. She had avoided being present at several of his evening visits by going to the play as often as possible. She saw her uncle doing his acrobatic tricks in *The Castle Spectre*, an entertainment she judged to be dull except for such moments as the spectre walked. Presently Lawrence was seen to be calling more frequently and finding more and better opportunities of catching Sally alone. Maria's letters took on a pettish tone. Lawrence's behaviour became so erratic, his moods so difficult, that Maria complained to her mother. Mrs. Siddons scolded the inconsiderate lover and the whole household was upset. Finally everybody got on everybody else's nerves to such an extent that there was one of those family rows, painful enough when they overtake normally self-controlled and reasonable people, but positively shattering when they burst on a hearth surrounded by those to whom the extremes of expression both in wrath and of outraged feelings are matters of professional accomplishment.

Mr. Siddons, though not a good actor, was actor enough to know how to release a grievance; Lawrence had at one time studied for the stage and had a fiend's temper in leash behind his angel's face; Maria, like any spoilt beauty, could storm and cry when upset, and Mrs. Siddons was the greatest tragic actress the world has known. Her performance on this occasion was said by those who witnessed it to give an inkling of what her King Lear might be. She derived inspiration from all the mothers at bay she had made her own on the stage and, with the indignant Claudia, felt able to justify her rage by remembering the expostulation : " What cares the lioness when robbed of her young in whose forest she roars ? "

For Lawrence, having thrown Sally over for Maria, was now quite quite sure that it had all been a mistake ; that Maria was a tiresome child ; that Sally was still, as she had always been, the object of his affections.

The position, difficult in itself, was complicated for Mrs. Siddons by her own conduct in having kept the first beginnings of the affair a secret from her husband and from her brother John as well. All that the family knew was that Lawrence, who had been engaged to Maria, was now in no mood to continue in his engagement. Siddons was furious, spoke of the defaulting Lawrence in those terms borrowed from the stable-yard which middle-aged gentlemen are wont to employ when enraged by their juniors, and forbade him the house.

Then ensued the greatest confusion. Maria and Sally both became ill with excitement. Maria was bled. Sally wrote no letters being, as she cautiously expresses it, " prevented by indisposition." Then, being persuaded that the maintenance of the greatest secrecy and reserve was the only way in which the affair could be properly hushed up, the sisters began to give their little evening parties again without Lawrence, whenever Maria was well enough for such excitement. After one of these poor Maria writes of a sad pain in her side adding " A relapse is always worse than the original illness and yet I think I shall not live a long while, it is perhaps merely nervous . . . but I see nothing very shocking in the idea . . . I may be sav'd from much misery." She was also a little perturbed because " The French will certainly come and kill us all or worse . . . they will be here in six weeks perhaps." Maria did not like the idea of being killed by the French and she had a sick girl's fancy to go to Clifton. " It is a lovely place, and I never was more delighted in my life than I was the first time I ever saw that walk there in between the rocks ; a river runs through it, and when we were there it was evening and there was one late boat coming home and music in it."

Summer was coming and with it the closing of the London theatre season. With two sick daughters and a husband more and more in need of the waters of Bath to relieve the pains and stiffness of his ageing limbs Mrs. Siddons had to face an increase in expenses by her own unaided efforts. Another tour was imperative. So off she set for Cheltenham from which town as centre she travelled to play at Gloucester ; at Worcester ; at Hereford ; at Birmingham ; in *The Gamester* and *Jane Shore* ; in *The Fair Penitent* and *Douglas*, taking with her a maid who was not used to the business of laying out and packing up the elaborate costume she wore in these parts, and sitting up late into the night, after her various performances, writing long anxious letters to Clifton where Maria was slowly getting worse; or watching by the bedside of poor Sally whom she had taken with her and who added to the fatigues of touring by falling ill at Hereford. A minor irritation in the midst of these serious troubles occurred in Birmingham where, during the course of a morning's shopping, she was offered one of those small plaster busts to be found even in our own day on cheap stalls where effigies of popular heroes can be bought for a shilling or two. This one was of herself and was so bad that the vendor did not recognize the original, any more than we who are familiar with her portraits can see any likeness to them in the statue by Campbell in Westminster Abbey and the bust in the National Portrait Gallery.

Having bought a specimen of this horrid publication Mrs. Siddons went off to Brighton for a week there to play before packed houses and to sup, much against her will, at the Pavilion with the Prince of Wales and Lady Jersey. She also paid a flying visit to London to play in a benefit for one of the Drury Lane actors, and, as Lawrence was in London and Maria, at Clifton, was no better, she sent Sally to join her sister. And she decided to model a bust of herself with her own hands.

For Lawrence was in London! There can be little doubt that one reason why Mrs. Siddons took Sally with her on tour was her determination to keep these two unlicensed lovers apart. The only engagement that had been admitted was Maria's: Sally's first understanding with the young painter had been a secret one. Lawrence had always found his access to Sally difficult: Mrs. Siddons was now determined, for the most plausible and motherly reasons, to make it impossible.

2

Some movement of resentment against the Kemble family had flared up in Lawrence's " Satan Summoning up his Legions " exhibited in the Royal Academy Exhibition the year before. There had been endless discussion about the origin and merits of this very theatrical picture. Fuseli seemed to feel that the idea of it was his own. Lawrence said he had seen Fuseli standing on the cliffs above the sea in just the attitude of his naked Lucifer, but that a prizefighter had actually posed for the torso. The face however was recognized as Kemble's in a mask of rage. And certainly the demon writhing upward from the pit at Satan's feet was given the unmistakable eye and profile of Mrs. Siddons herself. The painter, it seems clear, had transferred one of the Kemble family rows on to canvas for all the world to see and to recognize. The world was to some extent busy about other matters ; the battles of Cape St. Vincent and the Nile ; the state of Europe ; the news from Ireland ; the scandals of the Prince Regent's life and the daily gossip from Bushey House where the Duke of Clarence was giving performances of Haydn's oratorios presided over by Mrs. Jordan : it found small time to pry very far into the pique behind the scenes of this sensational picture which most people considered to be a very fine masterpiece. Presently Lawrence painted a cloud of smoke over Mrs. Siddons, but the original figure broke through a little with time, and can still be distinguished, when the light is good enough, by a really inquisitive and informed eye peering at it from the staircase that leads up to the Diploma Gallery in Burlington House. Mrs. Piozzi, unaware of the secret strain in the relationship between Mrs. Siddons and the young painter, glossed this indiscretion over in her sensible way. The rising young man, " the Painter of the Day," had tried to paint the actress as a *rising* angel in opposition to Lucifer the *falling* one, she reported. That was before Maria had caught his fancy ; now he was the suppliant at Mrs. Siddons's feet, and she did her utmost to keep him there.

In London, in Brighton, and again, in Birmingham, Mrs. Siddons saw Lawrence and told him that, even if the state of Maria's health did not make it improper for any engagement between him and Sally to be ratified, Sally herself had come to the conclusion that she did not want to marry him. It was common enough in those days for a mother to convey such a message from a daughter to the suitor she no longer wished to encourage, but Mrs. Siddons must have suspected an underlying wish to yield on Sally's part, so took upon herself to deliver Sally's messages. For other reasons too she was not able to cut off all communication with the frantic young man. Wherever she went, there she found him, and a scene ensued.

" It is nearly two o'clock," she wrote after one such interview " I am harassed, fatigued to death. . . . It is long since I have slept."

Lawrence threatened to commit suicide : he also

vanished for a time. His sister knew nothing of his movements and Mrs. Siddons, travelling up and down from Cheltenham to Brighton; to Worcester; to Hereford, half dead with fatigue and anxiety, also forgot to keep all her friends posted as to her shifting stations. In September Mrs. Piozzi complained that she "could no more imagine where Mrs. Siddons is than where Buonaparte is. The papers announce her at Drury Lane, a letter from a friend at Brighthelmestone tells how she is playing Mrs. Beverley for the amusement of the Prince of Wales, and another induces me to believe her at the Hot Wells."

And all the time, playing, packing, travelling, writing, she was driven by one tormenting thought. Sally must not, she could not, she ought not to marry Tom Lawrence. He was worthless; a trifler with young affections: he had turned from one sister to the other and back again; Maria was dying (though even Mrs. Siddons could not say this was of a broken heart); it would be indecent of Sally to do other than reject him.

The confidante to whom all these reiterated assertions were made was the very kind, but not at all sensible, woman to whose care Maria had gone in the early summer. Mrs. Pennington, a connection of the Whalleys, lived in Clifton, on rather straightened means, and was glad enough to take in Maria Siddons who was not apparently very ill in June 1798 when her mother started on tour. She was at any rate able to go for drives and to several evening parties though she was forbidden to dance. Mrs. Pennington was quite thrilled at the idea of becoming the friend and constant correspondent of the great actress, and, being an extremely gushing and kind-hearted woman, soon got a confession of Maria's love-story out of the girl. This she wrote out in full to Mrs. Siddons adding, as her own discovery, that the chief burden on the dear girl's mind was her dread lest Sally should ever be unhappy enough to become the wicked Thomas Lawrence's wife. Once the secret was out Mrs. Siddons experienced great relief. Here at last was someone to whom she could unbosom herself quite fully: someone grown-up who would be on her side. So far she had had to keep her wretched secret between her two daughters and the distraught young man who, whenever she told him that he could not marry one or other of the girls, simply froze the blood in her veins by threatening that "he would fly to compose his Spirit to the mountains of Switzerland ... Switzerland was still his resource." This threat, so tame in our ears, evidently covered abysses we cannot now explore. "Oh," cried poor Mrs. Siddons, reporting it to the attentive and responsive Mrs. Pennington, "Oh! that caprice and passion should thus obscure the many excellencies and lofty genius of this man!"

No sooner had the ice been broken between the two ladies in the matter of the triangular love affair, than Lawrence himself melted it for good by following Sally to Clifton. He called himself Mr. Jennings. He took rooms at an hotel. He wrote to Mrs. Pennington. He wrote to Sally. He saw both Sally and her guardian and then dashed off to Birmingham where he caught Mrs. Siddons after the play and " paced about here in agonies that brought me almost to fainting three or four times. I was so shaken by his wild transports that on rising to ring for some hartshorn and water, I should have fallen upon the floor if he had not fortunately caught me at the instant, and was totally incapacitated to play last night."

Nor was Mrs. Siddons the only person to be upset by his violence. In a letter written to Mrs. Pennington after his return to London Lawrence boasts of having conquered her enmity to him, and allows himself the queerest jesting at the good matron's own eagerness to be drawn into all the ridicule of unnecessarily clandestine meeting. For Mrs. Pennington, as silly as the most romantic heroine on the stage, had neither received Lawrence in her own house nor made him meet her in some room in his hotel but had trudged off to a rendez-vous under an oak-tree in a field behind the Bear Inn on a broiling afternoon, and had suffered considerable discomfort from the heat.

No woman could resist Lawrence. Poor, stout, sentimental Mrs. Pennington was now his slave. Sally had already complained to Miss Bird about her torrents of eloquence. " It seems to me impossible she can feel the sensations she finds such fine language to explain." These torrents now flowed from her pen in long, expostulatory letters to Mrs. Siddons about " our tormentor," as Lawrence has now become, and the dear angels Sally and Maria, and, in still longer, still more vehement streams of ejaculatory exhortation to Lawrence himself. In order that Mrs. Siddons might not miss one comma of this correspondence Mrs. Pennington recopied her own and many of Lawrence's letters and read them aloud to Sally, who also received her mamma's written encouragements to stand firm. Mrs. Pennington can have had very little time to do anything but write and rewrite and read all the letters that passed between her and Lawrence and Mrs. Siddons throughout August and September of that agitated year.

Early in October Maria Siddons died, and, on her deathbed, in the presence of Mrs. Pennington and Mr. and Mrs. Siddons, the poor, little, wasted but still passionate egoist exacted from her sister a vow that she would never be Lawrence's wife. Sally tried to compromise. " I did *not* promise " she protested, but Maria dying was inexorable. " Mother—Mrs. Pennington—bear witness—lay your hands on hers."

Sally promised her " dear dying angel," and Maria died triumphant.

The letter Mrs. Pennington wrote acquainting Lawrence with all the circumstances of Maria Siddons's death is a masterpiece of self-deluding cruelty : it almost drove him over the borders of insanity.

" It is only my hand that shakes not my mind " was the first line of the scrawl in which he answered her forbidding her to repeat her story to one human being. But Mrs. Pennington with all the vanity of authorship had already transcribed her marvellous letter and a copy of it had gone away with Mrs. Siddons who based her own necessarily modified description of Maria's deathbed on Mrs. Pennington's original. Both ladies were under the impression that the dying girl was actuated by Wisdom from on High. In a letter to Mrs. Fitz-Hugh, written after she had left Clifton, Mrs. Siddons declared that Maria's death " far surpassed the imagination of Rousseau and Richardson in their Heloise and Clarissa Harlowe, for hers was, I believe, from the immediate inspiration of the Divinity." But when she wrote Rousseau and Richardson Mrs. Siddons meant Penelope Pennington, and allowed herself, tired and full of grief as she was, to be persuaded that the iniquity of the vow she had helped to force on Sally was a fulfilment of the word of God.

Maria Siddons was buried at Clifton on the 9th of October. A fortnight later Mrs. Siddons reappeared in London as Isabella in *Measure for Measure*. She chose this part " because it is a character that affords as little as possible to open wounds which are but too apt to bleed afresh."

3

It would seem as if, at this point, any mother who had the faintest glimmer of understanding of a daughter's heart would have found some means of sending Sally, who still loved the man she was under so terrifying an obligation to forget, as far as possible from the scenes that must remind her of him and from the places where they were bound to meet. France was of course in too disturbed a state to warrant the girl's return for a few months to the school where she had been so happy, and Switzerland, as we have already seen, was inextricably connected with the excesses of despair. But Mrs. Fitz Hugh was at Brighton; Mr. Siddons was at Bath; Sally's health was growing worse (she had had another asthmatic attack soon after Maria's death) and yet she remained in London through the autumn. Perhaps she wanted to be near her mother; perhaps she longed to see Lawrence again. For a time however he kept aloof and Mrs. Siddons did not conceal her annoyance at this. " All is still quiet " she reported to Mrs. Pennington. " I am astonished at it, and so is Sally . . . I talked of the importance of their first meeting anywhere. She told him it was impossible for her to treat him with coldness or neglect." Mrs. Twiss, her sister, was now the go-between. Lawrence was said to be paying attention to another young lady. Mrs. Siddons felt this to be only a ruse. She was sure he would " break forth to torment us." There was no real attempt on anybody's part to get away from the situation. It was allowed to drag on, and, lest it should die out, or be superseded by fresh events, Mrs. Pennington spread the tale, by making a great secret of it to several people, so that by the beginning of November she was able to assure the Siddons family in London that people were far better aware of Sally's situation than they supposed.

By this time Lawrence had begun to make advances to Patty Wilkinson who was now an inmate of the Siddons household, half companion half adopted daughter, helping Sally to take care of the four year old Cecilia, an enchanting little girl of whom Lawrence had made more than one of his delicious child-studies. They took the little creature to see *Blue Beard* and all next day she did nothing but act Sister Ann upon the tower waving her handkerchief. And Patty Wilkinson carried a letter and a message or so between Great Marlborough Street and Lawrence's Studio.

Mrs. Siddons, paying a round of visits ; going off to play Mrs. Haller with a poor company to support her ; working with her brother to get out of the bottomless pit of Sheridan's brilliant mismanagement, and actually setting up with him in management at Drury Lane, was all the time restless and unhappy because in one way or another, for reasons good or bad, for no reasons at all, she must still be seeing Lawrence, thinking of Lawrence, striving by every pretence of thrusting him aside to prevent him slipping out of her life. Now it was Sally's letters she must persuade him to return ; now it was some message to him through the Twisses she must deal with ; always when she played she looked more beautiful than ever and wondered if, or was assured that, he was in the audience watching her. Sometimes, he came with others to make his purely formal but deeply significant bow in her dressing-room.

"There is a corner yet left in my heart" was her confession "that still feels for this unhappy creature, and still yearns towards him."

And when, at moments, an absence or another preoccupation drove Lawrence from the foreground of Mrs. Siddons's intercourse with her daughter, there was always Mrs. Pennington to write from Clifton to know if our tormentor were cured yet, or how Sally's own feelings about him were getting on. Poor Sally! With such a stubborn purpose devouring the elder woman who watched over her, what chance had she to forget the charmer for whose presence she watched at every party, from every box at play or opera to which she was taken? Her whole mind was given over to the thought of the fashionable painter; the gay and handsome man who had once belonged to her; who still claimed her, so she was forced to believe, across the vow she had been forced to make.

"Who now will tell me I am remembered, or say that I do not forget?" she wrote two years after Maria's death. "It should be my constant prayer to be always kept at this same distance from that being whose fascinations I have not the power to escape should I be drawn within the circle of his magic."

4

Three years passed thus and then, more tired and driven than ever, seeing that Sid had ceased to manage her affairs very well and, though retaining possession of all her earnings, had lost £10,000 in unwise speculation, Mrs. Siddons set off on a long tour in Ireland, accompanied by Patty Wilkinson. Sally went down to Bath in the company of her papa, who by now knew all about that rascally Lawrence and had no soft corner in his poor old gouty heart in which memories of him could be encouraged. There the poor girl tried cures for her spasms, and fell back once more on the laudanum which alone gave her relief. She grew rapidly worse, but Siddons, unwilling to cut short his wife's most profitable tour, forbade Patty Wilkinson to tell Mrs. Siddons the truth about Sally's condition, and Mrs. Siddons, delayed by this subterfuge, though struggling all the time under a presentiment of sorrow, reached England in March too late to see her daughter alive.

Three extracts from the Galindo letters show how little she had been really told of Sally's state, and how terrible the shock of the truth was when it came.

The first comes from a hurried note written at Holyhead in the mood when separation from the friendly companions of a long period of work and intercourse seemed to her a heavier affliction than the illness she thought she was returning to soothe.

"Holyhead, *Sunday the Twelfth of April* 1803.
"For some hours we had scarce a breath of wind, and the vessel seemed to leave your coast as unwillingly as your poor friend. About six o'clock this morning, the snowy tops of the mountains appeared, they chilled my heart, for I felt that they were emblematic of the cold and dreary prospect before me."

Four days later she has reached London, having travelled the last stages of the journey with the news of Sally's death driving her almost out of her mind as the anguish and confusion of her words betray.

"London, *April* 16*th*, 1803.
"What can I say to you? And why should I write to you, since the dark cloud that hangs over my destiny will not, cannot be dispersed, *and every ray of sunshine*

departed from it at that time I left you, never to return? If I am to write or to speak to those I love, I must speak and write from genuine feeling, and why distress you with my overwhelming sorrow? God knows the portion of each individual is sufficient for him to bear. I make the attempt to tell you many things that press upon my aching memory, but I feel myself unequal to it. I hope a little time will restore my tranquillity, at present my head is so confused it is not without difficulty I have said thus much, though I should write volumes, I could never describe what I have lost in you, my beloved friends, and the sweet angel that is gone before. Good God, what a deprivation in a few days!

"Adieu! Adieu!"

Then there is a silence for a month and, when she writes again, she is able to do so rationally, with kind words and remembered details of her Irish friends. She gives them an account of herself in the rural hiding place her friends had provided for her at Birch Farm near Cheltenham where she stayed with Patty Wilkinson and her daughter Cecilia and Sally's friend Miss Place, who had nursed her through her last days and now stayed on to comfort the distraught and exhausted mother.

The letter is dated May 15th 1803.

". . . Our little cottage is some distance from the town, perfectly retired, surrounded by hills and fields and groves. The air of this place is peculiarly salubrious; I live out of doors as much as possible, sometimes reading under the haystack in the farmyard, sometimes rambling in the fields and sometimes musing in the orchard, all of which I do without spectators, no observers near to say I am mad, foolish or melancholy; thus I keep the 'noiseless tenour of my way'

and you will be glad to hear this mode of life so well
suited to my taste. Rising at six and going to bed at ten
has brought me to my comfortable sleep once more ;
the bitterness and anguish of selfish grief begin to
subside, and the tender recollections of excellence and
virtues gone to the blessed place of their eternal reward
are now sweet, though sad companions of my lonely
walks . . ."

The following year Lawrence exhibited the picture of Mrs. Siddons reading from *Paradise Lost* that has already been described in these pages. It was commissioned by Mrs. FitzHugh, who by this time knew as much as any living person of the state of Mrs. Siddons's heart. Whether she herself realized the declaration of defiance he painted into her glowing, sullen smile we have no means of ascertaining. But another student of her beauty has left another record of the aspect she showed to other men at this time, and, in doing so, has unwittingly written the epitaph on her two daughters who died for love of the man from whom their mother could not save them because her subjugation to him was as abject, and more far-reaching than theirs.

" But beauty is a fading flower ; it faded from her
face ere one wrinkle had touched that fixed paleness
which seldom was tinged with any colour, even in the
whirlwind of passion. Light came and went across
those finest features at the coming or going of each
feeling and thought ; but faint was the change of hue
ever visible on that glorious marble. It was the magnificent countenance of an animated statue, in the still-
ness of its idealized beauty instinct with all the emotions
of our mortal life. Idealized beauty ! Did we not say

that beauty had faded from her face? Yes, but it was over-spread with a kindred expression, for which we withhold the name only because it seemed more divine, inspiring awe that overpowered while it mingled with delight, more than regal—say rather, immortal. Such an image surely had never before trod, nor ever again will tread the enchanted floor. In all stateliest shows of waking woe she dwindled the stateliest into insignificance; her majesty made others mean; in her sun-like light all stars 'paled their ineffectual fires.' But none knew the troubled grandeur of guilt till they saw her in Lady Macbeth, walking in her sleep, and as she wrung her hands striving in vain to wash from her the ingrained murder, 'Not all the perfumes of Arabia could sweeten this little hand!' The whisper came as from the hollow grave; and more hideously haunted than ever was the hollow grave, seemed then to be the cell of her heart."

This was John Wilson, writing English in retrospect. The earlier picture of her, made with him by Hogge as the Etrick Shepherd, during one of the "Noctes Ambrosinæ," is better known:

"Sarah was a glorious creature. Methinks I see her now in the sleep-walking scene as Leddy Macbeth! Her gran' high straicht-nosed face, whiter than ashes! Fixed een, no like the een o' the dead, yet hardly mair like them o' the leevin; dim, and yet licht wi' an obscure lustre through which the tormented sowl looked in the chains o' sleep and dreams wi' a' the distraction o' remorse and despair,—and oh! sic an expanse o' forehead for a warld o' dreadfu' thochts, aneath the braided blackness o' her hair, that had nevertheless been put up wi' a steady and nae uncarefu' haun before the troubled Leddy had lain down, for it behoved ane so high-born as she, in the midst o' her ruefu' trouble, no to neglect what she owed to her stately beauty, and to the head that lay on the couch of ane o' Scotland's Thanes—noo, likewise about to be, during the short space o' the passing o' a thundercloud, her bluidy and usurping King.

"Onwards she used to come—no Sarah Siddons—but just Leddy Macbeth hersel'—though through that melancholy masquerade o' passion, the spectator aye had a confused glimmerin apprehension o' the great actress—glidin wi' the ghost-like motion o' nicht-wanderin unrest, unconscious o' surroundin objects,—for oh! how could the glazed, yet gleemin een, see aught in this material world?—yet, by some mysterious power o' instinct, never touchin ane o' the impediments that the furniture o' the auld castle micht hae opposed to her haunted footsteps,—on she came, wring wringin her hauns, as if washin them in the cleansin dews frae the blouts o' blood,—but wae's me for the murderess, out they wad no be, ony mair than the stains on the spat o' the floor where some midnicht-slain Christian has groaned out his soul aneath the dagger's stroke, when the sleepin hoose heard not the shriek o' departing life.

"Whether a' this was natural or not, ye see I dinna ken, because I never beheld ony woman, either gentle or semple, walkin in her sleep after having committed murder. But, Lord save us! that hollow, broken-hearted voice, 'Out, damned spot', was o' itsel aneuch to tell to a' that heard it, that crimes done in the flesh during time will needs be punished in the spirit during eternity. It was a dreadfu' homily yon; and wha that saw't would ever ask whether tragedy or the stage was moral, purging the soul, as she did, wi' pity and wi' terror?"

5

There is another and an equally revealing footnote to this queer, complicated tragedy made in a spirit of more intimate portrayal and with a vivid wickedness that gives weight to the real feeling underlying the obliterated head of the demon in the Satan picture.

While Maria Siddons was still alive, Lawrence, pathetically enough, employed the pencil queens were anxious to retain in their services, in working at a head of the girl he had tired of, making it as lovely as he remembered her, sending it to Mrs. Pennington as a child might do in token of his willingness to be good ; to be reasonable ; to be friends, if only Sally would relent. There is something very attractive and disarming in his conviction that the gift of this most beautiful drawing, a work into which we may be sure he poured the whole flattery of his art, would please the vanity of the dying girl, and make her accept the friendship, the ardent, if now purely brotherly, affection he offered her. He was so used to pleasing : he could not bear that even Maria should harbour any resentment. Ever since his babyhood he had seen black looks turn to smiles and threatened punishments averted by the gift of a pretty picture he had made. The drawing was sent to Clifton, and has disappeared. Mrs. Pennington, goose that she was, may have destroyed it after Maria had been thoroughly upset by a sight of it. If it were lovelier than the two lovely sketches we still have of her it must have been a masterpiece ; and indeed it came

MARIA SIDDONS BY LAWRENCE

out of the kind of mood in which masterpieces are conceived and fashioned. No one, competent to judge it as a work of art, ever saw it before it was destroyed.

But there is another picture, the head of a fury, with snaky locks writhing above the black brows and fixed malignant stare of wrath that is also called Maria Siddons. The nose is huge, dominant, pinched above the nostrils, the lovely mouth is set, thin-lipped, unsmiling, stiff with an inexorable purpose. The head alone is finished : some loose indeterminate gown is thrown over the shoulders and the folds are indicated by thick and furious strokes of the painter's brush, twisting and curling together in an insane calligraphy. There is no need to ask for date or explanation of this terrible work. Thus he must have seen the face he once had loved after reading that beautiful, eloquent, abominable letter of which Mrs. Pennington was so proud ; of which Mrs. Siddons spoke with so much reverent gratitude and admiration.

III

DANGEROUS YEARS

I

IRELAND was something of a Tom Tiddler's Ground to the Kembles. There was a good theatre-going public in Dublin where the managers maintained companies equal to playing up to any visiting stars from London, and, so long as such stars were willing to travel into the savage wilderness Mrs. Siddons described as lying between the capital and the towns of Cork and Limerick where she undertook to appear, the rewards of a prolonged tour were worth the pains.

This time she left England with no husband to protect her interests, taking with her as sole companion Tate Wilkinson's daughter Patty, a devoted but rather lamb-like and youthful chaperon for the lioness who was in a difficult mood just then.

She was tired, she was wretchedly unhappy. Her grief for Maria; the uneasy strain of keeping up Sally's resolution not to yield to Lawrence; the dreadful excitement of meeting, and sometimes arguing with, the painter had exhausted her, and lately an even more exhausting suspicion had robbed her of the factitious excitement that had kept her more or less riding the storm. Loth as mother and daughter alike were to admit it,

Lawrence for some months had showed every symptom of being quite ready to take "No" for an answer. Instead of pausing when he met Miss Siddons and fixing thrilling looks upon her countenance; instead of trying to slip little notes for Sally into Miss Patty Wilkinson's ready hands, he had actually cut poor Sally dead one evening at the theatre, and had sent her, quite openly, an extremely chilly little note in reply to her request that she might be told wherein she had offended him. Miss Amelia Locke was not the cause of this change. She was encouraging the addresses of the rich half-Russian widower Mr. Angerstein, a great patron of the Arts; nor had Lawrence's threat of seeking consolation at Clapham, where a very pretty young lady took drawing-lessons from him, come to anything. Mr. Lawrence was busy, far too busy the gossips said, at Montagu House painting the Princess of Wales and the Princess Charlotte. Mrs. Siddons knew she had, for the moment, lost her hold on him. She may have believed the loss to be final. So to Ireland she went, much as a galley-slave might return to his bench and oar.

"I shall be here till Saturday,"

she wrote to Mrs. FitzHugh from Preston in July 1801,

"and after that time, at Lancaster, till Thursday the 28th; thence I shall go immediately to Bath, where I shall have about a month's quiet; and then begin to play at Bristol for a few nights. 'Such resting finds the soul of unblest feet.' *When* we shall come to London is uncertain, for nothing is settled by Mr. Sheridan, and I think it not impossible that *my* winter may be spent in Dublin ; for I must go on *making*, to secure the few comforts that I have been able to attain for myself and my family. It is providential for us all, that I can do so much. But I hope it is not wrong to say, that I am tired, and should be glad to be at rest indeed."

She arrived in Dublin, a woman of forty-five, still beautiful and at the height of her fame. For twenty-seven years she had lived the faithful wife of a dull husband, the unremitting wage-earner of the family. She had enjoyed friendships and adulation in the intervals of very strenuous work, and she had been able to sublimate a great deal of her emotional force in the exercise of her profession : but she had never been able to live at all for herself : she had never, in the parlance of peoples Cæsar never knew, had a good time. Her infatuation for Lawrence had brought her the maximum of distress. She had disguised its true nature from herself as from all those about her, making a show of quasi-maternal interest in the man she had known ever since his childhood. But she was not *quite* old enough to be his mother, and he, who made implicit love to every woman he met, was quite genuinely crazy about her beauty, as indeed he was about that of the whole Kemble family. There was, in the stately loveliness of Mrs. Siddons ; the monumental good looks of John Philip ; the beautifully chiselled expressiveness of Charles Kemble's features, a suggestion of the statuesque, a marmoreal quality that captivated the mischievous lightness in Thomas

Lawrence, giving him an assurance of weight, offering him the deep, psychological attraction of a compensatory otherness, so that he felt safe as well as happily sinful and audacious, though not a Roman Catholic, eating beefsteaks with Kemble in a coffee house on a fast day, and making picture after picture of Melpomene girlish and in love.

We cannot be sure how far Lawrence himself realized the nature of his own feeling for Mrs. Siddons. There is his quoted statement of a reason for preferring Maria to Sally : " she is the more like her mother." The fact that he was unfaithful by turns to both sisters seems to point to the deeply rooted consciousness that he was in love with neither and yet at the same time incapable of loving outside the Siddons, or more exactly the Kemble, family. Thirty years later the sight of little Fanny Kemble tottering to throw herself into her own mother's arms at her first entry as Juliet, while Mrs. Siddons herself looked on from a stage box, drew the sixty-year-old painter into his last enslavement to the Kemble eye and face and voice. But in 1802 the knowledge that he was unable to tear himself away from her side was only an exasperation to Mrs. Siddons's own tenderness, not an assuagement of it : for Lawrence must still disguise the mother in the daughter, and she must always defend her own self-esteem under the cloak of protecting her child from the unhappiness of a marriage with so volatile and inconsiderate a lover. At times, as we have seen, she even tried to save him from the discomfort and boredom of an invalid wife. All the most noble pretexts were called in to prevent

Sally from ever becoming a connubial burden to Lawrence. Once when Mrs. Siddons suspected Miss Bird of carrying letters between Sally and the painter she exploded into one of her terrific rages and blew her world to bits for a time. But, before she left for Ireland, even the outlet of a rage was closed to her. Lawrence, still successful, still dazzling, had tired of his part : it did not suit his vanity to be the ever-rejected suitor : it was, for the moment, absorbing enough to play the difficult, the actually dangerous game of portrait painter to the Royal Family and to spread his conquests, always on the most definitely understood basis of hopelessness, in a still more exciting field. Somewhere in the secret places of her heart, the places she never explored as a woman, Mrs. Siddons realized that, for her, and for the moment, the game was up.

2

So to Ireland she went, feeling old ; deserted ; burdened ; leaving her baby Cecilia behind her and with no one who really cared for her, or for whom she cared very much, to welcome her on the other side of the water. She had always had trouble in Ireland. William Brereton had gone mad there (some people seemed to think he had been in love with her and that her coldness had deranged him), and the troublesome business of Digge's benefit still stuck in the retentive Irish mind. She knew no good would come of the visit. She was quite right.

No sooner had she landed than Frederic Jones,

the manager of the Theatre Royal at Dublin, asked her if she would give a benefit performance for the Lying-in Hospital. Benefits were not Mrs. Siddons's strong point. She would rather pay £50 into the box office, as she did for Miss Kitty Gough's benefit a few months later, than act herself beyond her regular appearances, tired and stale as she then felt. But she could not and did not refuse to play for the poor mothers of Dublin and their new-born infants; it was Jones who mismanaged the whole business, so that no date when she was free to play was ever fixed and she was accused of being backward in the cause of that particular charity she was the most willing to support.

The days were gone by when a young equerry at Dublin Castle wore her miniature set in diamonds on his finger; the Duchess of Leinster no longer kept open house for her at Black Rock; Shane Castle, with its private theatre where she had once enjoyed hospitality that " almost inspired the recollection of an Arabian night's entertainment," had been burnt down these ten years and more. Certain distinguished people made her welcome on her arrival in Dublin; but, after the season ended, she was alone except for Patty Wilkinson: no brother John, no William Brereton, not even the semi-drunken Cooke to support her. She bore the whole burden of a solitary travelling star.

When, tired and unhappy and anxious, she wanted to cut short her tour, to be in London for her son Henry's wedding, Siddons wrote begging her to stay on. She could play to several hundred pounds a night in Limerick, in Cork, in Belfast;

the painter and decorator had been in the house at Great Marlborough Street and their bill was enormous; George, the son who had as a baby " looked so very like the Prince of Wales," had just received his appointment in the Indian Civil Service and needed an entire and very expensive outfit: there was every reason why poor mamma, who was still without that carriage of her own she had been trying to afford for years, should stay acting in the savage wilderness. So in Ireland she stayed, missing Henry's wedding, but not George's departure for India as he, dear boy, went over to Dublin to spend a farewell week with his mother before leaving Europe; missing also her father Roger Kemble's deathbed and funeral, and finally, as we have seen, urged by her husband to remain to fulfil a not really binding engagement to play once more at Cork, and so missing the last hours of her adored, mismanaged Sally's life.

That is one side of the picture, a picture of misery complete only when its last tragic colour has been laid on at Shrewsbury where Mrs. Siddons, at last on her way home, received the news of Sally's death and fell into a trance of grief and exhaustion from which it took her months of seclusion to recover. The other side of the picture has been preserved for us by the exertions of Mrs. Galindo in her *Circumstantial Detail of Mrs. Siddons's Life for the last Seven Years*.

3

When Mrs. Siddons reached Dublin in the early summer of 1802 the time was ripe for the Galindos and the Galindos were there. Mrs. Galindo's stage name was Kitty Gough. She was quite a bad actress but, being as a girl in comfortable circumstances, she had indulged a taste for private theatricals and, when her father met with a reverse of fortune, had followed the advice of friends and gone on the stage. At this point her own story is shrouded in some ambiguity :

> " I met with all the success I could reasonably hope for, in point of emolument certainly beyond what I felt I deserved. In a short time I realized a property sufficient for all the reasonable wants of life beside being able to allow my father a yearly income."

As she has previously assured us that her father's estate had been " charged with a moderate fortune for myself and sisters " out of which she gave her father all she could spare when he sold his own annuity and spent the proceeds, it seems probable that Miss Gough's earnings inside the theatre were not her only means of support. She had acted in Leeds and was acquainted with Patty Wilkinson, then living at home as Tate Wilkinson's child, and she had also played in Dublin with John Philip Kemble when he was the visiting star there ; but until 1802, she had never met Mrs. Siddons.

Taking advantage of her acquaintance with Miss Wilkinson, the actress pushed forward and pressed for a personal introduction to Mrs. Siddons with whom she was presently to act on the stage, and made herself very agreeable to the great woman. By this time Miss Gough, though retaining her maiden name as an actress, had acquired a husband, and even her own self-justifying pen cannot make this addition to her belongings seem altogether a credit to her.

> "The first winter of my Dublin engagement, I became acquainted with Mr. G..., whom I had known slightly at Bath, where I had performed the former winter. A strong and perhaps fatal attachment united us; on my part I do not scruple to acknowledge I sacrificed more than prudence can excuse: the resentment of my relatives was, and is to this day implacable, by which I have lost the share of a considerable property on the death of my beforementioned uncle. To the distressing circumstances which attended my union with Mr. G. I had nothing to oppose but that happiness which I possessed to the extreme. In my domestic enjoyments you found me, as you too well were convinced of, in the possession of as great a portion of content as this life can be supposed to have, yet it alone existed in the possession of one blessing, the affection of that object I had sacrificed so much for."

Galindo was an attractive-looking creature, younger than his wife, much younger than Mrs. Siddons. He was a fencing-master and his first usefulness to Mrs. Siddons was inaugurated when Jones either made, or accepted, the suggestion that the lady should revive her performance of Hamlet that had gone down so well at Manchester years before. The sketch reproduced here proves that she appeared as Hamlet during the Dublin season. She was forty-seven and growing stout. She certainly took

COSTUME WORN BY MRS. SIDDONS AS HAMLET

fencing-lessons from Galindo in the pretext of preparing herself for the part and thus was in constant association with the object of Mrs. Galindo's affections.

In addition to the object, called alternatively "Mr. G." by her throughout the rest of her narrative, the Irish actress possessed a curricle and pair. These with Mr. G. as driver she placed at Mrs. Siddons's entire disposal.

> "I requested you might use my carriage as if it were your own; you literally took me at my word, for from that time I was entirely excluded from it."

Here again Mrs. Galindo proves herself a most unreliable narrator, for a few lines further down the page she relates that when the company travelled to Cork or to Limerick, Mrs. Siddons and Patty Wilkinson did the first stage by mail-coach while Mr. and Mrs. Galindo drove in their own carriage, after which Mrs. Galindo joined Miss Wilkinson in the general company, where she was clearly far more entertained than by a *tête-à-tête* with her husband. Mrs. Siddons allowed herself to be driven slowly after them, obliged to follow at some distance to avoid the dust of the mail-coach and to stop on the road to give the horses a rest, whereas the coach took fresh horses at every stage. So it came about that Mr. Galindo, who had started early in the morning driving his wife on the first stage, reached the end of the day's journey, with Mrs. Siddons in the curricle, later in the evening than Mrs. Galindo and Patty Wilkinson who had travelled by the quicker coach. And since Mrs. Siddons, sleepy with driving all day in the open carriage, wanted nothing but to get to bed, and Mr. Galindo, who had driven all day, was too tired to pay much attention to his wife, Miss Wilkinson and Mrs. Galindo were left to finish the evening together, and Mrs. Galindo, unable to show off her intimate acquaintance with the famous actress, or to get any details of the day's conversation from her drowsy husband when she joined him upstairs, began to nurse a sense of injury.

Mrs. Siddons, glad of any distraction from her own troubles, took an interest in the Galindo family—the pair had two, possibly three, children at this time—and Patty Wilkinson, glad to find an acquaintance in the strange country, gossiped away her time with the chatty, common Irishwoman and persuaded Mrs. Siddons to see rather more of her than she would naturally have done. When they were in Dublin, Galindo took Mrs. Siddons for a drive almost every day and when travelling, as we have seen, she often preferred the longer, quieter hours in the curricle to the crowded swiftness of the coach. Aware that she owed some return for this kindness Mrs. Siddons not only acted in a benefit for Miss Gough in Cork, but also contributed £50 to the box office on another occasion in Dublin. She also, and here she made a real error in judgment, promised the Irish actress to get her brother to take her on for a season in London. Kemble was annoyed when his sister returned to town with this obligation. He did not see why he should share the expenses of returning the hospitality his sister had enjoyed. During his ensuing season in Dublin he treated Miss Gough with so much coldness that she began to feel less anxious to play in London than she had done when accepting Mrs. Siddons's offer.

But to London the Galindos went, and Mrs. Siddons began to realize the mistake she had made. For Mrs. Galindo was a very difficult woman at the best of times and, as by the time she reached London her Irish susceptibilities were all wounded, she was anything but a success behind the scenes at Covent Garden. Kemble had never wanted her : he said there were no parts for her in the season's programmes. It was all very awkward. Galindo, who had obtained a job, vaguely defined as " a military situation," had arrived in London before his wife, and had, quite naturally, claimed Mrs. Siddons as a friend. He was not quite so welcome in London as he had been in Dublin but he seems to have got round Patty Wilkinson and was in the habit of dropping in to supper whenever Mrs. Siddons was in town. For some months she had a small house at Hampstead, and thither, when Mrs. Galindo joined him, the whole family would repair and outstay their welcome. One night they stayed on so late after supper that Mrs. Siddons had no choice but to offer to put them up. Mrs. Galindo and her child shared the one spare-bed ; Galindo slept on the dining-room sopha. Six years later, Mrs. Galindo remembering this circumstance bethought her that, as the sopha could not have been a very comfortable bed, Mr. G., being what he was, and possibly drunk, might have tried to share his hostess's couch. The suspicion deepened and spread. " I accuse you," wrote Mrs. Galindo reviewing the history of Mrs. Siddons's kindness and her own jealousy, "that you asked my child for the purpose of separating Mr. G. and I at night."

So tiresome did the Galindos become that, when Mrs. Siddons left Hampstead for Westbourne Farm, her change of address was at first kept a secret from them. But they found out the place and one day, before Mrs. Siddons had moved in, had the curiosity to go and look over the empty house and were discovered in the act. This made Mrs. Siddons so angry that she tried to break off the whole connection: but Galindo got hold of Patty Wilkinson once more, and once more Mrs. Siddons was weak enough to let this handsome ne'er-do-weel call and apologize and flatter her into seeing him again, though, with pardonable foolishness, she drew the line at his wife.

Presently, her whole family, and such of her friends as knew of her entanglement with these tiresome people, being unanimous that she must cease from admitting them to her private life, she lent the pair £1,000 towards getting them a partnership with the elder Macready in Manchester. A friend, a gentleman friend, of Mrs. Galindo's, supplied a second £1,000: the third £1,000 was to remain a debt on which the Galindos would pay interest. Unable or unwilling to let Mr. Siddons know of the transaction Mrs. Siddons kept it a secret from him, though how she explained the disappearance of so large a sum to him is not made clear. Perhaps she said she had invested it herself: she certainly did let the Galindos arrange to pay her interest on it, though when they were unpunctual she does not appear to have pressed them. Her one idea was to get them out of London. Manchester was a long way off. It was worth the complete loss of £1,000 and another postponement of the carriage of her own to be free of the possibility of either of the Galindos turning up to spend a night on the sopha. For by this time Mrs. Siddons had forbidden *Mr.* Galindo the door.

However, Macready was no more pleased with his bargain than Kemble had been. Galindo seems to have told him that Mrs. Siddons would come and play at Manchester whenever she was asked ; but Mrs. Siddons refused to discuss any such arrangement. She did go to play in Birmingham however, and, when she reached the city, there was Mrs. Galindo established in rooms in the same house as her own ! Mrs. Galindo's own account of what followed shows her and her victim in the very colours the writer did not intend to suggest :

" Miss W. met me on the instant of my arrival, to my surprize, in the most friendly manner. After the treatment I had received from you, I wished to decline all conversation with her, but she would force it on me. I saw she wanted to do away the letter you had written, she endeavoured to blame me for having in my answer used the words, ' few women in my situation would have acted by you as I have done ' ; I supported the truth of my observation so strongly, that she had nothing to reply to it ; she then said you were sorry for what you had done, and requested all might be forgotten, she pressed, nay insisted, I should spend the evening with you. I reluctantly consented, you met me with more warmth and seeming kindness, than I had for a long time seen in your manner ; and repeated what Miss W. had said, I was affected even to tears, my mind was in a dreadful state, as I shall explain hereafter. In a few days we parted, when you took your leave of me, I told you I was very unhappy, and that you were the object of my uneasiness, but that when you next saw me, let it cost me even my life, all should be explained ; you seemed shocked and surprized at my words ; taking my hand in the most *affectionate* manner, you said, ' if you ever should believe me any other than your sincere friend, you will wrong me much.' From that moment I spared no pains to unravel the clue, which by the most extraordinary means I had been entrusted with, to develop the truth of your real character and conduct in respect to me, and your connection with Mr. G. the whole of which I was shortly after acquainted with. It is now two years past since I went to London for no other purpose than that of telling you I knew you now in your real character. I was so agitated on seeing you I could scarcely speak ; you said you were going to *church* ; I told you I should not detain you, as I had only come to fulfil the promise I had made when last we parted, and in a few words to tell you, I was no longer your dupe, as I was now perfectly informed as to the nature of your attachment to Mr. G. for these many years. You changed from red to extreme paleness, and with trembling lips and great hesitation of speech, after some time you said, ' you cannot believe what you say, and on what do you found your accusation ? ' I answered, ' that is of no consequence, you know what I say to be *true*.' I then walked out of your house, not chusing to prolong the conversation."

Poor Mrs. Siddons ! She had paid a very high price for the indulgence of a little vanity; the mistake of making friends with vulgar people; the fatigue that allowed her to accept a few drives from a handsome and plausible young man, urged to pay her this attention by the coarse-grained ambition of his pushing and venomous wife. It was a greater mistake to lend the £1,000; she never saw a penny of it again. But that would not have been a very serious blow to her for by this time the £10,000 limit she had set herself to reach had been secured in spite of Siddons's loss of exactly that sum invested in Sadler's Wells, and also of the disastrous fire at Covent Garden Theatre in which all her stage jewellery and rich lace and velvet costumes together with many valuable souvenirs were destroyed.

This loss was, in part, compensated for in 1808 when the death of Mr. Siddons placed her at last in full possession of her own money and also made it possible for her to reduce her establishments to one house where she and Cecilia, now a girl of fourteen almost alarmingly like Maria, could live watched over and tended by the devoted Patty. Though Sid had been a trial for many years he had never been so bad a husband as to make his wife anything but sincerely grieved when he died. The days of their youth and love came back to her memory: she mourned him as a rigidly faithful wife must mourn the man who has been lover and friend and the father of her children. Also, in those days a widow was a woman who had lost a natural protector, and though Kemble was there to safe-guard his sister's interests in the theatre, and though her eldest son Henry was now grown up, she was, in a more far-reaching sense than any widow in these days, alone in the world. In the following year the new theatre built for the Kembles by subscription was opened and the famous Old Prices Riots started. The public resented a new arrangement of seats and higher charges. Scandals from Ireland, that breeding-ground of malignant gossip, were revived. John Philip Kemble and Mrs. Siddons were under a cloud. The moment was ripe. Mrs. Galindo published her famous letter.

Its title-page alone was enough to insure a certain sale :

MRS. GALINDO'S LETTER
TO
MRS. SIDDONS :
Being a Circumstantial Detail of
Mrs. Siddon's Life
for
The last Seven Years ;
With Several of her Letters.

. . . Dark and unknown betrayer :
But now the dawn begins, and the slow hand
Of fate is stretch'd to draw the veil and leave
Thee bare, the naked mark of public view.

CONGREVE

LONDON :
Printed for the Authoress :
Sold by M. Jones, No. 5 Newgate Street ; and to be had of all the booksellers in the United Kingdom.
1809.
(*Price* 5*s.*)
W. N. Jones, Printer, Green Arbour Court, Old Bailey, London.

We have already quoted from the pamphlet's contents and given the salient features of the story Mrs. Galindo distorted with so much vehement malice : but no abridgment of the work can do justice to the native confusions of her style, as may be seen by a consideration of her opening and closing paragraphs :

" Madam,—

"Conscious as I am that the life and circumstances of an insignificant individual can create no interest worthy of public curiosity, yet, when joined with a name such as yours, they become an object of attention—a person so long eminent for your public talents, and *supposed private virtues* ; on that I found my hopes I shall be forgiven for intruding on the world the sad events of a life, the principal misfortunes of which you have caused. Destitute of all those advantages which you possess over me (your victim for near seven miserable years), I dare appeal even to the same public who have so long held you justly in estimation by the delightful gratification your great talents afforded them, convinced as I am that if justice or humanity reside upon this earth, it is in the breasts of Englishmen, capable by the solidity of their judgment to discern the truth, and from their love of justice, always ready to hear and assist the oppressed, through whatever medium they may be addressed ; the nature of my wrongs leaves me no other tribunal to which I can apply for retribution, no other punishment on my oppressor, but what may be obtained by letting the world know your true character, stripped of that veil with which hypocrisy has so long and successfully covered it.

. . . .

"After what I have now detailed, I appeal to a public, ever ready to hear with candour the complaints of the oppressed. Should the mother of three innocent and *as yet infant* children, crouch under such accumulated wrongs and not seek for redress ? Is there a mind that would not be roused by such injuries to unmask its oppressor? You shall not triumph over the grave, which perhaps your conduct may cause me shortly to descend into, before I shall endeavour to do myself justice. Neither your great talents, your hypocrisy, nor any of those advantages which you possess, can place you above the reach of truth, the greatest evil you have to dread, whose life is a falsehood. To the world I leave my cause: I have advanced nothing but what I can substantiate by the most certain evidence, if called upon so to do.

. . . .

"I aver, were I to descend to a particular detail of those circumstances which have come to my knowledge, that have passed between you and Mr. G. both in England and Ireland, no modest eye could peruse these sheets. But in the latter place your conduct being more accurately and minutely known, is execrated, as it must ever be when it is known, and I am the object of universal commiseration, as it is but too public what sacrifices I made for Mr. G. and what the return *you* have caused him to make me. I have by you lost all that could make my life valuable; my children and myself are reduced to comparative beggary, my friend (perhaps my only one) engaged to pay what is alone Mr. G.'s debt to you; my spirits so broken, and my health so much impaired by what I have suffered for these many years, that perhaps the publication of this will be the last act of my life. This is therefore the wretched legacy I now prepare to leave you.

"I have now, Madam, little more to add, but that I shall produce to the public a few of your letters, some written to me, others to Mr. G. which I was entrusted with, as I suppose, with your leave, the better to blind your *dupe*. Those *tender epistles* that were written, as I have before described, were carefully concealed from my view, only I once by accident saw them : the accumulated wrongs which I have been obliged to endure for your sake, the sacrifices which I shall still be forced to make, excuses me for renouncing that submission to the will of Mr. G. that hitherto I have practised. Though by this public disclosure of your conduct, the bonds which you vainly tried to break should be for ever rent asunder, that even shall not deter me from the fixed purpose of my heart. Without any claim upon the public, but what their pity and their justice may grant to an unfortunate being, who appeals to their tribunal against one of the most practised hypocrites that ever imposed upon the world ; unassisted, oppressed by illness and sorrow, with all the imperfections which I am but too conscious this story is filled with, still I dare hope for their indulgence, their consideration.

" I now take my leave, Madam, subscribing myself,
" With the greatest truth,
" Your wretched victim,
" CATHERINE GALINDO."

Unsupported by other evidence it is just possible that Mrs. Galindo's tale might be found to hold water by a reader prejudiced by natural cynicism against any successful and virtuous woman, or by some person ignorant of Mrs. Siddons's own life and character ; but, with the overweening folly that usually urges the villain towards ultimate self-destruction, Mrs. Galindo published twenty of the letters Mrs. Siddons had addressed to her and to her husband. The earlier ones are couched in terms of affectionate friendship and one letter to Galindo has a rather silly playfulness of phrase, but, towards the close of the correspondence, a tone of increasing exasperation, held in check by dignity and considerable patience, makes itself heard.

It is instructive when weighing Mrs. Siddons's case to consider three of the later letters.

1

"*February* 19*th*, 1804.

"My dear Mrs. G.,—

"I am sure you will do me the justice to believe I should have answered your kind letter long ago, if I could have snatched so much time from incessant occupation, but indeed I have never had so much to do in my life before. I almost live in the theatre, and am almost worn out with the duties of my profession, and other every day concerns, which, however frivolous, are (as you know) necessary to be attended to; in the mean time, it gives me great pleasure that Mr. G. looks very well, and his only uneasiness seems to be the want of his domestic comforts; I wish it was in my power to see more of him here, because I know it would make his time pass more comfortably: he is gone for a few days to the country, I wish he was staying there altogether, for the country air seems to do him good. All this he has told you no doubt. I look forward with great pleasure to the time I hope to see you settled near to us. Adieu! my dear Mrs. G., and believe me,

"Your affectionate,
"and faithful friend
"S. Siddons."

2

"*Sunday*, Manchester.

"My dear Mrs. G.,—

"Mr. G. has just been here ... about the plays, he offered me his hand but I had not duplicity enough to receive it. I need only tell you that he was as violent as usual, and wondered what he had done to offend me. I endeavoured, but in vain, for he had all the talk to

himself, to ask him what he thought of telling Mr.——
that *I lent* him the money, after I had his sacred promise
on account of M. never to let be known. I asked him if he
had ever heard me utter a word respecting you, that was
not dictated by esteem and cordial good will, and how
he could imagine that if I had an idea that his acquaintance with me could give *you one* moment's uneasiness,
that I should not in *that moment* have broken it off. God
knows, and he knows too, that I would, but I always
thought you were desirous of keeping it up, as being
sure of his at least being in society that could not be
disreputable. I tell you all this, WHICH IS ALL THAT
PASSED BETWEEN US IN THIS INTERVIEW, that you may
know from one who never yet told you a falsehood (and
as *he* professes to be unable to relate anything accurately), the truth, the whole truth, and nothing but the
truth, that you may not be misled ; he was talking so
much all the time, that I believe he hardly heard me,
when I assured him I was sorry to see him carried away
by the violence of his temper—that I harboured no
resentment against him,—and only hoped he would not
hereafter represent me as such a fiend, to turn a man's
wife into ridicule to her *husband*, as it was likely to come
to the ears of those, who are not so deeply impressed
with the duty of forgiveness, as myself ; he went away
in a rage, or perhaps I might have talked him into a
little reason.

" Adieu, and
" Believe me, dear Mrs. G.,
" Your sincere friend,
" S. SIDDONS."

3

" Mrs. Siddons's compliments to Mr. Galindo ; she
declines the favour of any interview and begs leave to
refer him to Mr. —— for any business he may have to
transact."

a prosecution?" she asked her family. "Damages or imprisonment I suppose, and in failure of the first what should I gain by inflicting the second? There are three children all under nine years old, too, that must be reduced in either case to a state of wretchedness and perhaps absolute want of bread."

And then, remembering, for a rather frightened moment, the scenes Mrs. Galindo was so well equipped to make, and with a swift and possibly shame-faced glance backward to occasions when her own conduct had laid her open to the easily roused jealousy of an ill-bred vulgarian, she scuttled rather hurriedly into the defences a woman can always throw up against the name of action.

"There is no species of suffering that I would not prefer to encountering the horrible indecency of that wretched woman, whom everyone supposes to be quite mad too."

So there was to be no prosecution: Mrs. Siddons was wise, even if she had been a little frightened: it was far better to ignore the whole business, to trust calumny to die of neglect.

It was to her very dear nephew Horace Twiss that Mrs. Siddons had addressed her final and most decisive refusal to be bothered with replying to Mrs. Galindo's letter. She wrote to him a great deal, and he was devoted to her. When, three years later she took her farewell of the stage, in the part of Lady Macbeth, it was Horace Twiss who composed the lines she spoke after the sleep-walking scene, when the audience, moved to enthusiasm and grief, refused to let the play go on, not wanting to hear anyone else that night, once Lady Macbeth had left the stage. The speech is a model of its kind; spoken by a great actress still in possession of her powers and lacking only the grace of youth it must have been as moving, in a tender and pensive way, as anything her voice had ever sent ringing to the galleries of the theatre she and her brother had rebuilt and restored. Many an actress, giving a farewell performance since that night, must have wished to speak them again, and, so modest is their tenour, that, except for the association, more than one English actress among her successors might have done so without vanity or presumption.

> " *Who has not felt how growing ease endears*
> *The fond remembrance of our former years ?*
> *Who has not sigh'd, when doom'd to leave at last*
> *The hopes of youth, the habits of the past,*
> *Ten thousand ties and interests that impart*
> *A second nature to the human heart,*
> *And writhing round it close, like tendrils, climb*
> *Blooming in age, and sanctified by time !*
>
> *Yes ! At this moment crowd upon my mind*
> *Scenes of bright days for ever left behind,*
> *Bewildering visions of enraptured youth,*
> *When hope and fancy wore the guise of truth,*
> *And long-forgotten years, that almost seem*
> *The faded traces of a morning dream !*
> *Sweet are those mournful thoughts : for they renew*
> *The pleasing sense of all I owe to you,*
> *For each inspiring smile, and soothing tear—*
> *For those full honours of my long career,*
> *That cheer'd my earliest hope, and chased my latest*
>   *fear !*

And though for me those tears shall flow no more,
And the warm sunshine of your smile is o'er,
Though the bright beams are fading fast away
That shone unclouded through my summer day—
Yet grateful Memory shall reflect their light
O'er the dim shadows of the coming night,
And lend to later life a softer tone,
A moonlight tint—a lustre of her own.

Judges and Friends! to whom the magic strain
Of Nature's feeling never spoke in vain,
Perhaps your hearts, when years have glided by,
And past emotions wake a fleeting sigh,
May think on her whose lips have pour'd so long
The charmed sorrows of your Shakespeare's song—
On her who, parting to return no more,
Is now the mourner she but seem'd before;
Herself subdued, resigns the melting spell,
And breathes, with swelling heart, her long,
  Her last Farewell!"

Copyright Diploma Gallery
THE CHAIR USED BY SIR THOMAS LAWRENCE'S SITTERS

IV

"THEIR FIRE IS NOT QUENCHED"

I

For eighteen years Mrs. Siddons lived, growing old in a retirement that was not for a long time a real seclusion. At first she stayed on at Westbourne Farm while Cecilia was still more or less a schoolgirl, giving small parties there and going for long visits to friends. She emerged from time to time for a few hours on the occasions when she played for charity or gave readings by royal command at Windsor. When times grew more settled she went to Paris : later, after John Philip retired, she stayed with him and his wife in their villa above Lausanne whence brother and sister contemplated " the horrible grandeur of the Alps," and were very active for their respective ages.

Then, as she grew older, and Cecilia, now out of her teens, was naturally anxious to go to and to give parties, Westbourne Farm seemed a little remote, so Mrs. and Miss Siddons moved nearer to London and took a house with a good drawing-room at No. 27 Upper Baker Street, overlooking the new concentric circles of Regent's Park. In this pleasant almost suburban home, Mrs. Siddons passed fourteen happy enough years, having all her comforts about her. She was able to give herself up to decent and quiet mourning there when, one after another,

her brother John Philip Kemble; and her son Henry Siddons; and Mrs. Piozzi; and old Mrs. Garrick, who bequeathed to her a pair of Shakespeare's gloves; and Mrs. Damer, who had inherited the castellated Gothic of Strawberry Hill from Horace Walpole, died and left her a little more lonely for each loss. She gave up modelling in clay. She took to wearing her spectacles all the time, instead of waving them gracefully in the air while she talked or recited. She began to wear a mob cap and to play the grandmother. Mrs. Charles Kemble, who could never quite control the infant Fanny, once took the small delinquent all the way to Westbourne Farm to be scolded by her terrifying old aunt. But Mrs. Siddons was incapable of frightening any child:

> "Melpomene took me upon her lap, and, bending upon me her 'controlling frown' discoursed to me of my evil ways in those accents which curdled the blood of the poor shopman of whom she demanded if the printed calico she purchased of him would wash. The tragic tones pausing in the midst of the impressed and impressive silence of the assembled family, I tinkled forth, 'What beautiful eyes you have!' all my small faculties having been absorbed in the steadfast gaze I fixed upon those magnificent orbs. Mrs. Siddons set me down with a smothered laugh."

It was years later that a touch of fear crept into the impudent young beauty's mind, when, as an actress already applauded by her venerable kinswoman, and tasting the first sweets of success, she wrote:

"What a price she has paid for her great celebrity! Weariness and vacuity and utter deadness of spirit. The cup has been so highly flavoured that life is absolutely without savour or sweetness to her now, nothing but tasteless insipidity. She has stood on a pinnacle till all things have come to look flat and dreary: mere shapeless, colourless, level monotony to her. Poor woman!"

That was the shallow judgment of a girl in the flush of her own first triumphs, unable to guess what memories stirred (and how) behind the silent reveries of age. Full of herself; expansive on that theme as she was in the pages of her journal, Fanny Kemble has unwittingly given us other more significant clues to the mind of the woman she described as "a magnificent ruin about to totter to its fall." A year before this last magniloquent reflection on the insipidity of age, the young actress had recorded her own shocked surprise at the sudden death of Sir Thomas Lawrence:

"Nor was it till I sat down to write to Cecilia, to request her to prevent any sudden communication of the event to my aunt Siddons, that I felt it was really true and found some relief in crying.... I understand that my aunt Siddons was dreadfully shocked by the news, and cried:
"'And have I lived to see him go before me.'"

We have seen how, ten years earlier, the report of his first presidential address to the Royal Academy, wherein he referred to Sir Joshua's Tragick Muse, not only as a masterpiece in itself, but as the greatest female portrait ever painted, had stirred Mrs. Siddons to the point of writing an almost incoherent letter to him. In it her pleasure was cloaked in a curious fumbling humility, an apologetic inconsequence, very unlike the lucid common-sense and commonplaceness of the letters she was still, at that period, writing to her relatives and friends.

The letter reads as though she had not seen Lawrence intimately for years. He had been at a party in her drawing-room in Upper Baker Street as late as 1821; but, between that date and the year 1810, when he had made a drawing of her wearing one of the new fashionable poke bonnets, worn unfashionably back on the head so as not to hide the profile, he had been whirled into circles that did not intersect those in which the now retired actress moved.

It was in that same year 1812, the year of Mrs. Siddons's retirement, that Lawrence had set about painting his portrait of John Philip Kemble as Cato, not as the actor, but as the great man reading the *Phædo* of Plato. " It is," he said, " perhaps the last I shall paint of him. I know it will be the best." Lawrence's infatuation for the Kembles seemed to have burnt itself out and he was preparing to turn away from the ashes of the fire that had lit his way to fame.

For Mrs. Siddons, too, the light had seemed to go out, extinguished, partly by the tears of her own half-realised remorse, and partly by the fumes of that more clouded and offensive flame she had permitted to burn, almost as if she had tried to raise a smoke screen between herself and the first disastrous conflagration.

But, in the long half-dream of old age, as she looked back on the phantasmagoria of a life, the most exalted moments of which had been, not make-believe only, but the creation of her own self-induced ecstasy, she may have recognized a parallel between the plays she acted in and the obscurer pretence of the drama in which she had played one character, and day-dreamed the other and more enduring part.

She may even have traced this double invention back to a day when, as a girl of nineteen, with the new-born Henry in her arms, she reached an inn one night on her journey, like Mary going into Egypt with the Child, and saw the proud hopes of her own young motherhood expressed in the beautiful, amazing boy who had dropped his hobby horse to draw her picture.

It may be that this meeting sealed her eyes, so that she confounded the son she nursed with the instinctive lover whose precocious genius, receiving the impression of her own beauty and overwhelmed by it, confessed himself innocently, spontaneously, in the flattery of his strange accomplishment. By the time his son was thirteen the strong business sense of the elder Lawrence had made this undiminished infatuation public to the " Nobility and Gentry in general and the University of Oxford in particular," by the simultaneous publication of two engravings made by J. R. Smith ; one from little Tom Lawrence's own portrait of himself and another of Mrs. Siddons, as she was then appearing in the theatres of Bath and Bristol wearing the turban and barbaric jewellery of Queen Zara in Congreve's *Mourning Bride*.

And still, at that time, Mrs. Siddons saw herself as an actress able to take a tragic rôle, but at her best in comedy. It was as Rosalind that the Duchess of Devonshire saw and adored her : it was as Portia that she offered herself to Garrick and was accepted to her undoing. Even in 1783 when she came to London the second time she still felt at home in the younger parts of innocence. She wanted to play in *The Grecian Daughter* ; she considered Medea and Lady Macbeth as out of her welkin, inhuman in their wickedness. She was still her Sid's quite actively faithful wife, unable even to see the admiration for her as a woman behind the homage she quite naturally accepted as due to her power as an actress.

But Sheridan, who gauged the sophistication of the town, had thrust the part of Isabella upon her. As she played it on that first unbelievable, unforgettable London night the identification of herself with the upright and much tried wife and mother who, to save an only child from want, accepts the honourable advances of a lover, and finds, when it is too late, that she has given him half her heart into the bargain, became complete, so that the audience lost itself in her no longer simulated anguish and wept and swooned with her. When she looked back upon that triumph, did she see it, as in a witch's mirror, bright with an ominous prophecy ?

A few months later, when she was glittering in the prime of her beauty on the very crest of the highest wave that has ever lifted an actress out of the trough of the waters, a new distraction was offered to the fashionable world. A youth of nineteen, beautiful as an angel, who made portraits of a fairy-like grace and prettiness, came to town, from Bath, the forcing-ground of artistic reputations, and in the twinkling of an eye, was all the rage.

Mrs. Siddons, who had been in London for two years now, found herself obliged to give parties in the larger rooms she had moved to from her first lodgings near the theatre, and the fact that Mr. Thomas Lawrence was to be met with in her drawing-room gave just that slight edge of freshness to the excitement of waiting on her that was enough to increase a popularity which had shown no signs of waning. It must have been then, with the boy of thirteen she had known at Bath become the young man whose conscious charm was none the less powerful that it was exerted on everyone he met, that she first realized the hold he had made and was to continue to make on her imagination.

Reynolds's Tragick Muse had been the sensation of the Royal Academy Exhibition three years earlier: Gainsborough had painted his masterpiece of her and it had been seen by all the critics and the gossips as well: the new young painter was quickly on the track of so much beauty, such incessant fame. For ten years she had sat to him, smiled at him, listened to him; had seen herself softer, more feminine, lovelier in his eyes than she showed to any other worshippers of her beauty. Hamilton and Harlow, painting her in her great rôles, glorified the actress; but Tom Lawrence, with sketch and

T s

pastel and intimate oil-painting of Mrs. Siddons in a cap; Mrs. Siddons in a riding habit; Mrs. Siddons; Mrs. Siddons; Mrs. Siddons; at home; enchanting; intimate; alive and approachable; had fed her deep, unacknowledged, unsuspected vanity, had shown her to herself as a woman soft and lovely and beloved.

When she had resolved to attempt Lady Randolph during the lifetime of the great Mrs. Crawford, Mrs. Siddons may have found the part in Nature, only so far as it portrayed the grief of a mother over her long-lost son, and the ferocious chastity of a widow who, remarried for convenience, remains faithful to the memory of a dead husband through nineteen tearful years. But at some later repetition of her triumph in this play, when old Mrs. Crawford, called from Ireland to outshine her at Covent Garden, had gone back to Dublin defeated, Mrs. Siddons in her very early thirties must have known that Lawrence, his seraphic eyes fixed on her every movement, was seated deep in the dark hollow of the fourth wall, rapt and breathless and too old to be her son. And, as she played, it must have heightened the glow and luminosity of her tender scenes to realize that, neither the author of the play nor the audiences who had applauded it for so long, thought it strange, or in any way out of Nature, that a woman still young and beautiful should be suspected of taking for a lover a man so much younger than herself that he was actually her son. The situation was fairly common on the stage and in novels then, as now; Jocasta had had innumerable daughters in fiction before the Rev.

John Home converted her into a Scottish Niobe and mitigated the terror of her fate. It may not have been in Mrs. Siddons's mind, but it may well have blossomed in the effulgence of her acting, this analogy between her situation in the play and the relationship of her private life as a lovely matron adored by a young man whose success in London was as swift, and as sensational, as that made in the play by the stranger who enters, an unknown boy, to become the hero and champion of an army resisting the invader.

It was the very strength of her propriety, the legend already accumulating about the rectitude of her private life, that led her into danger. Lawrence, in common with all young men in the thrall of an early infatuation, spread his enthusiasm wide, and adored the whole Kemble family. John Philip was his boon companion; Frances, now Mrs. Twiss, his indulgent hostess; Charles, some four years his junior, had a more classically regular profile than the elder Kembles, and was as eagerly drawn by their artist friend.

Mrs. Siddons did not monopolize the attention of the painter: she set herself to work with all the energy of a woman of comprehensive genius to forward his career. Within three years of his arrival in London Lawrence had been made an A.R.A. and on the death of Sir Joshua Reynolds found himself promoted to be Principal Painter to the King. He had other patrons, but it has never been disputed that Mrs. Siddons helped most powerfully towards his advancement. Looking back to the brightness of the meteoric career she had fostered so well, Mrs. Siddons could not fail to reflect on the affectionate fidelity with which her care had been rewarded for ten halcyon years. Whether fixed in her supremacy on the London stage ; or wandering as a star that astonished wherever it came to rest, Mrs. Siddons could always rely on the mutual flattery of the exchange of smiles and congratulation with which she and the man, who grew older so much more rapidly than she did, met one another after a few days', or a few weeks' separation.

One morning about this time she must have received a copy of verses, written by Lawrence when she was far away from London, and certainly, if we know anything of human vanity, sent after her by the author.

"*Does he paint? He fain would write a poem....*"

Easy, half tender, half joking, unfinished, flippant, they are characteristic of the man who was presently to break into a seriousness more like lunacy than ordinary human conduct under stress.

"THOUGHTS ON BEING ALONE AFTER DINNER

"*How shall I, friend, employ my time,*
Alone, no book of prose or rhyme,
Or pencil to amuse me ;
No pen or paper to be found,
No friend to push the bottle round,
Or for its stay abuse me ?

THE SITTER

The servants come and find me here,
And stare upon me like the deer
  On Selkirk in Fernandez ;
And, quite as tame, they wipe the chairs,
And scrub, and hum their favourite airs,
  And ask what my command is.

I wish one knew the way to change
Customs so barbarous and strange,
  So savage and inhuman ;
I wish the sex were kinder grown,
And when they find a man alone,
  Would treat him like a woman.

Well, here's to her, who, far away,
Cares not that I am grave or gay ;
  So now no more I'll drink,
But fold my arms and meditate,
And clap my feet upon the grate,
  And on grave matters think.

'Tis, let me see, full sixteen years,
And wondrous short the time appears,
  Since, with inquiry warm,
With beauty's novel power amazed,
I follow'd, midst the crowd, and gazed
  On Siddons' beauteous form.

Up Bath's fatiguing streets I ran,
Just half pretending to be man,
  And fearful to intrude ;
Busied I looked on some employ,
Or limp'd to see some other boy,
  Lest she should think me rude.

The sun was bright, and on her face,
As proud to show the stranger grace,
   Shone with its purest rays;
And through the folds that veil'd her form,
Motion displayed its happiest charm,
   To catch the admiring gaze.

The smiling lustre of her eyes,
That triumph'd in our wild surprise,
   Well I remember still:
They spoke of joy to yield delight,
And plainly said, ' If I'm the sight,
   Good people, take your fill.'

And can it be that 'neath this roof,
Whilst I sit patiently aloof,
   This watching form can be?
Quick let me fly—avaunt my fears!
'Tis but a door and sixteen years
   Divide this fair and me.

Alas! that beauty should grow old!
Alas! that passion should be cold!
   Alas! that rhymes should fail!
That no due coffee-bell should ring,

   . . . .

   To close my mournful tale.

Ye youths debarr'd your fair one's eye,
Ye that for love to memory fly,
   Attend this moral rhyme,
List to the pensive lay it pours,
The Devil take your doors and hours,
   Your carpenters and time."

There must have been other verses in this vein, and letters as well, but their recipient may have had some fleeting bashfulness about keeping them. None of them, so far as we know, has survived save this, in a duplicate copy either found among its writer's papers after his death or circulated amongst a few personal friends, and preserved for us by that industrious gossip Mr. John Timbs in his *Anecdote Lives*.

When this accepted and entirely innocent idyll had continued some six years or so, Mrs. Siddons gave birth to her sixth and last child Cecilia, in the same year as saw the opening of the new Drury Lane Theatre, on which occasion she played the Lady to her brother's Macbeth. The elder daughters Sally and Maria were still at school, and Lawrence, in the full tide of his success at Court and in Society, found time to come and draw the baby which its mother declared to be " a wit and a beauty " before it was even weaned. There is a drawing in a private collection of Cecilia Siddons at the age of three, in an embroidered cap, with dark eyes and a mischievous smile on her already handsome little face, as lovely as any picture of a baby ever drawn even by Lawrence himself. If it remained in her mother's possession for many years it must have seemed to stand as the full stop, not only to her married life, but also to the unadmitted course of the romantic affection that had, for so long, mingled its dangerous sweetness with the stream of duty and the business of day by day.

For, the business of getting Cecilia comfortably

born being over, and Mrs. Siddons being on her feet once more, the whole movement of her private life changed its time and tune. Sally and Maria came home, grown up and lovely, to be rivals of their beautiful mamma in the drawing-room at Great Marlborough Street and at the routs and concerts and picture shows where the fashionable world congregated.

Their arrival was too much for Lawrence. Two more Kembles—this time young women, younger than himself, eager, tender, innocent young women who looked at him, not with the amused indulgent eyes of friends and protectors who could be flattered, but with the questioning timid glances of maidens who must be protected always, and wooed if possible, changed the nature of his idolatry. He ceased for a time to be the spoilt favourite of the great, and became, still spoilt and wilful, the ardent young man ardently, if a little confusedly, in love. We know the story. We have seen how Mrs. Siddons's first indignant realization that her own reign was cut short, that she must, whether she would or no, abdicate in favour of her delicate and gentle Sally, produced a clash of wills. We know that Lawrence rose out of the dust and turmoil, paintbrush in hand, and half-way through his triple love-affairs, painted Hell as the habitat of the elder Kembles who had thwarted him.

As she looked back on those three tortuous, feverish years; recalling all the turnings and twistings of her own and Lawrence's dealings with one another, and with the two girls they destroyed between them; facing scenes, of which there is now no record, in the cold light we all turn on past events when it is too late to readjust our own reactions to them, did she, we wonder, fully realize the full extent of her self-deception, the real character of the bond that kept her daughters' suitor so fixed in his pursuit? Or had she, in some purposely unexplored corner of her heart, known it all the time?

When, during the progress of Maria's illness, while countenancing Lawrence's engagement to the younger girl in spite of his earlier and more natural attachment to Sally, Mrs. Siddons was asked by Sheridan to read the part of Mrs. Haller, what was it, in the play we have considered in detail, that really induced her to take the subsidiary part? At the time, it is clear, that, just as she played the Lady to Kemble's Macbeth, she was ready to support him in this untried piece that offered him a release from the ignominy of his appearances in *The Castle Spectre*. But she was to play this secondary part with so much conviction, such a convulsive shedding of tears, that in time it became Mrs. Haller in *The Stranger* who attracted audiences. As we have seen, even so early as 1798 Mrs. Siddons was touring in the play with Palmer in John Philip Kemble's part. There, what she found in Nature still remains for us to pick out from what was then the fashionable sentimentality of the age: but the thing that shocked the censorious hypocrites of the day, the spectacle of a guilty wife being still, in all other respects save one, a model of virtue and capable of an efficacious repentance, may have broken in as an almost blinding revelation on some secret consciousness to the woman who read the part. Technically virtuous, strenuously faithful and devoted she knew herself to be: and yet, for a moment, she may have seen and turned away from the possibility in herself of a weakness she must have understood or she could never have made the part of Mrs. Haller so completely her own. It was the contention behind Kotzebue's plot that, because a woman is beautiful, industrious, good to the poor, fond of children, well-mannered and repentant, she is (with the schoolboy's well-known exception of " a slight tendency towards adultery ") a heroine to be admired and rewarded, that horrified a public inured to the age-old fairy-tale morality of chaste Beauty in distress. It was precisely this irregularity and false argument that fitted the unacknowledged but none the less real craving for justification that must have haunted the secret places of Mrs. Siddons's heart.

How eagerly she must have read the critic's pronouncement: " It is the criminality of Mrs. Haller that makes the piece interesting. Mr. Sheridan is right when he says that to kill her would be to kill the play." The knowledge that she accepted that point of view must have been, in real life, the main-spring of her anger against Sally and of her almost devilish plausibility in devising reasons for keeping Sally the bait, dangling before Lawrence's eyes and for twitching it sharply away each time the poor fish made a sudden, hungry rush towards it, and so, towards the unhappy angler who could not let him go.

It is noteworthy that, immediately after the death

of Maria, Mrs. Siddons's friendships with people of strong common sense fell away and she became the close correspondent and companion of the silly Mrs. Pennington; the vulgar Mrs. Galindo, and the blindly adoring Mrs. FitzHugh. Did she, in her ruminating years, we may wonder, close the eyes of memory on those miserable self-deceiving months when she and Sally wrote to Clifton every time they had caught a glimpse of " our tormentor " and put themselves into complete subjugation to the kind but foolish Mrs. Pennington's judgment? Did she realize, now, all passion spent, that she had substituted the spurious attractiveness of a handsome Irish fencing-master for the loss of the real charm and distinction she had for so long enjoyed in Lawrence's company and devotion? Was she able to sit opposite the huge black-velvet dress; the crimson curtain; the glowing ruby and cornelian jewels of the portrait that hung in Mrs. FitzHugh's dining-room for the last twenty years of her life, and never see how shamelessly the beautiful face admitted a weakness and acknowledged a defeat? She must have posed to Lawrence many times for that picture: he was a slow and most painstaking worker: a score of sittings were not enough to satisfy him when he was trying to catch a perfect likeness. In 1804 he had not begun to leave the accessories of his pictures to pupils and underlings, though the painting of some of this particular picture is dull enough to allow us to suspect him of the delegation here: but no one else could have been told off to paint that sullen, smiling, passionate face; and to no one else could she have looked, as she still looks out from the canvas in the cellars of the National Gallery when the attendant has drawn up the blind and let the shadowed daylight in to fall on the enormous bulk of the figure that carries the still lovely, glowing head.

Sally was dead before that portrait was commissioned ; William Siddons was an invalid detained in Bath ; little Cecilia was away at school. Mrs. Siddons herself had almost died of grief and shock at Shrewsbury early in the previous year and had spent many months in seclusion recovering from the blow. So ill had she been that some gossip, half aware of the facts, started a report that she was out of her mind : a report so ill-founded that no one ever appeared to claim the reward of £1,000 Siddons offered for a disclosure of its originator's name. Kind Mrs. FitzHugh may have thought there could be no better cure for her adored friend's melancholy than to bring her into daily touch with the brilliant and amusing painter who had always been so devoted to her and to her whole family. For it is quite possible that Mrs. FitzHugh knew so little of the real state of affairs that she imagined it a tactful thing to arrange for these sittings.

Perhaps, in her armchair by the window, overlooking the young trees of the Outer Circle and the shallow waters where the ducks swam in the lake of Regent's Park, old Mrs. Siddons in her mob cap, nodding a little over *Paradise Regained*, took off her spectacles and smiled to herself, a ghost of that melting, half guilty, wholly passionate smile. She may have believed that she had allowed or even connived at her kind friend's willingness to be the confidante of one of those picturesque, and often quite platonic, flirtations so fashionable at the time on the Continent that no French or Italian or German woman of distinction could feel herself properly married unless she had a devoted and recognized adorer as an extra member of her household.

It was in the autumn of the year this portrait was finished that John Philip took a holiday and carried his sister out of town, before going abroad himself, for that tour of Wales and the Wye Valley in the course of which they are said to have visited the grave of the martyred Father Kemble.

There may have been some glimmer in the old lady's remembering thoughts of an idea that, by sparing money to tend the martyr's grave (and it was never a very easy thing for her to spare money for any object not directly concerned with her family's welfare), she had possibly obtained a little grace for the fault she never actually committed. She had, after all, been brought up in a family where all the men were Roman Catholics and it is inevitable that some of the more comfortable doctrines of the most human of all systems of enabling the soul to keep its accounts balanced must have presented themselves to her as acceptable, and possibly efficacious, in the long hours of old age when she was at leisure to make her reckoning.

When her thoughts turned away to the theatre again, there were other parts, besides Mrs. Haller and Lady Randolph, that must have come back to her as she sat dreaming of her triumphs and looking into her own heart : Jane Shore the wanton whose sufferings she had depicted with so much nobility that the spectators suffered too, but for the deserted woman not for the king's mistress ; Mrs. Beverley, a part she played superbly to the end, so superbly indeed that when she was fifty and stout for her age she acted it to the Beverley of Macready, a boy of nineteen, and not only took the house by storm but inspired the nervous young actor to a memorable performance of his own. And, always, greater even than her great interpretations of them, the majestic figures of Shakespeare's tragic women ; Queen Katharine, Volumnia ; Constance ; Margaret of Anjou, must have risen towering against the backcloth of the dim scenes she no longer trod, giving her assurance of the power that, having used her as its channel, was no longer making itself manifest in human form. Miss O'Neill might win golden opinions ; that little puss Fanny Kemble might play Juliet and Belvidera to an indulgent town ; but neither of them could ever freeze the marrow in the bones of those who heard and saw their pretty antics, as she had done, even so late as that June evening in 1817, when she had come out of her retirement, a woman of sixty-two, to play Lady Macbeth in the week of her brother's farewell performances. It was as Lady Macbeth that her genius had carried her further into the hidden places of human experience than in any other part. Each time she played it she added some shred of knowledge, some fresh gleam of the imagination's pride to the figure she built up and presented and exposed. In her, remorse became incarnate, rising from the union of ambition and crime. She showed the dream, unchecked, turn to red-handed action: she flayed the soul that survived its own destruction and knew itself for carrion.

Artists, statesmen, poets all wondered at and acknowledged her genius in this supreme exposure of the human spirit. They collaborated in it, as great minds must, adding by their plaudits and comments fresh material to the actress's own conception of the part. It was Reynolds who, after her first London performance of the part, suggested white for the sleep-walking scene. Burke and Gibbon saw her act and came to talk to her of her performance afterwards. Each time she played it the spark struck from the finest minds of the age flashed back to her and enriched her reading. When she was twenty she had tried it and had failed, terrified by the horror that had pursued her one solitary night when she had sat up into the small hours getting the dreadful, guilty, lines by heart: at thirty she gave to the banquet and the sleep-walking scenes such an extension that no actress in any country or any language since her day has come near to giving a more than tolerable interpretation of the part.

John Wilson, ignorant of the cause we may surmise, saw her give this terrifying portrayal, late in her career. We have read his final word: " None knew the troubled grandeur of guilt till they saw her in Lady Macbeth . . . more hideously haunted than ever was the hollow grave, seemed then, to be the cell of her heart."

2

So, with her suppressions sublimated in her acting, Mrs. Siddons passed through the great emotional crisis of her life, and lived to see its fires dwindle to a glow that, from time to time, sent up a pale tongue of flame to leap across the darkness of memory showing her her life as she had supposed it to be, if never quite life as it actually was.

Her public appearances grew rarer : her sons and her younger brother Charles were anxious that they should cease altogether, partly because they became too great a strain on her failing powers ; partly because her powers *were* failing and they could not bear any hint of disillusionment to mar the legend of her greatness. She still gave parties : sometimes she gave a reading or a recital during the evening : even as late as 1828 she dined out occasionally. At one of these dinner parties she met Thomas Moore and told him that many a time during her life she had " got credit for the truth and feeling of her acting when she was doing nothing more than relieve her own heart of its grief." More and more in retrospect she confounded her art with her life, and, in doing so, saw that life as a play of which she was now become the rapt and wondering spectator.

" I drive out to recover my voice and my spirits, and am better while abroad ; but I come home and lose them both in an hour. I cannot read . . ." So she had written to Mrs. Piozzi while she was still active enough to be amusing herself with trying to model a full-length portrait of Cecilia. But year by year she lost some part of her strength, though her mind remained clear, and her patience grew as the need for it increased.

One October evening in 1829, she was made to bestir herself and was dressed very carefully in a black velvet gown and driven from Upper Baker Street to Covent Garden and led into a box at the right moment for the audience, waiting for the curtain to rise on *Romeo and Juliet*, to recognize and applaud her entrance. Little Fanny Kemble in her Juliet costume waiting in tears and shudders for the play to begin, heard the tumult behind the scenes, and feared there would be no enthusiasm for her own first entrance on the stage. All through the young actress's account of her aunt's old age there runs a tiny, piping shrill of jealousy—a hint of a rivalry she never began to attain. But Fanny Kemble's success as Juliet was great enough that night, and her aunt Siddons applauded from her box with admired grace and real enthusiasm.

Within a week, the President of the Royal Academy, who had been in the auditorium, was begging the latest and prettiest of the Kembles for a sitting.

Up in her drawing-room in Baker Street the news of Lawrence's enslavement at sixty to the child of nineteen was told and received without much comment. But, under the mob cap, and the folded muslin of the old lady's quiet dress, the mind and the heart of the lioness stirred again. Presently she put forth a paw, to mark her own, and for the last time. She said she would dine with her brother and sister-in-law one evening, dark and cold as the autumn evenings were.

"And how is the portrait of Fanny getting on?" she asked.

They told her but she made no comment. The poor old lady was growing very absent-minded, they said, rambling even. But the old lady was not rambling. Lawrence had not had Maria; he had not had Sally; and did Fanny Kemble think she was going to carry him off now? Laying her hand on her brother's arm she said:

"Charles, when I die, I wish to be carried to my grave by you and Lawrence."

She had thrust the thought of death between the girl and her elderly adorer—her own death, as she believed. But it was in another way that she kept him from this last unfaithfulness with a girl of her own blood. Before his portrait of Fanny as Juliet was completed Sir Thomas Lawrence himself was dead: dead so suddenly that at first the gossips supposed he might have destroyed himself.

She survived him for a year and five months.

On the morning of June 9th, 1831, Haydon wrote in his diary:

"Mrs. Siddons died this morning: the greatest, grandest genius that ever was born! Peace to her immortal shade! She was good and pious and an affectionate mother. What a splendid Pythoness she seemed when reading Macbeth."

Five thousand people attended her funeral, and Macready had a terrible time over getting her statue by Campbell into Westminster Abbey. For a time there was nobody to take her place : then a new generation arose and she was forgotten. But while London was crowding to be amused by Mrs. Bancroft and stirred by Mrs. Kendall, and to adore the blonde magic of Ellen Terry, the people who lived in the Regency House in Upper Baker Street from the drawing-room of which Mrs. Siddons had looked out on Regent's Park, would occasionally think they saw a tall old lady in a flounced black skirt going slowly up the winding staircase. They did not seem to mind her. Mrs. Siddons was a pleasant and a quiet ghost.

3

Fanny Kemble, in her excitement over her sudden leap into popularity as Juliet, and in her quite natural delight at the interest taken in her, both as a pretty girl and as a charming actress, by Sir Thomas Lawrence still urbane and gallant and in the fashion at the age of sixty, states categorically that after the death of Sally all communication was broken off between the painter and Mrs. Siddons and that " from that time they never saw or had any intercourse with each other."

But Fanny was not born until six years after Mrs. Siddons had returned from Ireland to find Sally dead. In 1821, when Mrs. Siddons and Cecilia were giving parties in Upper Baker Street, one of which Lawrence certainly attended, little Miss Kemble was away at school in France, and nobody would have considered it worth while writing to tell the child who did and who did not call on her aunt and cousin.

Sir Thomas Lawrence had returned to England in 1820 from his long triumphal progress through rows of Princes, Kings, Emperors, Cardinals, all of whose portraits he painted at Aix-la-Chapelle, or in Vienna, until his glory culminated in a command from King George IV to proceed to Rome there to make a painting of Pope Pius VII. This picture, still in the Royal Collection at Windsor, has been ranked among the painter's masterpieces : it also records one of the few defeats sustained by the courtier in Lawrence : for the old man, seated almost humbly in the pontifical chair, had refused to meet the artist's eye and to give smile for smile. He was painted looking sideways and out of the picture, gentle, but sardonic too, and unrelated, except in the painter's scheme of composition, to the Roman warrior who approaches the sunlit Laocoön group through an arch of the Vatican galleries beyond the inevitable drapery of the curtains looped apart behind the sitter's chair. There is a portrait of Lord Castlereagh, now in the National Gallery, showing the half unwilling yet indulgent smile of a sitter who could not, or did not resist, as the Pope could do, the charm and the careful impudence of the painter of whom the phrase " his enamelled smile " was first coined by the witty and unfortunate Benjamin Haydon.

Lawrence was to meet another defeat, and almost to accomplish another masterpiece in his unfinished sketch of the little Duc de Reichstadt, Napoléon François Charles Joseph Roi de Rome, who looks out from the canvas, a blond and exquisite child. The son of Buonaparte with his mother's tender colouring, posed, a little sullenly, refusing to smile at the Englishman who had come to make a portrait of his grandfather to place among the trophies that proclaimed his father's defeat.

There was another portrait, made at this period from a sketch of the Princess Clémentine Metternich, a girl so lovely in the bloom of her sixteenth year that Lawrence, seeing her walking with her governess in the streets of Vienna, followed her home and obtained permission to draw her. Within a year of this meeting the young princess was dead, of the same disease as had carried off Maria Siddons. But Lawrence could not be publicly disconsolate on so slight an acquaintanceship. Hearing that the girl was ill he finished a portrait from the sketch he had carried back to London with him and sent it out to Vienna in time for her to see it before she died. There was no reason why it should not be shown to her : but, when she had seen it, the poor child called for a mirror and cried out at the change in her still living face. When he heard this it is impossible to suppose that Lawrence did not cast one backward thought to those other portraits he had made of an equally lovely and, once, far more deeply beloved face. But, just as a happiness cannot be recaptured once it is over, so a sorrow cannot repeat its circumstances without dulling the edge of grief.

By this time Thomas Lawrence had formed the habit and perfected the technique of loving in vain. Miss Amelia Locke, long before the royal and princely portraits of Aix-la-Chapelle were commissioned, had married Mr. Angerstein ; Miss Jennings, whom he drew so beautifully, married Mr. Locke ; the anonymous lady at Clapham faded from memory ; the never authenticated scandal that once coupled his name with that of the unfortunate Princess of Wales died away ; the beautiful and sympathetic Mrs. Wolff was a wife and the mother of a son of whom Lawrence had made a picture before he went off to Aix : even she did not apparently occupy his exclusive attention when he was in his fifties, for an unnamed lady is reported to have put on widow's weeds after his death saying that, had he lived, he would have married her. This of course may have been a delusion on the lady's part fostered by the President of the Royal Academy's often quoted habit of accepting an invitation to dinner in the terms of a love-letter ; and there must have been many other women who were not without cause for supposing that he regarded them with something more than the warmth of platonic friendship.

Philanderer though he was Lawrence was no sensualist. His fine house in Russell Square was a place of business, and a workshop ; only, very unimportantly, a home. The two drawing-rooms were used as studio and picture gallery ; six of the bedrooms had been thrown into a vast workshop where he arranged the draperies for his backgrounds and set his pupils and assistants to paint them. For his own use, a small bedroom, sparsely furnished, with a narrow bed in it, and one small parlour sufficed. He dined out so often, and worked so unremittingly, that he needed very little space in which to be alone and to rest. These were not the typical bachelor quarters of the fashionable amorist. In private life he was frugal, but so generous and reckless that, when he died, his estate barely sufficed to meet the claims made upon it. He was a most open-handed friend, and supported his parents and sisters out of his earnings from the time he was seventeen. Though the days of his fame were long and the fees he could demand were high, it is clear that he painted many of his greatest works for love, and as in the case of the Calmady children, spent far more time on the difficult delicious pair than was represented by the hundred and fifty pounds which was all Mr. and Mrs. Calmady could afford to pay for the little masterpiece. When this was finished it was shown to the King who offered £2,000 for it ; but the parents would not sell their treasure, so it was engraved, and Lawrence paid the engraver £20 more than the fee agreed on for the work, so pleased was he with the result. His impulsiveness was as genuine as it was sometimes inconvenient but it harmed him himself as much and as often as it disturbed others.

All that has been proved against him is that he never quite meant the love he made so eloquently by letter and in the dazzling flattery of the portraits that showed each sitter at her loveliest while still remaining perfect likenesses. It was a regrettable trait, a vein of spuriousness in a character otherwise charming : some hint of it must have appeared in his general behaviour to cause a wit to remark of the slightly too gushing, and too beautiful young man at the time when he was making his first successes that he could never remember to be a gentleman for more than three consecutive minutes.

4

For a time, and in appearance, Lawrence may have forgotten Mrs. Siddons. We know that he drew her as late as 1810 : we know that, when he came back to London loaded with honours and diamonds and the snuff-boxes given him by Emperors and Kings, he was at one of her parties and behaved rather badly there.

On the 10th of March 1821 Haydon the painter went to hear Mrs. Siddons give a private reading of *Macbeth*. In his opinion Mrs. Siddons read the part of Macbeth himself better than either Kemble and Kean had ever acted it. In the interval after Act III. the gentlemen left the drawing-room and were served with tea and toast.

" While we were all eating toast "

wrote Haydon in his Journal that night,

" and tingling cups and saucers, she began again. It was like the effect of a mass bell at Madrid. All noise ceased ; we slunk to our seats like boors, two or three of the most distinguished men of the day, with the very toast in their mouths, afraid to bite.

" It was curious to see Lawrence in the predicament, to hear him bite by degrees and then stop for fear of making too much crackle, his eyes full of water from the constraint ; and at the same time to hear Mrs. Siddons's

> '*Eye of newt and toe of frog*'

and then to see Lawrence give a sly bite, and then look awed, and pretend to be listening."

The point of the story is that Lawrence felt able to behave in this childish manner, and that he did so unrebuked. Mrs. Siddons went on reading : perhaps the sound of her own voice deadened the crunching so that she did not hear it : perhaps she was still so moved by the remembrance of that wonderful speech Lawrence had made about the Tragick Muse ; so pleased that her letter of thanks had brought him once more into her circle that she needed all her self-possession to be able to read at all, and, once having started, was as impervious to any crackle from the audience as if she had been actually on the stage at Drury Lane ignoring the winter coughs that then, as now, raised their barrage across the performance. Perhaps she did hear and did know that Lawrence was behaving badly, and, either wounded, or too shy to draw attention to him, as she might have done to any other misdemeanant, let him nibble on in his corner, trusting to his fellow-guests to keep him in check.

We know that he visited her later : for in 1828, long after Fanny Kemble had come home from school in France, Mrs. Siddons sent by hand a note to Lawrence asking his interest on behalf of a friend who required a post, in terms which make it clear that their intercourse was still friendly and fairly constant. This letter ends : " I have no more to say but Farewel ! and God bless you ! " and is signed " Sarah Siddons." No wonder he kept it, though he must have destroyed many longer and more intimate epistles in the same hand.

Fanny Kemble did not know what she was writing about when, three years later, she thought she had been told that her elderly admirer no longer visited her aunt Siddons in Upper Baker Street.

But, under the enamelled smile ; under the orders and decorations ; beneath those financial and other difficulties of his life that made his old housekeeper cry to Haydon : " Poor Sir Thomas ! always in trouble ! always something to worrit him ! " the one, inextinguishable flame still smouldered. There was, there never had been, any woman quite so wonderful as Mrs. Siddons. Time had divided them : he was born too late, and she was grown too bright when he first knew her for them ever to have been lovers, and yet it was as lovers that they both might have reached an earthly happiness more satisfying than the fame they each enjoyed. A great part of this loss transformed itself in both cases, and more significantly in hers than in his, into the expression of their chosen arts. But, when her art failed her and she had empty nights to face, with all the actor's long habit of wakefulness till the small hours in her brain, she complained sometimes of missing the reverberations from the excitement of the lighted theatre and of the tears and cries she once had given and taken back again from the public. Beneath that emptiness she must have grown aware of another, a never fulfilled ecstasy, that still troubled her mind though its torment had long ago died away from her tired blood. We have seen her put forth her hand to claim the man who had passed out of her life, demanding that he stand with her own brother when she should be buried. We know that the thought of this stirred in her on the night when she sat and watched the youngest Kemble playing on the stage of Drury Lane and was told that Sir Thomas Lawrence, who had for many years given up the theatre, had not only come to see the play, but, for some days beforehand, had visited the budding actress and her mother, and had given his advice about Juliet's dress.

It was unwise of him, now close upon his sixtieth birthday, to plunge so eagerly into the excitement of seeing a young and gifted actress every day. "Her face is not regularly handsome" he wrote to the Angersteins "but she has eyes and hair like Mrs. Siddons in her finest time . . . the genius of Mrs. Siddons is recalled to us by Miss Fanny Kemble . . . her voice is sweet . . . it is peculiar to her family . . . her manner in private has that modest gravity which in Mrs. Siddons was strictly natural to her, though, from being peculiar in the general gaiety of society, it was often thought assumed. For years I have not gone to the theatre above once or twice in the year but this fine genius has drawn me often to it. . . ."

It was dangerous at sixty to drink of the fountain of youth again : the more dangerous since it brought him back to the original source of passion. Fanny began to sit for him : Fanny could sing. So, in the days he thought he had forgotten, did Sally Siddons: so had a later and a more lately perished flame, for Mrs. Wolff had been a singer, and one evening Lawrence asked Miss Kemble to sing one of her songs for him. But Mrs. Wolff was forgotten on the day when, looking at the newly finished portrait of Fanny Mrs. Kemble was moved to ejaculate : " It is very like Maria Siddons ! " and Lawrence was at once plunged into a paroxysm of emotion and almost choked out his agreement : " Oh, she is very like her ! She is very like them all ! "

On another occasion Mrs. Kemble, who had a Frenchwoman's logical and unimaginative ideas of what should please a hearer, sought to gratify the painter by telling him of Mrs. Siddons's wish that he and Charles should carry her to her grave. Lawrence was too moved to go on painting. Neither Mrs. nor Miss Kemble quite understood why. " This strange man " wrote Fanny " fell into one of these paroxysms of emotion."

It was too odd of the famous Sir Thomas Lawrence, who, old as he was, was avowedly more than half in love with Fanny, to be so upset at the mention of old aunt Siddons " tottering on the brink of the tomb " away in Upper Baker Street. Fanny was more than half in love with Sir Thomas herself. He had hinted that the stage would lose a fine tragic actress were she ever to be persuaded to leave it, and he had not only designed her dress for Belvidera, but had actually come and heard her lines and advised her upon them, which was more than her aunt Siddons had ever offered to do. Fanny had it in her mind to try Lady Macbeth

THE SITTER

presently. Why not, even though she were a short little person, more properly equipped for comedy than tragedy? Lawrence had seen her aunt play the lady many a score of times. She saw no reason why he should not coach her in the part. She saw very few reasons, though she was only nineteen and her admirer was a portly but fresh and handsome sixty, why she might not, for a few dignified and brilliant years, be Lady Lawrence, even if this did mean a temporary retirement from the stage. She was, after all, almost as much in love with him as he seemed to be with her.

But Fanny did not see very far. She did not see fifty years backward into time, into the parlour of an inn at Devizes, where a boy as beautiful as an angel sat drawing a girl, no older than Fanny herself, who held a child in her slender arms, and smiled, and blushed a little, and was at once Virgin and Mother and Queen to the eager child-artist who worshipped as he drew with the innocent, self-forgetting adoration of first love.

First love! Last love! In his elderly pursuit of little Fanny Kemble, Thomas Lawrence was drawing near and nearer to his past. It was dangerous to look backward thus; dangerous to remember the storms that had divided him from the one adorable and adored mistress of his vision. Once before, and how disastrously, the glamour of youth and maidenhood had fallen on his senses and hidden the grand figure of his adoration in the veils of the beauty she had stamped with her own inimitable seal. It was the mother he had loved in the daughters whose love he had so disastrously won and lost. And now, once more, Mrs. Siddons ! Mrs. Siddons ! Mrs. Siddons ! he kept repeating as he watched a fleeting glance, the ghost of an ineffable smile cross the pretty little face of Fanny Kemble, and caught in her clear young voice the echo of the most marvellous speech the world has ever heard.

One day he ordered a magnificent proof-plate of an engraving after Reynolds's Tragick Muse. When it came home he took his pen and in his graceful, feminine handwriting inscribed it :

> " This portrait by England's greatest painter, of the noblest subject of his pencil, is presented to her niece and worthy successor, by her most faithful humble friend and servant, Lawrence."

Fanny had let her admirer know that she would be twenty on the 27th of November, and this was his birthday card for her. He had the engraving framed, beautifully framed too, and sent to Buckingham Gate with his compliments. Fanny was pleased, but not at all overwhelmed by his compliment. Her mother, with some stirring of forgotten associations, wondered a little at the flattery of the comparison, but accepted it, as a mother excused for doing, as the right of her wonderful child.

But Lawrence, sleepless in his narrow bed, on the top floor of the great, bleak house in Russell Square, was unhappy at his treachery. He had broken the ice that had borne him so long and so safely over the dark waters of memory. He knew that Fanny Kemble was only an excuse, the stimulus that had sent him dreaming backwards to the days when he had lived and suffered and loved with the one indestructible passion of his unsatisfied, questing heart.

He went to Buckingham Gate and told the pretty girl that he wanted to have his present put into a better frame for her. She had to let him take it home again.

For some days it lay on the table in his parlour, and then his secretary was told to take it out of its frame. Lawrence took his pen and obliterated the words " and worthy successor." He had retracted his heresy. There was only one Mrs. Siddons. Fanny was nothing but the wraith of the glory that came dazzling back to his remembering eyes. The picture was returned to its frame.

" Cover it up," said Lawrence to the man who showed it to him for his approval. " I cannot bear to look at it."

A few days later he was dead.

THE END